Microsoft Rising
...and other tales of Silicon Valley

Ted G. Lewis

IEEE
COMPUTER
SOCIETY

Los Alamitos, California

Washington ● Brussels ● Tokyo

Library of Congress Cataloging-in-Publication Data

Lewis, T. G. (Theodore Gyle), 1941-
    Microsoft rising – and other tales of Silicon Valley / Ted G. Lewis.
        p.   cm.
    A compilation of columns previously published in IEEE Computer
(1994-1998), Internet Computing, and Scientific American.
    Includes bibliographical references.
    1. Microsoft Corporation – History. 2. Internet software industry –
United States – History. I. Title: Microsoft rising. II. Title

HD9696.65.U64 M535 1999
338.7'610053'0973 — dc21

                                                                    99-052735
                                                                    CIP

IEEE Computer Society Press Order Number BP00200
Library of Congress Number 99-052735
ISBN 0-7695-0200-8

Additional copies may be ordered from:

IEEE Computer Society Press
Customer Service Center
10662 Los Vaqueros Circle
P.O. Box 3014
Los Alamitos, CA 90720-1314
Tel: +1-714-821-8380
Fax: +1-714-821-4641
Email: cs.books@computer.org

IEEE Service Center
445 Hoes Lane
P.O. Box 1331
Piscataway, NJ 08855-1331
Tel: +1-732-981-0060
Fax: +1-732-981-9667
mis.custserv@computer.org

IEEE Computer Society
Watanabe Building
1-4-2 Minami-Aoyama
Minato-ku, Tokyo 107-0062
JAPAN
Tel: +81-3-3408-3118
Fax: +81-3-3408-3553
tokyo.ofc@computer.org

Executive Director and Chief Executive Officer: T. Michael Elliott
Publisher: Angela Burgess
Manager of Production, CS Press: Deborah Plummer
Advertising/Promotions: Tom Fink
Production Editor: Denise Hurst
Printed in the United States of America

Contents

Preface

One day while I was putting together this book from columns published in *IEEE Computer* (1994–1998), *IEEE Internet Computing,* and *Scientific American,* it suddenly dawned on me that this is the story of Microsoft and how it rose to become the first monopoly of the Information Age. I had not intended it to turn out this way. My original idea was to produce an eyewitness account of the changing computer industry. I wanted to rewrite the story of Silicon Valley and how it works. Yes, this book was to be a revisionist history of computing, circa 1990–2000. As it turned out, it was a revisionist history of Microsoft. *Microsoft Rising* is a tale of greed, emotion, and techno-marketing hype in one of the fastest growing, mainline industries of the world.

When viewed up close, as I have had the opportunity of doing while living on the outskirts of Silicon Valley, the world of hi-tech is a dog-eat-dog swirl of jousts and counter-jousts. Companies, ideas, and people come into focus and disappear in a human drama that is unlike the drama of other industries. Most of the wheeling and dealing, ego flexing, and marketing hype seems unnecessary, and maybe it is. But, when viewed from 30,000 feet or five years later, the actions of companies and people look more purposeful. They look more predictable. In fact, there is a rational basis for Silicon Valley, even though it is governed by chaos most of the time! This was my epiphany after organizing and rewriting the columns I had written over a 5-year period from 1993 to 1998. *Microsoft Rising* is ultimately about Microsoft's domination of the computer industry. But to get there we need to follow the path that most people of the mid-1990s followed. Many twists and turns of technology led Microsoft to its envied monopoly position, but as recently as 1994, it was not readily apparent that Microsoft would rise to its current position of dominance. Certainly no one in 1994 imagined that Microsoft would become the subject of a U.S. Department of Justice anti-trust lawsuit. Even fewer would have imagined the outcome.

Microsoft provides a lesson in something else besides greed and power. In fact, what we learn as the journey unfolds is that minor insignificant ripples in the past can grow into major accomplishments of great significance. We learn that a small, insignificant company in Redmond, Washington, which began by writing software and licensing it dirt cheap to hobby computer manufacturers, could grow to dominate an industry that almost nobody had heard of two decades earlier. Microsoft's minor ripple became a major roar in less than 20 years. Still more troublesome—Microsoft's emergence was totally unpredictable—especially troublesome for old-line companies like IBM.

Nowadays we have adjusted to a new business reality. Whenever a high technology company sprouts from a garage in Palo Alto, California, it is not clear where it will end up. It could become the next Microsoft, or it could become a quiet failure. Nonetheless, it has to be taken seriously—at least for a while—because there is a non-zero probability that it will become the next Microsoft. Netscape Communications may have been a disappointment to stock speculators who paid $170 per share for it in August 1995, but who could have known? Companies like Yahoo! and Excite are repeating Netscape's pattern. Excite's journey largely ended when it was brought into the AT&T family (AT&T bought TCI, which owned most of At Home, which bought Excite. So the big fish eat the little fish, which in turn eat the even smaller fish). Only Yahoo! is left standing and yet to play out its cycle—from obscure startup to powerhouse. Will it grow to dominate E-commerce, or succumb to a buyout by a bigger fish? At the time of this writing, we don't know the answer, but we do know that the Next Big Thing drives Silicon Valley.

The Next Big Thing always starts out as an insignificant thing. Hence the theory of emergent behaviour explains how hi-tech industries come and go. From humble beginnings come a few revolutionary ideas—and lots of failures. Separating the successes from the flops is what makes the game of hi-tech worthwhile playing. The risks are high, but the rewards are staggering. I am still kicking myself for selling Microsoft's stock in 1985, after it doubled its IPO price!

Upstart-to-Big-Shot and boom-to-bust are repeating patterns in hi-tech. It is an exciting game that attracts techno-society's equivalent of the chronic gambler—the Venture Capitalist (VC). Uniquely peculiar to the business world, the Silicon Valley VC is the spark plug of American Capitalism. Without them, innovation, economic growth, and American entrepreneurialism don't work. Venture Capital is Silicon Valley's secret advantage over the rest of the world.

Here is how the VC game is played. Someone in a garage somewhere (technical type) hatches an idea, and combines it with an even bigger surge of ambition—usually by partnering with a talented marketing personality (marketing type). The two shop their idea around the Valley for a moneyman, a parasitic VC who makes his or her living by exploiting both the technical/marketing types and the public. VCs swarm all over the start-up with money, advice, and fast talk. Their goal: take the startup company public at 100 times the price of their initial investment.

The VC game is legendary. For example, Steve Wozniak (technical type), Steve Jobs (marketing type), and Mike Markkula (moneyman type) took the public on a decade-long ride with the creation of Apple Computer. Even at its lowest point, Apple Computer was worth more than $2.5 billion, turning the two Steve's and Markkula into celebrity millionaires in less than a decade.

Marc Andreessen (technical type), with the assistance of a number of marketing types, and James Clark (moneyman) milked the investing public for $2.8 billion in August 1995 when Netscape Communications went public. Netscape had revenues of less than $12 million at the time. After only four years, Netscape Communications fetched a sale price of $4.2 billion from America Online. From zero to more than $4 billion in less than 5 years isn't bad for any VC. The objective of the VC game is to turn perception into reality by going public as soon as possible. Let the public be damned, because everyone in Silicon Valley knows that success lasts only as long as the Next Big Thing lasts. And even after the Next Big Thing passes, as it did for Netscape, there is always the merger.

Emergent behavior is a powerful force in shaping the future, but it is unsettling. It is bottom-up, unpredictable, and unmanageable. The fact that hi-tech has adapted to emergent behavior as an everyday occurrence is at the root of Silicon Valley's success. The future cannot be planned. It cannot be invented. Rather, the future can only be exploited. Indeed, we learn that the future can be most effectively exploited by the fleet-of-foot. In Silicon Valley, only the swift survive. We can see this in any number of examples, but the most dramatic case study is Microsoft. The world's most successful software company to date has achieved its success by being fast.

Being fast means you must be able to execute. Once the moneymen have come and gone, and once the public has bought into the perception force field of a certain company, the key to long-term survival is execution. This means implementation. A winner must be able to implement its vision. Fast implementation is everything in Silicon Valley. Without fast implementations, a company soon loses the initiative and falls prey to Davidow's Law, which states that a company must obsolesce its products before someone else does. Failure to do this leads to ruin. Intel Corporation and Microsoft have been masters of Davidow's Law. In fact, Davidow was a vice president of Intel at one time, before becoming a moneyman.

Companies like Intel and Microsoft live in fear of Davidow's Law. But nobody is perfect. Sometimes even the quickest companies fall behind. Someone else beats them to the Next Big Thing. This happened to Microsoft in the late 1990s. Sun Microsystems surprised Microsoft when its product—Java—unexpectedly gained traction in the programming language marketplace. Java, and its supporting technology, made it possible for software developers to write applications that could (theoretically) run on any computer. Such simplicity quickly captured mind share among the developers who write the applications that sell computer systems. Developers are a kind of gatekeeper—a choke point in the value chain that links hi-tech companies like Microsoft and Intel to the consumer. Without applications, Microsoft cannot sell software which means Intel cannot sell hardware which means the whole industry collapses. Java was like a toothpick holding up a bridge. And Microsoft wanted to own that prop. Java—a totally insignificant product in 1993—suddenly threatened Microsoft's domination. Once again, emergent behavior began grinding through its cycle. As the stories in this book unfold, we learn that strong companies like Intel and Microsoft must "absorb and extend" competitor's products whenever Davidow's Law threatens to take away their dominance. They must make resistance futile! Thus, absorb and extend is a strategy of the strong, while Davidow's Law is a strategy of the weak. This spectacle played out in public when Microsoft faced the U.S. Department of Justice in 1998–1999. Netscape, the weaker player, attempted to dislodge Microsoft, the stronger player. But, Microsoft quickly absorbed the features of Netscape's products (Navigator), and quickly moved to extend it in nonstandard ways, rendering it obsolete. This technique plays out daily in the dog-eat-dog world of hi-tech, but because Microsoft was big enough to deserve attention, it attracted the attention of the U.S. Department of Justice. The U.S. Department of Justice case against Microsoft would set legal precedent, regardless of the outcome.

Microsoft's absorb and extend strategy of the strong portends a decade of litigation for the company, because it leads the company into many segments of the market where Microsoft will be scrutinized and charged with anti-competitive behavior. This squeeze play is inevitable for Microsoft, because of its monopoly status. While it is not against U.S. law to be a monopoly, it is illegal to monopolize. What is the difference? A monopoly is not illegal, but monopolizing by a monopoly is. Specifically, Microsoft, or any other monopoly in the United States cannot use its monopoly position to obtain second, third, or additional monopolies. Achieving a monopoly position in an industry is a one-time deal. The fact that Microsoft used its monopoly power to attempt to gain additional monopoly power is what got the company into trouble.

Microsoft's growth has bounds because when it became a monopoly, the rules changed for the company. It can no longer behave like a startup. Rather, it must now behave like a mature company. The question is, "What will become of Microsoft?"

Microsoft's days may be numbered. As I write this, the company's future is tied to an unfinished product—Windows 2000. This mondo project is so big it is already 2 years late to market. And it may be too big. Some analysts estimate that Windows 2000 will break Microsoft. Indeed, at 30+ million lines of code, Windows 2000 may be a bridge too far. It could mark the beginning of the end for Microsoft. After all, Microsoft's history follows the familiar pattern of emergent behavior. From dust, to dust, in one quick cycle. It is the way of the hi-tech industry. Microsoft may not be the exception.

This book reports the author's personal history through the early 1990s to the end of the decade. These stories often try to predict or explain the chaos of Silicon Valley by making rash claims. Sometimes my prognostication is right on target; sometimes it is way off. The end of Microsoft? You be the judge after reading the following episodes. I have used hindsight to analyze where predictions have failed to materialize, and where they have come true. Hindsight, you see, is the tool of a revisionist historian.

First, the Industry is analyzed, and we come to realize that hi-tech industry is constantly churning—in turmoil and upheaval—an exercise in chaos theory. But this is OK, because chaos spells opportunity. Opportunity attracts the moneymen, and the cycle begins. Then, we witness the rise of the Internet—the gonzo opportunity of a lifetime. Moneymen and technical and marketing types fill the void like gossip at a graduating class reunion. The Internet creates waves of instability that sweep through the telecommunications industry—a regulated industry that has been asleep for decades! The 1996 Telecommunications Act is the most revolutionary regulatory law in 60 years, replacing the 1934 Telecommunications Act, and creating havoc in the telephone business. More chaos is piled on top of the seething semiconductor, software, and Internet businesses. More money pours in.

Next we examine the low art of software development. Software is the propellant of the Information Age, and yet nobody knows the best way to manufacture it. It is like building the automobile industry on an uncertain supply of oil. Even to this day, and probably into the distant future, software remains an art form. Software—the shifting sand that an entire empire is built on—adds more uncertainty and risk as it forms an unstable foundation for just about everything. Software uncertainty, chaos, and opportunity nip at the Venture Capitalists heel, and they love it! More money pours in.

The last two chapters deal with innovation and the emergence of a techno-society. Here, I try to place the foregoing chapters into perspective. Is innovation something that can be captured, nurtured, and recycled? Will techno-society last? I cannot promise any answers, but rather, conclude this short journey into the brief past with a number of provoking ideas about the future of hi-tech. But please, don't hold me to my word for more than 18 months, because Silicon Valley is designed to exploit emergent behaviors, not explain them!

Ted Lewis
May 1999
Tedglewis@friction-free-economy.com

Note: All product and other names
mentioned throughout this book are
the trademarks or service marks
of their respective holders.

PART ONE

The Valley of the Kings: Inside the Computer Industry

CHAPTER ONE

Reversals of Fortune

It was a warm, breezy day in the early summer of 1994 as I drove south on Middlefield Road in Mountain View, California, on my way to a new startup named Mosaic Communications, Inc. I had arranged to meet some old Apple Computer friends who had bailed out of Apple to join the new company only a few days earlier. My nethead friends were overly enamored, for my tastes, with the recently commercialized ARPANet, now becoming the Internet. In fact, Apple Computer hadn't paid much attention to their Internet dreams, so they left. Apple was never going to care about networks, so why not move to a networking company? Even I thought the "Internet business" was far too techie for consumers. But when my friends were offered stock options to play with the Internet, they bolted.

I thought my friends crazy for jumping the Apple Computer ship to swim with an unknown startup. After all, Apple Computer was going strong, growing its worldwide share of the personal computer market to nearly 10 percent, making it second only to all-powerful IBM. The personal computer market was up for grabs as nobody had more than 11–12 percent of the blooming global market. Things could only get better for Apple. Mosaic could be gone in 6 months.

A classic rock station blasted from my radio as I waited for a red stoplight to turn. The emblem of a polished horse glistened from the car next to me. These Ferrari's are a dime a dozen in Silicon Valley, I thought. They are usually the first things a software engineer buys when his or her stock options mature. It is a common story. First, a college grad takes any old job long enough to get a foot in the door. Then he or she works 80 hours per week, makes a mark, and quits to join a startup! Visions of fat stock options dance in the youngster's head. I was jarred back to reality when the Ferrari roared off into the distance—layering more dust onto my grimy Ford Bronco. My Mosaic friends, you see, were seeking their own Ferrari's. So much for corporate loyalty in Silicon Valley.

Life was good in the summer of 1994. Venture capitalists poured $5.3 billion into 1,036 startups and second round companies. Most of the money went into network equipment companies. Mosaic Communications seemed to be at the right place at the right time. In the case of Mosaic, the return was fantastic. A year later, the startup would change its name to Netscape Communications, and the VC moneymen would cash out at IPO time to the tune of $2.8 billion. Not bad for a company that was worthless 15 months earlier. I didn't know this, however, as I made my way to the front door. But I was fully aware that this is the way the Valley works.

Silicon Valley commands a 37 percent market share of all U.S. hi-tech businesses. With $500 billion in market value, Valley companies employ nearly 15 percent of all computer-related workers in the U.S. Hollywood controls 55 percent of the U.S. entertainment business, for example, but its market value is only $50 billion—one-tenth that of Silicon Valley's. Detroit's auto industry is approximately $100 billion (64 percent market share), New York controls 26 percent of the financial services market, but it still falls $100 billion short of Silicon Valley's valuation! Nestled almost entirely within Santa Clara County, ground zero of Silicon Valley is an economic powerhouse. I pondered the chicken-and-egg question, "Does greed chase after money, or does money come soon after the onset of greed?"

My turncoat friends escorted me into the cafeteria where we spent the next hour catching up and discussing why they had left the plush Apple campus for this scrappy startup. It wasn't the money they declared—it was the challenge. They were eager to knock off Microsoft. They had failed to kill Microsoft while at Apple, so Mosaic was their second chance. After all, Microsoft wasn't even a Silicon Valley company. How could it steal the limelight from companies like Apple, Oracle, Sun, Intel, Cisco, and the other legends of the Valley? Such daring was so preposterous, I thought, that it might make a good story for an article. The article would be about how Microsoft and Intel would loose their grip on hi-tech.

In 1994 Microsoft was an unknown to most ordinary people. Its stock price, and hence its power, was still fledgling at $45 per share—about what it had been 2 years earlier. Windows 3.1 was no match for the Macintosh operating system, and few decision-makers in corporate America took Microsoft products very seriously. Personal computers would never become the fabric of the enterprise. Perhaps they could be used as terminals connected to the big machines, or maybe they could replace typewriters. But, the thought of turning control over to a

Microsoft product rarely gained much credibility. It was simply too risky for the bean counters.

The hardware side of the computer industry was a different question. Intel was already the darling of the stock market. Most people had at least heard of the company. Intel was respected for its revenue growth and was clearly pushing its way to the top of the computer hardware pyramid. Intel faithfully tracked Moore's Law, which required a doubling of performance every 18 months. And Intel had sustained its torrid pace for over two decades. Incredibly, single-chip processors were beginning to challenge the big guys. Intel was so successful that it invited major competitors.

Motorola, IBM, and Apple Computer had their own idea of who should be King of the Valley. The AIM (Apple-IBM-Motorola) consortium intended to stop Intel in its tracks. The battle storm clouds were forming as I sat with my friends and planned the downfall of Intel and Microsoft—what soon would be known of as the Wintel monopoly. Who would win, and who would lose in the next round? What fortunes remained to be gained, and what reversals of fortune awaited laggard companies?

The following essay offers three futures of the computer industry, circa 1994. In hindsight, the first two scenarios were completely wrong. But, the third scenario turned out to be exactly what happened between 1994 and 1998. AIM quickly collapsed—its fortunes were reversed—not Wintel's. The Wintel partnership was about to become a major swell as AIM and other challenges faded. But, I didn't know this in the warm and breezy summer of 1994 as I said goodbye to my friends and drove home, contemplating the purchase of more Apple Computer stock.

Article by Ted Lewis, Computer, August 1994

A Reversal of Fortunes?

If business is war, the computer business is thermonuclear war. Consider the latest battles of the decade: IBM's PowerPC versus Intel's Pentium, and Microsoft's Windows 4.0 versus everyone else.

In 1976, IBM sowed the seeds of its decline by canceling the 801 Project after several years of heavy R&D. The 801 was the original RISC project based on John Cocke's ideas. Because it would have led to the obsolescence of IBM's own products, 801 was killed by the White Plains bean counters. As often happens with powerful organizations, a decade passed before the seriousness of this decision sunk in and IBM began reporting embarrassing balance sheets. But die-hard technologists at IBM hung in there to rise again, in the form of the workstation products group. Fortunately for IBM, fanciful RISC daydreaming resurfaced a decade later.

Then a funny thing happened while slumming with those wild-and-wacky upstarts at Apple Computer. Besides peddling disk drives to the Quiche Eaters of Cupertino, the IBMers discovered a shared taste for palace rebellion. In addition to putting IBM disk drives in Macintoshes, they concocted the PowerPC strategy to blunt the advances of the Huns of Microsoft and Intel and save Motorola and the American Way of Free Enterprise. The basic idea was that any challenge to Intel's dominance of the merchant processor market had to be commodity based. Millions of chips would have to be embedded in everything from personal computers to toasters. That is, the PowerPC had to be cheap and fast.

IBM and Apple made the game even more interesting by challenging the software platform responsible for selling massive quantities of Intel chips. Taligent was created to win the software platform wars, and Kaleida to win the multimedia application wars. Again, the strategy was simple: Flood the market with commodity-priced operating system software designed to knock off market leader Microsoft. With true competition returned to the marketplace, IBM and Apple would once again be able to play on a level field. Product quality rather than dominance would once again be rewarded. At least, that was the theory. Now, after billions of dollars and several years, what has changed?

It appears that the PowerPC is headed toward modest success, and the fortunes of Intel are challenged for the first time in a decade. We are on the verge of a new world. But which one? The following parallel universes suggest a major rift in the computer industry to rival the fall of mainframes.

A Tale of Three Companies

Encirclement is a game of strategy, and operating system roulette provides the battleground. The PowerPC chip opens a short-term door for resetting the basic platform of desktop computing. A blitzkrieg of PowerPC boxes running the many dialects of Unix, MacOS, Microsoft Windows, and OS/2 stream out of Austin and Cupertino. Add some side skirmishes, like porting the MacOS to Sun, Hewlett-Packard, and other Unix boxes, and loyalty to Microsoft begins to crumble. The other shoe drops when Apple licenses the MacOS to third-party clone manufacturers in Taiwan who flood the market with low-cost PowerPC boxes. IBM licenses OS/2, and the clone-makers surge. Later in the decade, everyone wants the Taligent OS, and the panzer divisions close in.

Intel finds the shoe on the other foot connected to Motorola's body instead of its own. Intel boxes begin to look like closed proprietary systems that run only Windows 4.0 and Windows NT. In an attempt to recover, Intel races against time to get on the RISC bandwagon, adopting Hewlett-Packard's PA (Precision Architecture) RISC architecture. Intel and Microsoft attempt to quickly convert the base of software that needs an Intel engine and try to reconvince MIS managers at Fortune 1,000 companies that it is still the standard. The MIS managers are not convinced, since every operating system conceived by man runs on the new commodity-priced PowerPC clones. They now have a choice.

Microsoft becomes just a run-of-the-mill multibillion-dollar software company, and the housing market in Redmond takes a dive. Cairo, Chicago, Daytona, and subsequent counterattacks by Microsoft fail because those zippy applications (including Microsoft's) run on a PowerPC box under your favorite OS, and from your favorite vendor. The operating-system war ends, and vendors compete on the basis of quality, price, and value added. The story ends happily for the Quiche Eaters who divide a much bigger (quiche) pie because the clone-makers are now working for IBM and Motorola.

Gone with the Wind

The personal computer industry wipes out the Unix workstation business with a slew of ultrafast boxes based on the PowerPC chip. Solaris, OSF/1, and the many dialects of Unix become too expensive to manage and maintain. Instead, Fortune 1,000 companies opt for the simplicity of PowerPC boxes that run Taligent frameworks or Windows NT on top of the Mach microkernel. Some diehards adopt OS/2 because it is even less costly to manage and maintain, and it provides a bridge from legacy Windows systems to the new world of frameworks. Novell NetWare also becomes a legacy system to be phased out (Novel and Lotus become application software vendors).

Seeing the handwriting on the wall, Intel converts its product line to the PA-RISC architecture over a period of years—becoming half its 1995 size. Microsoft also loses half its revenue because DOS and Windows lose out to Taligent and it takes too long for Microsoft to port Windows 4.0 to the PowerPC architecture. Bill Gates becomes the second richest person in the universe, after John Malone of Tele-Communications Inc. IBM once again dominates the computer industry, commanding 70 percent of the market. Apple becomes just another clone-maker, with most of its revenues coming from consumer electronic products like pagers and TV set-top boxes. Much smaller versions of Sun and HP enter the superPC business running the Taligent OS (and some Next OpenStep applications). Silicon Graphics dominates the supercomputer market with revenues approaching $20 billion per year.

Ironic Wipe-Out

Consumers ignore PowerPC, Taligent, IBM, Motorola, Adobe, Novell, HP, and Apple, and instead follow Microsoft, Lotus, Compaq, Dell and Intel as they lead the world down the x86/Windows 4.0 path. In the year 2000, Intel brings out the PA-RISC chip. Customers loudly complain as Microsoft and Lotus take two years to port their applications into the RISC world. While Bill Gates celebrates the purchase of Italy (for vacations), Apple, IBM, Motorola, and their followers file for bankruptcy. Customers display bronzed Sun, DEC, and HP workstations in glass displays as a reminder of the good old days.

Microsoft's Windows 6.0 running on Intel RISC chips dominates the personal computer industry. It features drag-and-drop e-mail just like Apple PowerTalk, rapid application development frameworks just like Taligent, multithreaded multitasking just like OS/2, and network-loadable modules just like Novell NetWare. Windows 6.0 supports built-in networking, SQL database access, and other plug-and-play features pioneered in 1984 by Apple. Ironic.

CHAPTER TWO

The Tombs of Tech

By early 1995 the outlines of a market shift that would dwarf all other shifts were beginning to appear. Personal computer processors were getting faster and cheaper and the software industry was increasingly being drawn to the masses. Like loaves of bread, computers were rapidly becoming commodities. This spelled trouble for just about everyone in Silicon Valley.

In particular, traditional computer manufacturers were rapidly losing ground to the unknown upstarts who offered toy-like devices at toyland prices. Michael Dell started making computers in his dorm room in Texas, using parts manufactured in Taiwan, software from Redmond, Washington, and mail-order marketing. Dell's approach contrasted sharply with the Brooks Brothers suited direct sales force of IBM, HP, Sun Microsystems, and SGI (Silicon Graphics, Inc.). Dell understood the shift from premium to commodity pricing. IBM, HP, Sun, and SGI would struggle to learn this lesson. The shift was especially subtle for top-of-the-line companies like Cray, Unisys, and CDC. Actually, most of these blue bloods never knew what hit them. As they retreated into the rarefied atmosphere of the multi-million dollar supercomputer market segment, their relevance faded. Eventually, they went the way of the dinosaur. When SGI swallowed Cray Computer a year later, it joined the list of dinosaurs about to go extinct.

In the fall of 1994 it was already becoming apparent that big iron was on its way out. However, I overestimated the cleverness of SGI, thinking it to be a savvy reader of the technology tea leaves. In this next story, I savage the supercomputer industry, but tread far too lightly on SGI. Perhaps it was because the company courted my business.

My cohorts at the Naval Postgraduate School run 3D graphic simulators on SGI hardware, which consumes processing power like it was Kool-Aid. This made me an important customer for SGI. So SGI's

Forrest Baskett invited me to the seat of the SGI Empire to hear the company's vision of supercomputing. I suppose they thought that if SGI impressed me with mega-hertz and bandwidth, I would surely buy more of its $100,000 to $1 million systems.

SGI is spread across a number of campuses in and around Mountain View, California. Its main headquarters building is off of Highway 101 at Shoreline Boulevard. So, I headed north on 101 to SGI's complex, where I listened to the future, as envisioned by the last of the great super-computing companies. As it turned out, I accurately predicted the demise of DEC and others, but I must have been charmed by Forrest Baskett and his co-workers, because I failed to predict the fall of SGI. In hindsight, I should have known better. SGI had no way of protecting itself from the tsunami about to hit the shores of Shoreline Boulevard. Supercomputing was already dead, but it took SGI another four years to realize that Microsoft was rising. This was far too long for SGI's own good.

Article by Ted Lewis, Computer, November 1994

Supercomputers Ain't So Super

This month celebrates Supercomputing 94, when speed junkies gather in D.C. to schmooze and sell their latest iron. But is this the happy-camper crowd of five years ago when parallel processing, super-computing, and Grand Challenges were in the hype? I'm afraid not. These days, Kendall Square Inc. wonders where the money went: Thinking Machines is gone; Cray Computer is living on Seymour's mortgaged wealth; and Intel has been wounded by reports that its machine doesn't really work. So what is wrong with America's lead in high-performance computing?

For one thing, the vendors soaked up government money to build fantastic iron, but forgot the software. With a wink of an eye, super-salespeople claimed peak gigaflop performance without mentioning how to program the things. But Gartner Group (Stamford, Connecticut) rated the top vendors according to "software availability" (applications code, not compilers and operating systems), rather than gigaflops, revealing the embarassing truth about life in the fast lane. Thinking

Machines, Kendall Square, Intel, and Cray Research received failing scores ranging from a dismal 1.0 to 3.5 (out of 31 "killer apps"), while top-ranked Silicon Graphics, Digital Equipment, and IBM received scores of 19.75, 14.50, and 7.25, respectively. Does this correlate with failure and success in the market? You bet.

Another factor is price/performance. I could never understand why a 30-processor multicomputer costs as much as 130 workstations when both contain the same commodity chips. Yet many early big-iron vendors—again with a wink of an eye—cashed in on the speed craze at premium prices. The truth is, you can use a network of workstations to simulate a large-grain parallel computer without ripping out operating system software, breaking and resetting programmers' coding arms, or hocking that prized collection of Peggy Lee recordings. Recently, more than one enterprising computer scientist has referred to this kind of parallel computation as "heterogenous computing." It's not new, but it is news. Expect to hear a lot about heterogeneous computing at Supercomputing 94's watering hole.

Smaller Footprints

Yet another reality is that computing happens on the desktop these days, and not in some fluorescent, air-conditioned, raised-floor computer center. Almost every National Supercomputer Center has free time to give away, if only someone will take it. But, hey, I can let my workstation run all night long, pick up the answer the next morning, and still beat the queue on a Cray C90 or Intel Paragon at the local Center for Really Fast Iron.

What we are talking about here is gigaflops on a budget. After the hype fades, the bottom line is whether or not your system can be programmed, is on your desktop, has a future when you want to scale up to lots of processors, and, by the way, runs your application fast. Sounds like a Silicon Graphics Challenge, doesn't it? I don't normally take sides in these matters, but frankly, SGI has the most sensible strategy to make supercomputing work (DEC and IBM come close, but no cigar). Before you send all that crank e-mail, let me explain.

First, big memory is more important when running "challenge problems" than lots of processors. Academics like me have had a decade to figure out how to partition a big problem into little pieces that can fit into distributed memories, only to discover that message passing is very slow. This means (virtual) shared memory and—to keep the processors busy—large-bus cache memory to boot.

Next, you need to run each processor as a workstation (to do real work, like your budgets and e-mail) and then be able to turn around and spread your application across a farm of boxes. Thus, you need to hide the difference between a network of machines and a single machine (by virtual shared-memory across a network, for example). And of course this means you need a fast network. Throw in a 300-Mflops chip (MIPS R8000) with 64-bit architecture. (OK, OK, it could be DEC Alpha or IBM RIOS-2 as well, but D.H. Brown Associates in Port Chester, New York, ranks MIPS slightly ahead in terms of SPEC92 benchmarks.)

Finally, you need a software strategy so that the installed base of Cray Computer devotees can port their Cray Fortran code onto a new machine with 90 percent lower maintenance fees. (Are you still with me? If not, call SGI, DEC, IBM, or Convex and ask for this stuff.) You need all of this to work today, as well as in three to five years when vendors upgrade to newer hardware and operating system platforms.

The Numbers Crunch

But technology is still not enough, because the market for supercomputers is so small compared to the desktop commodity chip market that you need to slum with the PC and game-machine bunch. Sales of your powerful processor must support high engineering and marketing costs, so you need to cut deals with Sega, Nintendo, Ford Motor, and various set-top-box manufacturers to reach production numbers of millions per year. This makes it all possible, because the next generation of fab will demand an investment of $1 billion just to stay in the game.

The numbers support the strategy. SGI's Koontz (director of marketing) claims 2,500 Challenge systems are in the field. Compare this with about a dozen Cray T3Ds and a handful of just about everything else that strays off the "formula" adopted by SGI. So beware the fast-iron sales engineer. Maybe that wink is usually a nervous twitch.

CHAPTER THREE

Operating System Roulette

SGI was not the only Silicon Valley company among the living dead in late 1994 and early 1995. Indeed, consumers could choose from among many varieties of computer products. There were many alternatives to the Wintel toy computer: UNIX workstations from Sun, HP, and IBM; departmental networked computers running Novell Netware; and desktop machines running IBM's OS/2, not to mention the super-cool Macintosh running the MacOS. But, this was before Microsoft's Windows 95 hit the streets. In early 1995 consumers still had faith in the market. They still believed quality products would always have an advantage over buggy, difficult-to-use, big, and slow products. Consumers would pay a little more for the all-in-one Macintosh ease-of-use, or sleep a little easier when IBM backed a product. Macintoshes sold to millions of independent thinkers in small businesses and at home. It matched the BMW car in the garage. IBM sold OS/2 and Sun sold Solaris to corporations who depended on IBM and Sun to back up their products with relentless service. Millions of companies—large and small— were convinced that Novell would be around forever. NetWare defined the local area network standard. It was the obvious choice of millions.

In, "Is the Macintosh dead meat?" I illustrate a common misconception held by many businesses in the mid-1990s: Companies can be judged by their strong profits. Novell, SGI, and Apple made fists full of profit during 1994–1995. Most people naturally concluded that they were strong companies. But by the end of the year, this misconception would prove a fallacy.

When Microsoft Windows 95 appeared in August, the world would soon learn two things: Profits don't matter—market share does, and

Quality doesn't count as much as quantity. Companies like Apple, SGI, and Novell, that sacrifice market share for short-term profits soon die. Companies like America Online that defer profits in order to gain market share survive and often become dominant in their industries.

The second shock to the system was more difficult to explain. Given a choice between solid goods and shoddy cheap products, consumers will buy the cheap product before the premium-priced superior product. This behavior is well known in the soap and toothpaste business, but it came as a surprise to computer manufacturers. By 1995 the computer industry had become just like any other commodity business.

In 1995 the world had a choice: consumers could continue to pay more for high-quality products and services, or they could settle for lowest-cost bidder goods. They could pay premium prices for the reliability and convenience of a Macintosh, OS/2, or NetWare-based system, or they could buy the cheapest Wintel machine they could find. Consumers voted with their pocketbook, and ordered Wintel products by the truckload. No matter how much money Apple made, its high-margin Macintosh was doomed. No matter how much better Novell's NetWare was in comparison with Microsoft's Windows NT, buyers opted for the lowest cost network system. Like someone dropping into a SpeedyMart for a six pack of beer, computer industry consumers embraced mediocrity.

The industry slide into mediocrity was assisted by Microsoft's monopolistic practices. Microsoft was exercising monopoly power behind the scenes as it rigged its operating system's licenses and Internet Service Provider contracts to favor Microsoft technology and products. The company had been under investigation by the FCC and then the DOJ for several years. But government interest in the company heated up in 1995. U.S. District Judge Stanley Sporkin tried to put a stop to Microsoft's monopolistic licensing agreements when he rejected the proposed 1995 Consent Degree, stating in February 1995 that it did not go far enough in restraining Microsoft. Microsoft's agreement with hardware manufacturers required them to pay an operating system's licensing fee on every machine made, regardless of which operating system actually shipped! It also gave Microsoft preferential treatment by manufacturers—treatment that competitors could not match. Microsoft was making similar deals with the emerging Internet Service Providers, too. The 1995 Consent Decree prevented Microsoft from forcing its customers to buy other Microsoft products in order to get access to Windows. Judge Sporkin was pushed aside by a three-judge appeals court on June 16, 1995, but the U.S. Department of Justice continued its pursuit of Microsoft. Yet the company was sowing the seeds of its own destruction as the world would learn in late 1998 when the U.S. Department of Justice sued Microsoft for violations of the Sherman Antitrust Act of 1891. But in 1995, Microsoft was still just a spoiled child playing the hi-tech game—perhaps too well for its own good.

In the meantime, Microsoft was gaining market share so rapidly that it found itself a household name by late 1995. Its stock price, and hence its market valuation, would quadruple over the next 3 years. Financially, Microsoft created its own Moore's Law, doubling its market cap value every 18 months! Thus, Microsoft proved that market share was worth more than profits. Its competitors proved the folly of taking profits at the expense of market share.

Operating system roulette spun for the last time in 1995 as consumers opted for Windows 95 in their desktop machines and Windows NT in their businesses. Apple Computer and Novell joined the living dead even while the money flowed in because of high margins and a loyal customer base. Both margins and customers were beginning to wither as Microsoft played the increasing returns game to the hilt. The more market share Microsoft accumulated, the more it got.

At the beginning of 1995 I was not overly concerned that Microsoft would win the race. Like Apple Computer itself, I was not willing to admit defeat. But then reality slowly set in. But by the end of the same year, I purchased a Macintosh computer simply to have it bronzed and stored away for a future generation. My bronzed Macintosh was a collector's item.

The answer to my rhetorical question, "Is the Macintosh dead meat?" is "yes." Even though Steve Jobs victoriously returned to Apple and soon turned the company around, the Macintosh would never become a leader again. As the iMac design swept the Apple product line in five flavors and Wintel-beating performance, Apple became more and more a niche player. The Macintosh became a tool of the most discriminating connoisseur, not the masses.

Apple Computer's experience was a symptom of a fundamental shift in the industry. The computer had become a commodity like apples and oranges. When confronted by a commodity, consumers can only judge by one measure—price. The era of quality products was gone, and here is why.

Article by Ted Lewis, Computer, February 1995

Is the Macintosh Dead Meat?

If you're a gambler, 1995 should offer plenty of interest in operating-systems roulette. Is it going to be OS/2, Windows 95 1/2, Novell NetWare, Macintosh System 8, Windows NT, Solaris, Unix, Taligent, Chorus, or NeXTstep? I'm going to wing-walk this month and give a surprise answer. (May I have the envelope, please?)

If you believe what you read, Microsoft will scorch a path to desktop domination. Shortly after Windows 95's late-1995 release, everyone else will surrender to the WinTel (Windows on Intel) juggernaut, or so says the press.

Windows 95 isn't the only reason for Microsoft's domination. According to *Information Week* (December 12, 1994, p. 26), "Microsoft Windows NT will be the standard operating system for database and application servers within two years." The reason? Lower prices and sheer bulk—NT has more ISVs than Unix. Strong words; I guess Sun, HP, SGI, Digital, IBM, Novell, and NeXT may as well give up.

Not!

It's irresponsible for anyone to claim victory months or years before a product is released. So I will add my two cents' worth to the pot and stir it around: The 32-bit operating system wars mean *everything,* and they mean *nothing!*

Price Plays a Role

Panelists interviewed by *New Media* magazine (December 1994, p. 41) generally do not believe that Windows 95 will succeed in wiping out the competition. It will neither kill the Macintosh nor put an end to Unix, they say, pointing to the superior quality and capability of non-Windows 95 products. There are still lots of Mercedes-Benz buyers in this Toyota world. (Phew, it's nice to know somebody else in The Fourth Estate is willing to work with the handicap of straight, honest facts.)

But there's more to the hype than Microsoft envy. Hewlett-Packard rattled its sword by saying it might not license Windows 95 unless Microsoft lowers its price. Vobis Microcomputer (Europe's fourth largest PC distributor) said it will replace DOS and Windows with OS/2 in most of its machines. Again, the reason is that Microsoft is pricing itself out of the market.

Consumer	Corporate	Sleepers
MacOS	Solaris	OpenStep
OS/2	OSF/1 (HP, DEC)	CommonPoint
Windows 95	Windows NT	Microsoft Cairo
	Novell/SuperNOS	

Table 3.1   OS market segments and sleepers promise to make operating-systems roulette more fun than Las Vegas in 1995.

IBM is claiming strong support for OS/2, citing a 20 percent demand for OS/2 Warp among OEMers. The PowerMac is selling like umbrellas in a monsoon, rocketing Apple to the number-one spot in US desktop box sales. It seems that killing Apple will be more difficult than the press pundits would have us believe.

Bigger Players Throw around Their Own Weight

Novell's NetWare/UnixWare is converging on a microkernel technology that will compete very nicely against Windows NT. HP just reaped huge revenues and is now five times larger than Microsoft. Digital is making inroads into client/server shops, and SGI is growing at about a 25 percent annual rate. If you believe the hype, everyone but Microsoft and Intel may as well pack up his or her tent and move on to the next revolution. The numbers, however, don't support the feeding-frenzied press.

This complicated scenario will become even more convoluted. Table 3.1 shows who the players are in each of two segments. The following scenario shows it is not too late to even the playing field by layering frameworks on top of all major operating systems, thus rendering them irrelevant. OpenStep is ready to make a move on the Sun, HP, and possibly Windows platforms, while Taligent's CommonPoint is about to add framework capability to OS/2, Windows, AIX, and MacOS. One or more of the sleepers shown here is positioned to shift the emphasis away from operating systems toward frameworks.

Companies Want One Thing

First, the corporate segment is consumed by client/server mania, which Unix rules. If Windows NT continues to be cheaper and easier to install and maintain than OS/2 and Unix, then it will probably squeeze out OS/2. So OS/2 will lose the departmental-level server battle because it lacks the applications, but Unix is another story. NT lacks the supporting cast of middleware, interoperability, and high-end application software to totally blow away the other vendors in this category. You need TP monitors and enterprise-wide management tools to knock off Unix, and NT doesn't have them.

Consumers Want Another

Now look at the consumer segment in Table 3.1. Clearly, Windows 95 will be dominant here because it is the only Intel alternative for Window 3.1 users, and they are thicker than flies on a camel. The limiting factor here is going to be upgrade costs. The Gartner Group estimates the average upgrade cost to be $1,200 per box. The large installed base of 286 and 386 machines will temper the rate at which users jump onto the Windows 95 bandwagon. Given Apple's strong position with the PowerMac and its upcoming System 8, some consumers will find it more attractive to buy advanced technology from Apple than to invest in the hefty upgrade. A PowerMac 6100 with Windows emulation sells for only slightly more than an upgrade. It is no coincidence that Microsoft is continuing to release new versions of DOS and Windows 3.x even after the introduction of Windows 95. While forging ahead, Microsoft must continue to wage a rear-guard action.

So Who'll Be the Big Winner?

Now comes the surprise ending. The sleeper column of Table 3.1 is full of players who can upset the platform cart. If NeXT, Taligent, or Microsoft successfully covers all major operating systems with a thick layer of application frameworks, as each is attempting to do, then the underlying OS no longer makes any difference. When Windows 95 hits the street, NeXT hopes to have OpenStep running on top of operating systems from Microsoft, Sun, HP, and others. Taligent will have its platform-independent framework called CommonPoint ready for Apple, IBM, Microsoft, and other Unix vendor machines in 1995. Microsoft lags this group because its object-oriented Cairo will not be ready until 1996. Any one of these products could shift the balance of power to any of these framework vendors, rendering the underlying operating systems as staid and boring as they were for decades before Microsoft came along and made things interesting.

CHAPTER FOUR

Silly Valley

By mid-1995 a new idea was hatching in Silicon Valley. The movers and shakers decided it was time to exploit the consumer market space. There were enough computers in homes to support edutainment on CD-ROMs, for example, and the Internet was one big wide screen just waiting to be exploited. There would soon be enough bandwidth—one way or the other—to pipe digital content into the living room of millions of couch potatoes. The special-effects industry would merge with the movie production industry, and the computer industry would be in the best position to exploit the confluence of art and technology. This was the mantra of the wheelers-and-dealers on Sand Hill Road, home of the moneymen.

Silicon Valley could become the twenty-first century's consumer product production studio. After all, the neighborhood around Oracle, SGI, and Apple began to realize that the really big money was in entertainment. A combination of greed and a desire to see oneself on the big screen turned into zeal as Larry Ellison of Oracle, Steve Jobs of Pixar, and Ed McCracken of SGI began to pitch their visions of computers and entertainment.

By the end of 1995, Silicon Valley was going Hollywood. Venture Capitalists were throwing money into startups like Cloud 9 ($3 million in June 1995), Humongous Entertainment, and Digital Domain (James Cameron's *Titanic*). It was the Next Big Thing.

The place was turning into Silly Valley, as far as I was concerned. Like its flamboyant sister in L.A., San Jose, California was getting weird. Technology was giving way to event marketing. Event marketing was giving way to a "hits" mentality. Most of the companies were missing instead of hitting, however. Within 2 years numerous startups went belly up, and the buzz had passed to the Web. The whole idea was stillborn.

This episode illustrates how fallible Silicon Valley is. When it flops, it flops big time. But, the Silly Valley epidemic provided a year of living dangerously. It also provided a lesson in humility, but not for long!

The foray into entertainment emphasized once again, the importance of having a large installed base of users for your products. Combined with the rising tide of the Internet, the urgent need to capture large audiences drove the computer industry into flights of fancy. Computer companies began to attack the living room with exaggerated claims that they could provide consumers with video-on-demand, pervasive home entertainment computers, and Internet bliss. The hyperbole was thicker than Java hype—the marketing buzz surrounding Sun Microsystem's new programming language, which was unveiled in the midst of this ballyhoo in May of 1995. Perhaps a bit of Hollywood rubbed off on Java, which explains why Java reality fell short of Java hype that year.

I went out on a limb and predicted that the consumer device of choice would be the plain ordinary (multimedia) computer—not some exotic set-top box, or glorified video game. In hindsight, I was right. After a lull in home adoptions, the home computer market regained its momentum in 1998, and was expected to reach the magic 50 percent penetration level by 2000. While actual penetration was a few years behind my forecast, nothing appears to be slowing the PC-as-consumer-device trend. The question remains, "How will content reach the home computer?" With such a huge potential, content will find a way into the home computer, no doubt. Exactly how, remains to be seen.

As this goes to press, the DVD standard has been settled and DVD drives are available for PCs as well as stand-alone consoles. These digital devices are the first to hold an entire movie. Combining them with home computers will provide an infrastructure for the dissemination of books, movies, and music—exactly where the money is. And DVD overcomes the Internet's bandwidth limitation.

We are on the threshold of yet another era in the expansion of various hi-tech industries. Only this time, Silicon Valley will seduce Hollywood—not the other way around. But in 1999 Silicon Valley still felt the sting of failure to become one with Hollywood. Alex Gove, writing in *The Red Herring* (January 1998, pp. 62), says, "Digital Hollywood continues to puzzle VCs," and titled his article, "There's no business like no business." The transition to digital edutainment is taking longer than Silly Valley expected.

Article by Ted Lewis, Computer, June 1995

Where the Big Money Is

Someone once told me that toy manufacturers had greater influence over computer design than computer scientists. I was young and brash and ignored this sage insight until decades later when the evidence mounted. The really big bucks are in consumer software products (about $90 billion per year), not information processing ($30–40 billion), client/server software (a few billion), scientific computing (maybe $2 billion), or multimedia (tens of billions). I'm no good at driving a hard bargain, but I could probably *buy* the Internet for a few months of revenue from the consumer software market as defined in Figure 4.1. As the saying goes, "If you've got the gold, you rule."

May I Have This Dance?

The PC industry has been seduced by all that glitters in Hollywood. I'm talking about the latest dance craze to hit Silicon Valley. Everyone knows about Bill Gates and the Dream Team, but the little guys in San Jose, Mountain View, Sunnyvale, and Palo Alto are also standing in line to autograph fat contracts with the "content kings." Content means edutainment—from million-unit best-sellers like *Myst* to personal libraries like *Encarta*. Join the technical staff of Silicon Graphics, Oracle, or any of the hundreds of companies listed in the *San Jose Mercury's* Monday business section, and your next assignment is likely to be consumer software development for the masses. Good times have returned to the valley with a vengeance, only this time you'll need to know who Rosebud was.

It Doesn't Have to Make Sense

What little logic there is to the dance craze gets twisted into Hollywood fables about the consumer's insatiable appetite for content and about how movie moguls have more marketing and distribution know-how than computer nerds. But even twisted logic has little to do with it. The edutainment business doesn't have to make sense, because it makes money. That may sound unfair, yet there's more than greed behind this stampede; there's the track record of revolutionary products to blame.

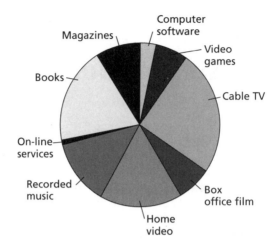

Figure 4.1 *How the $84-billion consumer software pie was divided in 1993. (Source: Jeffries & Co. Inc.)*

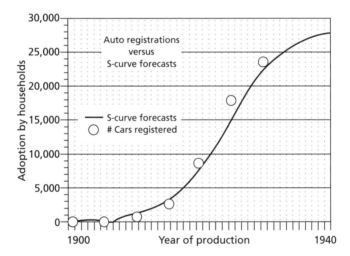

Figure 4.2 *Rapid growth of automobiles per household between 1915 and 1930. More than 14 million Model As were sold, which was a record until Volkswagen edged past Ford in the 1960s.*

Take, for example, the rise of the automobile, more fashionably known as the personal car (the original PC) revolution (see Figure 4.2). In a mere 15 years Henry Ford revolutionized transportation and nearly everything else about the American Way. He simultaneously wiped out the horse-drawn-carriage industry; put a dent in bus, train, and riverboat industries; and also made a few billion for himself. Sound familiar? History is repeating itself, only this time the product is going into everyone's living room, not garage. Figure 4.3, you'll notice, is amazingly similar to

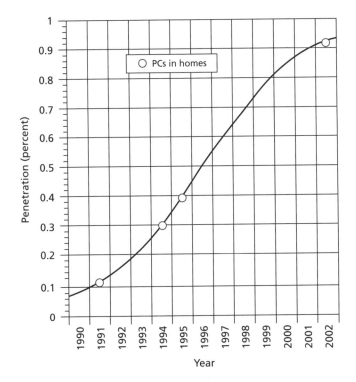

Figure 4.3 *Projected growth curve (based on Dataquest estimates) for installed base of home computers from 1990 to 2002.*

Figure 4.2, even to the time scale. (If you really have to know, the two logistics growth curves differ by a small amount—the exponential component of the curve for cars is 0.2271 and that of the PC curve is 0.388.)

We Don't Need No Stinkin' Set-top Boxes

I think the computer and communications industry can forget the set-top box, HDTV, and video-game-players like Sega, Nintendo, and 3DO: They're the Stanley Steamers of the Information Age. The game-player, set-top box, TV, telephone, VCR, and office are already wrapped up in the home PC. In the next two years, home computers will surpass video-game-players in terms of home market saturation.

The battle lines are already drawn, not around PCs, but around the slices shown in Figure 4.1. The next king-of-the-hill in magazines will be the outfit that electronically packages magazines for playback via the family PC (or PCs—who says there'll be only one?). Ditto for books, music, film, games, and on-line services.

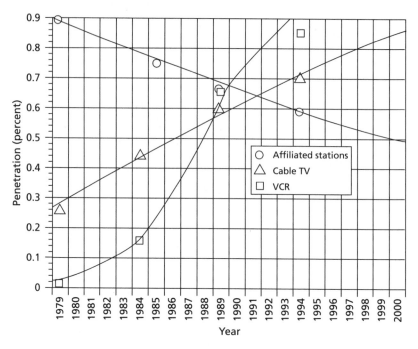

Figure 4.4 *Impact of narrowcasting on edutainment for the years 1970 through 1990 (Source: Nielsen BBDO Media Update, April 2, 1990), then projected through 2000.*

Being Digital

Read Nicholas Negroponte's book, *Being Digital,* (Knopf) if you want the details. Basically, being digital means using technology to personalize consumer products and services (and a bunch of other things there isn't room for here). Personalization in the media business means narrowcasting instead of broadcasting. Narrowcasting fits individuals, not masses. Negroponte is right on target, as shown in my final figure of the day, Figure 4.4. The trend is obvious: Mass media is sinking into oblivion, while products based on narrowcasting (for example, VCR tapes) are surging onto the market, just like Henry Ford's Model A. Whenever you see one of these S-curves, look out!

Being Cool

The size of the VCR tape rental market far exceeds the box office theater market, and just about everything else. This "content" will quickly find its way onto long-playing CD-ROMs for your home computer. It's one step away from being really cool with your friends; everyone who is anyone in 2002 will own a multifunctional PC. That, my friends, will influence the design of microprocessors more than all the computer scientists in the firmament.

CHAPTER FIVE

A Monopoly Is Born

A visitor from another land might think Windows 95 was a life-prolonging elixir or perhaps a remedy for famine, pestilence, and war, judging by the marketing hype that surrounded its introduction in August 1995. In hindsight, the impact of Windows 95 on the world of computing was no less than the hype. Windows 95 changed everything, and consolidated Microsoft's position in the computer industry.

Microsoft had tried for over a decade to duplicate the Macintosh's legendary ease-of-use. In fact, in 1988 the company won a landmark court decision in a contest with Apple Computer over who owned the GUI (Graphical User Interface). Apple lost. The decision established Microsoft's right—or any other company's right—to copy the graphical user interface of the Apple Mac. It opened the intellectual property floodgates for imitators.

Microsoft's first two attempts at imitation failed. Windows 3.0 was limited and buggy. Windows 3.1 was much improved, but still no match for the Macintosh. After almost a decade of trying, Microsoft finally got it right. Microsoft's Windows 95 turned Intel's hardware into a Macintosh—or at least close enough that many consumers could not tell the difference.

But the success of Windows 95 was no accident. Microsoft worked its way to the top through a series of never-say-die trials and tribulations. Its first editions were often barely usable by customers. Still, the company kept coming back. Version two usually showed more promise, but it took Microsoft three tries to get it right. Windows 95 was number three. It was the beginning of Microsoft-as-monopoly.

By Christmas 1995 it became obvious that Microsoft had gotten it right, even though Windows 95 failed to deliver on many of its promises. Plug-and-Play became an unfulfilled pledge, for example. Regardless, Windows 95 became a household name, and Bill Gates became a celebrity.

Windows NT was supposed to be the corporate version of Windows 95, but the market had difficulty differentiating the two. No matter, Windows 95's success made the company forget its game plan—at least for a while. As Windows 95 sold over 50 million copies, Windows NT took on a different competitor—UNIX. By early 1996 a strategy emerged for dominating the world. Windows 95 would kill off the Macintosh and IBM's OS/2, and Windows NT would go after UNIX. This two-pronged attack on the entire computer industry worked so well that Microsoft eventually attracted the attention of the U.S. Department of Justice.

To the outside observer, Apple Computer seemed complacent throughout this period, but behind the wall of its Cupertino buildings, it was rife with chaos and strife. Management vacillated between extremes: sometimes it positioned the company to be bought out, only to back away when pursued; other times it put its head in the sand, pretending that Microsoft Windows did not exist. All the while, the company was in re-organization hell.

Co-founders Steve Jobs and Steve Wozniak were long gone, and the bean counters from consumer product companies like Procter and Gamble overran the place. Morale dropped, and by the time Windows 95 was six months old, most of the smart people at Apple had taken off for greener pastures. The line of Apple escapees at Netscape's door grew as Apple Computer sunk under siege.

After suffering through a series of CEOs who really did not understand the computer industry, and posting several quarters of losses, Apple Computer woke up to the reality that Windows 95 had turned the commodity PC into a premium product that competed very well against the Macintosh. Time began running out for the premier personal computer company as its product direction floundered and Mac loyalists began to wander off into the Wintel camp.

The next essay evoked extensive criticism, because many readers thought me overly biased against Apple. Even Wintel readers accused me of slamming the hopes and aspirations of an entire industry. Unfortunately, history turned out to be even darker.

Within three years of Windows 95's introduction, all of my predictions became reality, and computer industry reality was darker than my tongue-in-cheek characterization. Looking back, reality has been tougher on Apple than I was! If anything, Windows 95 was bigger than nickel beer, and my dire predictions completely underestimated Windows NT's success. The essay erred on the conservative side: I was oblivious to the monopolistic undertow of Microsoft rising.

Article by Ted Lewis, Computer, August 1995

Windows 95: Next Step to Desktop NT?

This month marks the scheduled, and long-anticipated, release of Windows 95, one of the most hyped and overpreviewed sofware products in the history of software marketing. The cat has been out of the bag for a long time. Still, some people are wondering whether Win95 is a golden fleece or just a feline hair ball. The verdict? It's golden.

Still under Construction

Not everything is golden for Win95, however. *Computerworld* (May 1, 1995, p. 1) cautions, "Plug-and-play will be more promise than reality. Older PCs will be unable to take full advantage of Plug and Play . . . in fact it could be at least two years before Windows 95 users can count on full Plug and Play capabilities. . . ." The article goes on to tell Mac and OS/2 users what they suspected all along: "We're changing 10 years of nightmares. . . ." But this is just a detour marked "under construction."

Just Like Selling Razor Blades

One of the highest praises I have heard is, "Win95 is as good as a Macintosh." Actually, it looks to me like Win95 is even better than a Macintosh. *PC Computing* (July 1995, p. 186) paints a rosy picture and quotes Tim Bajarin: "Although OS/2 and the MacOS are excellent, Microsoft has already won the battle." Dataquest quantified the demise of competition with projections of extinction for OS/2 and dwindling market share for everyone else (see Figure 5.1). Lou Gerstner better dump OS/2 and get on the CHRP (Common Hardware Reference Platform) bandwagon in a hurry. Mike Spindler better start giving MacOS licenses away in cereal boxes. According to software industry observers, Win95 will halt OS/2 sales and drive the MacOS to its lowest ever market-acceptance level.

Microsoft will make a cool $1 billion from Win95 in 1996, rising to $7.5 billion in four years (see Figure 5.1). At $50 per pop, and with 20 million first-year buyers, Win95 will reach double-quadruple platinum in short order. Think of it as the software equivalent of razor

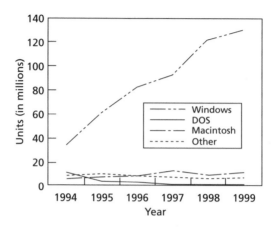

Figure 5.1 *Projected shipments of PC operating systems through 1999. The Windows projections include Win95. "Other" includes OS/2 (the 1995 installed base of OS/2 was estimated at 5.9 million). (Source: Dataquest Inc., as published in* MacWeek, *April 17, 1995, p. 20.)*

blades. In addition, Win95 will stimulate heavy demand for Pentiums, RAM, and bigger color monitors. Win95 is not a product, it is an entire industry. But is it the real thing? First, a short explanation of why Win95 will squeeze out everyone else.

So Long, Macintosh

The biggest initial impact will be felt in corporate computing, because Win95 is aimed at the rabid client-server market as well as at the Christmas gift-buying herd. This is because Plug and Play almost works, Wizards lurk everywhere to reduce training costs, and the kernel can multi-task. Rather than reboot each time a faulty Microsoft application hangs up, simply press Ctrl + Alt + Del to kill it. (Microsoft still thinks a user interface is a keyboard with F1 through F20 on it. Many DOS-like gestures remain in Win95.) IS managers love this kind of end-user assistance. It reduces calls in the night. It used to sell Macintoshes. Good-bye, Macintosh.

Adios, Novell

The corporate homogenizers will also be pleased to learn that Win95 is more than network friendly. Win95 understands peer-peer networking. In addition, a single desktop can control all other desktops connected via the LAN. Security issues have been thought out too, so your company jewels are safe. You can use Novell's ODI driver, but Win95's NetWare client software is faster and doesn't use as much memory. Along with Microsoft's Windows NT server, this little driver is aimed at forcing Novell off the road and into the ditch. Scratch Novell off the OS shopping list.

Good-bye, OS/2

Because Win95 is "just like a Macintosh," and OS/2 was as close to a Mac as IBM could make it, we no longer need "Mac on an Intel platform." OS/2 sales will be derailed like a train wreck. Too bad; it could have been a contender.

Don't Worry, It Won't Last Long

In spite of the frenzy over Win95, Microsoft says it is all for no good reason. Win95 is just a warm-up for the real OS. *Computerworld* (April 17, 1995, p. 6) reports, "Microsoft is going to reposition NT as Windows for desktop users in the 1997–98 time frame." Microsoft quietly announced in March that after its release Win95 would be added to Windows NT. "The plan signals the merger of the two systems into a single code base, which means Microsoft will phase out the current architecture of desktop Windows in favor of NT, a company official confirmed last week." In fact, before a software developer can claim Windows 95 compatibility, Microsoft requires that its applications run on both Win95 and NT boxes. This will clear the path for NT. If you have trouble getting excited about Win95, don't worry. Win95 will pass like a breeze in the night.

So why bother? Why not simply skip Win95 and start replacing those Windows 3. × systems with NT systems now, in anticipation of the NT onslaught due in 24 months? Just say "no" and wait until NT-with-Win95-GUI-and-Win95-applications is officially released.

While Cupertino Burns

Jon Swartz (*MacWeek,* April 17, 1995, p. 20) predicts, "IBM will kill off the [OS/2] platform sometime next year because of poor sales." This leaves Apple and the MacOS as the only remaining hope for free enterprise. So what is Apple doing about Win95? Copland (a.k.a. System 8) will ride to the rescue in 1996. It will incorporate end-user customization of its GUI, multitasking, and hardware independence (portability).

This is pathetic. Who cares about reconfigurable GUIs and portability? Surely not the consumer. To successfully compete, a product has to be 10 times better than the one it tries to displace. Reconfigurable icons and menus won't impress business and home buyers: GUI customization is simply not an order of magnitude better. Apple's fascination with GUI design is distracting the company from its number one objective: gaining market share. Only a radically superior OS, or uncommon marketing, can save Apple. Once a technology leader, Apple is on the defensive; it must play catch-up, or die. Meanwhile, back in Cupertino, someone is redrawing the org charts. Two thousand years ago, someone in a similar situation played a fiddle.

CHAPTER SIX

Ellison's Folly

Winter 1996 was an extremely wet season for northern California. Flood and mud was the standard of the day as I crept through traffic on Highway 101 on my way to Moscone Center in San Francisco. I had gotten up at 4 A.M. to beat the traffic, but ended up taking nearly 4 hours to drive 90 miles through the rain. There were casualties on all sides as commuters played bumper-car. This is worth it, I thought, to see and hear Oracle's CEO, Larry Ellison, speak.

I had become a willing victim of hype—Larry Ellison's NC (Network Computer) hype. Ellison's Redwood Shores, California company dominated the enterprise database segment of the software business, but it was a distant second or third in size and influence when compared with Microsoft. This irritated Mr. Ellison. It irritated other captains of the computer industry, too. Many of them thought it would be nice to recapture the lead that Bill Gates and Microsoft had stolen from them. So the hype machine began its work—agitating for a revolution. And like so many others in Silicon Valley, I was itching for a revolution.

Silicon Valley was energized for a while as it looked like the crown might pass to a new King of the Valley. Could Ellison and his Silicon Valley cohorts wrest control of the computer industry away from Bill Gates? While the very idea drew thousands of techno-geeks to Moscone to listen, it seemed like a long shot. Microsoft simply had a stranglehold on the whole industry. But the hype continued as Ellison entertained the conference attendees. I forgot about the flood and mud as Ellison hyped the crowd that dark and damp morning in San Francisco.

What started out to be the Next Big Thing would soon fizzle and become Ellison's Folly. But before he slipped into anonymity, Ellison's colorful diatribes drew plenty of readers to editorials of valley trade magazines. Ellison called the PC a "ridiculous device," because it cost too much, was too difficult to use, and ate maintenance budgets like his jet fighter airplane ate windshield bugs.

Ellison was reacting to Microsoft's alarming success with Windows 95, and Wintel's growing dominance of the computer industry. By 1996 it had become clear that Microsoft was monopolizing the entire computer industry. But he had a plan for reversing Microsoft's runaway success. His NC would become the Next Big Thing. It would be much cheaper, simpler, and easier to use than Windows 95. It would cost less than $500 because storage would reside on a server somewhere; it would be simpler because software would be automatically downloaded whenever needed; and it would be easier to use because . . . well Ellison wasn't very clear on that!

The NC never made it to prime time in Silicon Valley. By the time Oracle, Sun Microsystems, Wyse, and others made their scaled down boxes work, the "NC scare" had passed. In Silicon Valley you are either quick or toast. The NC manufacturers were toast. As it turned out, Microsoft and Intel could make NCs faster and better than Ellison and his counter-revolutionaries could. All they had to do was turn Moore's Law upside down. Instead of doubling performance every 18 months while holding prices level, Wintel vendors merely cut the price in half while holding performance constant. By mid-1998 over 42 percent of all PC sales were for machines costing less than $1,000.

Also, Ellison had difficulty convincing his troops that the NC was the golden opportunity they were looking for. His own people were skeptical, so he commissioned Frog Design to build a mockup, which he unveiled during a trip to Japan. He evangelized the concept at every opportunity. He seemed to especially enjoy trading insults with Bill Gates at industry conferences. Ellison shamelessly promoted the NC to President Bill Clinton while riding in the back seat with the president during a visit to Silicon Valley. Ellison was everywhere for a while, and then suddenly, he was gone. Easy come, easy go. The NC phenomenon was a bust.

The NC turned out to be more useful as a rallying cry for the anti-Microsoft forces than as a useful product. Strategy was center stage, while substance was somewhere out in the audience. The whole NC phenomenon turned out to be an embarrassing mistake. But, it could have turned the tide against Microsoft rising.

Ellison's Folly was not to be. Instead, another company would challenge Microsoft, at another time. Only, it would require the U.S. Department of Justice as a partner. Still, it is fun to speculate on what would have happened if Ellison had been right. In the next essay, written at the beginning of the NC debacle, I describe three scenarios: NC kills PC, The ridiculous PC wins, and NC as Trojan Horse. In hindsight, scenario two is close to what really happened. The computer industry would have evolved in a much different way if one of the other two scenarios had come true.

Article by Ted Lewis, Computer, February 1996

The NC Phenomena: Scenes from Your Living Room

Scene I: NC Kills PC

The industry is bracing for the slim possibility that the NC will go over bigger than the Beatles revival. The $500 NC (processor with 32 megabytes of RAM, modem, and CRT/keyboard) is rumored to boot up directly from the Internet without much help from Microsoft. All you have to do is brush away the environmentally incorrect foam packing, plug it into a power outlet, flip the "on" switch, and give it your credit card's vital statistics. There is some hallway scuffling about whether it will connect via a telephone or a CATV (cable) modem, but this debate will be resolved in time.

Then the NC logs you into the Internet access provider and starts Netscape Navigator 98. Cyber Simpsons are too dumb to set their VCR clocks, so they won't notice the absence of Windows 95, MacOS, or Motif/Unix. Instead, they will see the simple home page of Netscape and a version of Navigator that can handle e-mail, Adobe Acrobat PDF files, audio and video (picture-phone) files, and billing (to ensure that everyone gets paid out of your Mastercard account).

Two kinds of companies will be affected by this sea change: those that go out of business after a few years because they built $500 Internet terminals, and those that will make even bigger profits by giving away razors so that they can sell razor blades. The razor blade companies will teach us another lesson in Info Age marketing. How so?

The survivors will be the old-line PC companies that retool to sell stripped-down PCs (think of Apple's Pippin or the original Macintosh with a built-in screen and a cable modem in place of a disk drive as a model of the first NC). These machines will be able to boot from the Internet, of course, but they will have other capabilities, too. For example, they will have a large socket in the back where the Internet-jaded consumer can plug in a CD-ROM disk drive for an additional $300. This allows the kids to play MUDs (Multi-User Doom) with dozens of other kids in Asia and Europe.

The successful NC will also have a port for a 10-gigabyte read/write optical disk drive. Thus, the appliance-challenged consumer can add applications software purchased over the Net. Products like Fractal Design Painter 4.0 will eat up 2 Gbytes (sample works of art), and

MathCAD will devour another 3 Gbytes by holding various math models. (Both applications work across the Internet.) The market for razor blades—correction, peripherals and software—will mushroom as delighted consumers buy their own storage devices so that they don't have to rely on the "virtual disk" of the Internet. Freedom has its price—adding another $500 to the $500 NC.

Credit-card-wielding consumers continue to add peripherals (scanner, printer, graphics accelerator card) and software (hand recognition, voice recognition, telephony, art and architecture software) until the typical home has a full-powered PC in the living room, another in the office, and two in the kids' bedrooms. The typical family ends up owning several PCs, each costing far more than the all-in-one $2,500 PC. The NC adds billions more to the coffers of the PC industry through the sale of add-ons, which would never have been possible by way of a more logical approach. This concludes the lesson in Info Age marketing.

Bottom line: Bill Gates announces his candidacy for president, and Andy Grove runs for vice president. Apple Computer ships its 100 millionth Mac (achieving 5 percent market share, for the 20th time) and fueling rumors that the company will be taken over by a consortium of Japanese companies (also for the 20th time).

Scene 2: The Ridiculous Device (Wintel PC)

In this imaginary scenario, predictions of the PC's decline turn out to be NC hype as the techno-buzz spewing from Oracle, Sun, and the seven dwarfs joins a long list of "next big thing" fairy tales like the pervasive personal digital assistant, the electric car, and smaller government. The "ridiculous device" is not so ridiculous after all. It rules the living room as television sales decline and Andy Grove's outlandish billion-processor sales prediction becomes a reality.

Ignoring Larry Ellison of Oracle, millions of mail-order-catalog consumers flex their credit-card muscle as if buying trash romance novels at Borders Book Store. The bloated PC rules, and sales of CD-ROM software climb, per Figure 6.1. Crazed by relentless Windows 95 hype, lured by the prospect of dirty talk on CompuServe, trafficking in explicit GIFs from *Playboy's* home page, and rationalizing hours spent unlocking the keys to wealth via AOL's stock market services, living room lemmings consume $2,500 PCs at an even faster rate, running up record consumer debt.

Things get worse everywhere. Wintel sucks up the video game business (after Microsoft finally catches up with the graphics capability of the Macintosh) and makes bigger and bigger inroads into work-at-home, learn-at-home, shop-at-home, bank-at-home, and stay-at-home. Microsoft

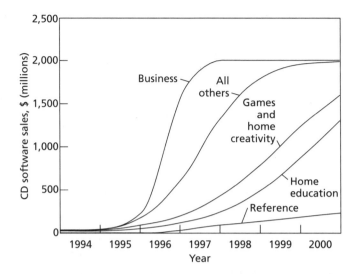

Figure 6.1   *Sales forecast for CD software. (Sources: Software Publishers' Association; NewMedia magazine, Dec. 1995, p. 24.)*

and Intel get bigger, richer, and more arrogant as sales of overpowered Super Pentiums with 10-gigabyte disk drives, 1-million-polygon/second graphics engines, and 10-megabit/second cable modems flood living rooms with the billiard-room glow of multimedia.

In fact, by the time you read this, the NC scare may already have become such old news that it leaves this writer with egg on his face for lending credence to the possibility of NC as the next big thing. In this scenario, the NC revolution lasts about as long as standard agreements among Unix rivals.

Bottom line: Bill Gates announces his candidacy for president, and Grove seeks appointment as secretary of state. Apple achieves 5 percent market share, again, and takeover rumors abound. Larry Ellison is never heard of again.

Scene 3: The Trojan Horse Ploy

I n this scenario, Microsoft's worst nightmare springs from the shadows of the multiheaded Nethead Gang. This gang (see December 1995 column) realizes its vision of world domination through a combination of slick marketing and a replay of the ancient Trojan Horse scenario. In fact, their game plan is so diabolical that it makes the Trojan Horse gambit look like George Bush's presidential campaign.

You may have noticed that Netscape Navigator plays a major role in all future Wired World fantasies, because anti-Microsoft forces will do just about anything to destroy Wintel dominance. Netscape appears to be the only weapon these anarchists have, especially since most computer company managers lack imagination, technical competence, or both. As a consequence of this dull-mindedness, the whiz kids at Netscape are basking in attention. But they are neither stupid nor just plain lucky, as some folks think: They have a plan. Here is how their plan could unfold.

The first salvo was the appearance of Navigator 2.0's plug-in architecture. Plug-ins are the gates of Troy standing wide open, a fact of life that has not been lost on most software developers. These savvy software companies are busily supplying Netscape plug-ins for doing everything from translating a home page from English into Japanese to modernizing OLE so that it can work over the Internet. The Navigator plug-in market is the real componentware of the decade. Forget Java, OLE, OpenDoc, and Corba and cash in on the plug-in rush before it's too late.

Now, to make this fantasy even more interesting, suppose a small unknown company in Europe constructs a version of Netscape that I will call NOS, or Netscape On Steroids. This is Navigator 98 with megabytes of plug-ins. They do everything that Windows 98 does, plus more. In fact, this version of Netscape obviates the need for Windows 98, Unix, and the MacOS. Anyone with a $2,500 NC (the ones with the big disks, CD-ROM drives, and other peripherals) can run any application, from the Internet or not, with a single copy of supercharged NOS. The little company in Europe sells out to Netscape Communications for a measly $100 million (they never get out of their garage). The principals in this company move to Mountain View, where they are immediately put to work writing a small network operating system kernel that supports the Windows 98 API. The belly of the Trojan Horse opens and out come free copies of NOS. Users throw away Windows 98 and run all of their applications on top of NOS. Before Microsoft realizes it, 50 percent of its income is diverted into the Netscape treasury. Novell puts its NetWare business up for sale, and IBM gives Lotus back to Manzi.

Bottom line: Netscape's Jim Clark runs for president, and Bill Gates retires and runs for mayor of Redmond. How does Apple achieve 5 percent share? Since 1996 its Cyberdog has been doing what NOS finally does. So once again Apple captures 5 percent of the market, and leading industry watchers predict a buyout.

What's Wrong with These Pictures?

Each of these highly cynical scenarios has something wrong. After all, it's entirely likely that nothing much will change and the PC industry of 2006 will look a lot like the industry of 1996. One argument that supports the status quo is the notion that the $500 NC is not unlike existing video game products, and the video game segment is almost as large as the PC industry. Today's coexistence of the PC and video game markets may be a model for the future coexistence of the PC and the NC.

Microsoft's dominance is nearly ensured for the next 100 years (OK, OK, this is a boast, but how long have DuPont, Standard Oil, AT&T, IBM, General Mills, and the other Industrial Revolution pioneers been in business?). The Info Age moves faster than earlier ages, but I don't see any reason to think the replacement of one ridiculous device with another will break Wintel's lock on a segment of the largest industry in the world.

CHAPTER SEVEN

How Hits Happen

By 1997 the U.S. economy was doing so well that company evaluations soared, taking the stock market with them. Low inflation, low interest rates, and high profits turned investors on to hi-tech portfolios because hi-tech was where they anticipated rampant profits. Even my grandmother speculated. This confidence was rewarded as profits exceeded the wildest projections, leading to more speculation. Greed and hi-tech became even greater coconspirators as the market sizzled and venture funding topped all records.

Greed is the great equalizer in Silicon Valley. Nobody cares if you are black, brown, white, male, female, European, Asian, Latin, or plain old WASP, as long as you are smart and ambitious. The average worker is well educated (college degrees are a dime a dozen with lots of advanced degree holders providing the brainpower), and of course, motivated by the American Dream of owning one's own company and a Ferrari. This combination of education, intelligence, and greed is explosive.

With such a high value placed on cleverness, it is inevitable that Silicon Valley would become home to the knowledge economy. The concepts underlying this economy began to be known as the "new economy," or what Bill Gates called "frictionless capitalism." The main idea underlying the friction-free economy was simply that the old rules of supply-and-demand no longer applied. Instead, hi-tech companies exist in a surreal world where prices go down as products get better, resulting in a spiral of increasing sales. As sales increase, so does demand, and as demand increases so do sales! Thus, the friction-free economy obeys the economic laws of increasing returns.

Increasing returns theory runs counter to traditional economics. It says that the more of something there is, the more consumers tend to buy it. Microsoft Office increases its sales simply because more people own Office than some other product. Thus, Office sales (and market share) increases—the very idea underlying increasing returns. This feed-forward mechanism reinforces demand, which accelerates even more sales. Skyrocketing demand for a product that continues to become more plentiful is the theory behind Microsoft's success.

Increasing returns is the opposite of diminishing returns, whereby a commodity loses its value as the market becomes saturated. When everyone has two chickens in every pot, the demand for chicken soup diminishes. Not so with software. In the friction-free economy of software—and services as well—demand is stimulated by product upgrades and services. The demand for Microsoft Office is periodically stimulated by obsolescing earlier versions of the popular package. Software doesn't rust—it just becomes obsolete. Therefore, upgrades keep the friction-free economy humming.

The key to world domination in the new economy is to lock-in customers during the early stages of a new market. Once customers are locked in, upgrades and new releases of the product feed off of increasing returns. This, of course, leads to a monopoly. It explains Microsoft rising.

The goal of any market leader is simply to create an early lock-in to its products. Netscape did this by giving away its Netscape Browser for free. McAffee (now Network Associates) started life as a freely distributed anti-virus program. Most modern Internet shopping sites give something away—if nothing more than stock quotations—to attract customers and lock them into the services provided by the site. Everyone in Silicon Valley is looking to ride the increasing returns wave. The question is, "how?"

How does the Next Big Thing get started? This brings us to the theory of emergent behavior. In general, this is how Silicon Valley works: some clever and greedy entrepreneur thinks of a new technique, process, product, service, or mechanism that customers will buy—at the right price. The innovation is usually a half-baked idea and the entrepreneur is usually moonlighting while working 60 hours per week for an established company.

The entrepreneur "shops the idea" by talking to everyone he or she encounters. The idea is to create a buzz around the product or service, which eventually attracts the attention of the moneymen. The moneymen sell or license the idea, or use it as the basis of a startup. In many cases, the entrepreneur's day-job employer buys the startup. In other cases, the idea is big enough to support a startup company. The goal of all startups is to be bought, either by a bigger company or by the public, through an IPO (Initial Public Offering). In either case, speed is essential, because every good idea has a finite shelf life. Someone is always right behind you with the Next Big Thing.

I have just explained the theory of emergent behavior. It is the process used to create wealth in the friction-free economy. It is so important to Silicon Valley that it is becoming a technique, which can be modeled and used in a premeditated way. Companies that try to predict the future or anticipate the Next Big Thing are institutionalizing it.

In the next essay, I explain the theory in more detail, and apply it to several interesting processes: the stock market itself, and project management—a core capability of all hi-tech companies. Of course, the idea is much more general and powerful than portrayed here. In hindsight, emergent behavior is stronger today that it was in 1997 when I first wrote about it.

Article by Ted Lewis, Computer, July 1997

Emergent Behavior, Emergent Profits

Emergent behavior may be one of the principal driving factors in future businesses. Through a new kind of simulation called agent-based simulation, forward-thinking companies are discovering the laws of a new economy—the "friction-free economy." Let me illustrate some of the principles of agent-based simulation and how it can be used to build scenarios.

For example, stock market fluctuations illustrate one nonclassical phenomenon that occurs every day. To better anticipate stock price fluctuations, it pays to understand something about chaos theory. Indeed, chaos reigns in much of the economy, so much so that I have coined the phrase "friction-free economy" after a hint in Bill Gate's *The Road Ahead*: He titled one chapter "Frictionless Capitalism."

Strange Attractors and the Next Billionaire

Along with American Online's actual stock price, Figure 7.1 shows the "strange-attractor" price associated with AOL stock. According to chaos theory, nonlinear systems like the stock market often tend to a fixed point, the strange attractor. Usually, we can find a strange attractor by computing for an infinite amount of time, but when betting on stocks we don't have that much time. Notice how this value—labeled the

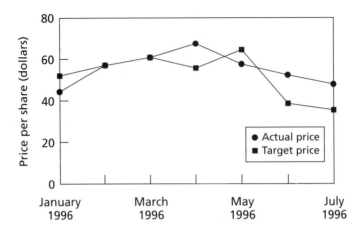

Figure 7.1   *Actual and target prices of America Online common stock before, during, and immediately after the July 1996 stock market crash.*

target price for reasons I will soon reveal—often foreshadows the actual price. In fact, if you had bought AOL when the actual price fell below the target price (in January 1996), and sold it when the target price fell below the actual price (April), you would have reaped a tidy profit. Your neighbors would have asked how you knew which way the stock would move. (Yes, you would have lost money between May and June, but overall you gain.)

Here's how: The target price is where the stock wants to go. Targets act like compasses that point up when the actual price is below market expectation and down when the market overheats. Thus, target price is a barometer of herd instinct. You can calculate it by finding the emerging pattern in the stock; that is, computing the strange attractor (from chaos theory).

As a test of this idea, consider what happened in July 1996: The Dow Jones Industrial Average dropped 165 points in one day. The target line for the Dow pointed downward a full week earlier. This gave me plenty of time to sell my penny stocks and then buy them back in August. I amassed $12.48, a $2.48 (25 percent) gain in less than six weeks.

Chaos drives many businesses these days and can explain much of what appears to be random behavior. A strange attractor like the one in Figure 7.1 can be used to predict when stocks are about to become unstable, how much market share a company could capture, and who will win the software monopoly game.

Chaos-based principles are becoming essential to future fortunes. In fact, strange attractors and the next billionaire may go together. What are these principles, and how do they work?

Ordering Steak

The big-money players in hi-tech already know how to exploit the friction-free economy's subtle principles—such as Davidow's law, emergent behavior, and reinforcement learning—to fatten their profit margins. Intel, Microsoft, Sun, Netscape, and Cisco Systems translate these principles into corporate mantras. Davidow's law (the company that releases a product first will dominate the market especially if it is the first to obsolesce its own product), drives market share to monopolistic levels. But, like the other two, Davidow's law is a learned behavior, not a genetically inherent trait of CEOs like Grove, Gates, McNealy, Barksdale, and Chambers. Anyone can learn them.

Learning the principle of emergent behavior, for example, is just like ordering steak at a restaurant.

Here's the scene. You are with a group of hungry diners. The first person orders steak, and guess what? Others also order steak. By the time the server has completed the rounds, a higher than expected percentage of people ordered the same thing as the first person—steak. Coincidence?

In emergent behavior, a small perturbation in the environment leads to a larger than expected outcome simply because subsequent choices reinforce the first choice (an example of reinforcement learning). This snowballs until an unexpected number of party animals have ordered an unexpected number of steaks.

Emergent behavior is a powerful market force and does two things: It selects one from many and eliminates optional choices. Add reinforcement learning to this formula, and a herd instinct takes over. The (random) first choice becomes the favored choice of others. Once this ball starts rolling, it's hard to stop. It's why Microsoft is so powerful, and it may be a key strategy of the next billionaire.

Whether making big bucks by timing the stock market or turning a small company into a market leader, competitors in the friction-free economy must master emergent behavior and reinforcement learning. If you don't apply these principles, your competitors will. In fact, you have to model every strategic move by computer; otherwise, someone with a better computer model will outflank your company.

Finding Outlaws

Emergent-behavior simulation can not only save a company's bottom line, it can generate novel solutions to complex business situations. In fact, scenario generation is really where this kind of simulation and modeling differs from past methods. The power of emergent-behavior modeling is that it finds "outliers"—solutions that fall many standard deviations from the average. Outliers are unexpected results; outlaw solutions that should never happen or are so highly unlikely to occur that an ordinary simulation cannot find them. Because they are so rare, outlaws can take too much computer time to find by traditional simulation. But emergent-behavior modeling can find these outlaws using much less computer time. Such modeling also incorporates an element of chance that produces interesting outlaws. Sometimes an outlaw solution is exactly what you want—the best solution because your competitor never thought of it.

Figure 7.2 shows unlikely and likely scenarios and thus reflects what happens in the real market and in the real world, where unexpected things happen every day. In Figure 7.2a, all three competitors misjudge the market and everyone loses. Figure 7.2b shows a tie and Figure 7.2c, a runaway success.

If only reinforcement learning is in play, the three competitors take turns stepping up their market shares, as shown in Figure 7.2b. The struggle between Microsoft and Netscape in 1997—a market share browser war—falls in the category of reinforcement learning.

Adding emergent behavior effects to reinforcement learning leads to the Figure 7.2c scenario. The first customer orders a particular competitor's product. This represents a slight advantage, since other customers have a slight tendency to buy from the same competitor. A competitor's chance of adding market share in the next time step is also proportional to its market share in the current time step. Thus, small advantages snowball into bigger advantages. Before you know it, one competitor has 90 percent of the market and the others are grasping for a game plan.

Fear Versus Greed

The trick to predicting market share is to select the right method for simulating emergent behavior. But predicting the stock market is more difficult; it takes math.

A computer using a software agent can approximate a stock market investor. You could program such an agent to behave like a 55-year-old seeking his retirement fortune—a conservative trader vacillating between fear and greed. It is this tension between fear and greed that makes the agent-based simulation chaotic. To make a long derivation short, the fear-greed equation is nonlinear, hence the simulation program approximates the real stock market's nonlinear behavior. As we all know, nonlinear systems can become unstable at the slightest provocation, just like the stock market crashes of 1996–97.

Now that we have an agent-encapsulated, nonlinear equation that describes each investor, we unleash thousands of agents inside of a computer and let them buy and sell thousands of times. Sooner or later a pattern will emerge—one analogous to the steak-ordering pattern. This pat-

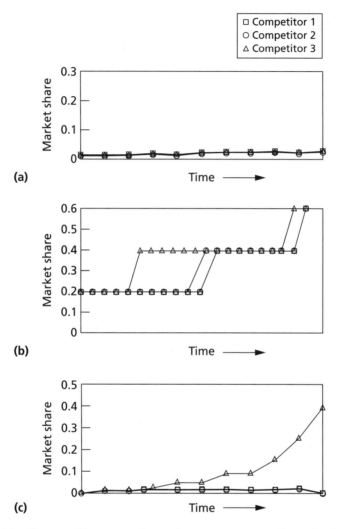

Figure 7.2 *Three possible outcomes from a three-way competition for market share in a specific market segment: (a) everybody loses, (b) a near tie, and (c) one competitor dominates the others.*

tern of emergent behavior defines "what the market wants," a kind of strange attractor or target price.

So now you know how to beat the stock market. Well, not exactly. Remember that agent-based simulations generate scenarios—lots of them, some more likely than others. In the case of stock timing, an agent-based simulation of emergent behavior may or may not yield a scene compatible with Alan Greenspan's announcements.

Tools That Think

Emergent behavior is becoming such a powerful technique that out-of-the-box thinkers at the Santa Fe Institute, a private research center, and Thinking Tools, a startup, are turning it into a business. Because emergent-behavior simulations generate outlaw scenarios, they are a perfect tool for training strategists and planners. *Forbes* quoted Thinking Tools' founder John Hiles (April 7, 1997, p. 107): "The world of business has lots of agents. It's beyond our power of imagination. A simulation lets us practice." And practice makes perfect.

The first shrink-wrapped software product from Thinking Tools, Project Challenge is an agent-based simulation of project management for any kind of project. It employs a video-game-like user interface over a simulator that uses techniques like emergent behavior and chaos theory to train managers. Mostly, Project Challenge humbles its players with scenarios from hell: cost overruns, people problems, hiring fiascoes, and bosses like those in Dilbert. Clearly, Project Challenge is true to life; a flight simulator for suits. More seriously, however, it uses sophisticated agent-based techniques to hone project leadership skills.

Unlike other simulation and modeling techniques, applying emergent behavior, chaos, and genetic algorithms to business competition is just starting. There is a lot to learn about how to tame chaos. In the meantime, fierce competitors are already using agent-based simulators to generate uncanny scenarios. It is almost like using a tool to think. Could this be the real AI?

Probably not, but the future of hi-tech marketing may require MBAs to spend time with simulators like Project Challenge rather than in stifling lecture halls. If experience is the best teacher, then time-compressed experience in front of a simulator may be the only way for the next billionaire to learn in Internet time.

CHAPTER EIGHT

The Techno Treadmill

The reward for failure in Silicon Valley is that you get to roll the dice, again. This may seem strange, but entrepreneurs get better as they go through more startups and rise to greater heights within established companies. Keep fast company by jumping on emergent ideas before anyone else, and when it flops, move on to the Next Big Thing. This is the mantra of Silicon Valley.

Of course, nobody yearns to fail. It is much better to have a string of successes than a mixed batting average. This is why it is so important to quantify the mantra. And because Silicon Valley has so many smart people, quantification doesn't intimidate anyone. Everyone understands mathematics.

The reader may want to skip the following essay because it contains mathematical equations. But if you want to really understand how the industry works, it is worthwhile to plow through the equations. And if you want to vie for leadership in the friction-free economy, it is essential that you hone your mathematical skills. After all, if you want to swim with the sharks without becoming shark bait, you will need repellant.

In December 1996, *Upside* magazine rated Marc Andreessen number 22 in its "Top 100 Elite" of Silicon Valley. The magazine editors described the co-founder and vice president of Netscape Communications as, "The epitome of nerd revenge . . . when he isn't doing doughnuts in his white Mercedes coupe, you can find him raving rapidly about Intranets at important industry events." Andreessen, of course, is the boy wonder who led a team of students at the University of Illinois in the development of Mosaic—the first web browser for personal computers.

Andreessen was in the right place at the right time to catch the emergent behavior wave called the Internet. The Internet was born in 1992 when the U.S. National Science Foundation commercialized the ARPANet. A few visionaries like Tim Berners-Lee realized that the Internet would be too difficult for ordinary users unless the user interface could be improved. In 1992 access to the Net was by CLI (Command Line Interface). It was the Microsoft DOS of networking.

People like Berners-Lee and Andreessen worked to put a graphical user interface (GUI) between users and the raw Internet. They envisioned the Internet going the way of the GUI. Mosaic was to the Internet what the Macintosh was to personal computers.

The timing was just right. When Jim Clark came to visit, looking for the Next Big Thing in networking, Andreessen convinced him that it already existed in the form of the retreaded Internet. Clark went to Illinois thinking the future was in on-demand TV, and returned to Mountain View, California completely turned around. It's the Internet, stupid!

By October 1997 when I recorded Andreessen's Laws, Netscape Communications had been in business for 30 months. This was enough time—in Internet Time—to sit back and reflect. Andreessen's Laws are simply a condensation of the rules governing Silicon Valley. While they are mathematically precise, their meaning is very clear:

+ Moore's Law sets the clock speed of the industry: If it cannot be brought to market in less than 18 months, it will be too late. Thus, the window of opportunity for the Next Big Thing is 18 months.

+ Metcalf's Law is a rephrasing of the Law of Increasing Returns. The value of a network increases as the square of the number of computers connected to it. This concept applies to all increasing returns businesses. The value of a magazine, on-line service, radio or TV channel, university alumni club, etc. increases as the square of the number of users. The value of a product increases as the square of its market share.

+ Sidgmore's Law governs the rise of the Internet: The number of packets flying around the Internet doubles every three months. Hence, Sidgmore's Law is equivalent to Moore's Law, except it applies to networking.

+ Cost of bandwidth is dropping as fast as the number of packets being sent across the Internet is increasing. This rule summarizes the impact that the Internet is having on the globe: The Net is driving out costs and in so doing, driving goods and services to a commodity level.

+ Network capitalism, namely, the friction-free economy is changing everything. The friction-free economy has infinite shelf space and zero marginal cost. Thus, traditional businesses that depend on consumer ignorance or high cost of goods are doomed.

Network capitalism shifts control from vendor to consumer. It also shifts the middleman—a process called reintermediation—to a new kind of middleman—the Internet.

These five laws dictate how the economy will shape up in the twenty-first century. They are also the laws that govern life and death in Silicon Valley.

---

*Article by Ted Lewis, Internet Computing,
September–October 1997*

Andreessen's Laws vs. the Techno Treadmill

Earth-shaking Laws

I thought the Big Five were nationalism, multiculturalism, globalism, capitalism, and the crash communism. But Andreessen's Laws are a much different set of *isms*—laws that govern Silicon Valley. And what drives Silicon Valley also drives the economy of California, one of the largest economies in the world.

What are these earth-shaking laws, and what do they mean? If you will permit poetic license, here are Andreessen's Laws rephrased as a set of isms:

+ *Moore-ism.* Moore's Law says processor performance, P, increases according to the formula

$$P = P(0) [1 + B]^t$$

where $P(0)$ is a constant of proportionality and B is that old favorite learning parameter of mine that determines how fast a product, service, or idea mainstreams. Moore used $B = 0.5$. (Actually, this formula is the popular version—not the original law—but even Moore revises it once in a while.)

+ *Metcalf-ism.* Metcalf's Law says the value of a network, N, is proportional to the square of the number of nodes, n, connected by the network:

$$N = N(0) \, n^2$$

This also explains the next ism.

+ *Sidgmore-ism.* Sidgmore is the chief honcho at UUNET. Sidgmore's Law says that traffic, T, on the UUNET backbone doubles every three months, according to the formula

$$T = T(0) \, [2]^{(4t)}$$

where t is time in years. Of course, traffic is defined as the number of paying IP packets passing over UUNET's wires. This observation is also related to the next law.

+ *Bandwidth-ism.* The cost of bandwidth is dropping like Apple Computer's market share, with no end in sight. Andreessen is mathematically vague about this, so I have taken the liberty of making this ism much more analytical.

In classical wired-world economy style, the cost per IP packet transmitted over the Internet is inversely proportional to Sidgmore's Law:

$$C = C(0) \, [1/2]^{(4t)}$$

where C is cost and $C(0)$ is a constant of proportionality. (How else could we expect traffic intensity to soar?)

There are two reality checks here: (1) government regulation may not permit such drastic changes in pricing, and (2) switching and routing devices are inherently computers, which means their price-learning curves must obey Moore-ism. This has a moderating effect on practical bandwidth-ism. (More on this later.)

+ *Network capitalism.* Andreessen is even less analytical about this law. He asserts that the Internet makes new concepts easier to roll out than ever before; and in fact, network capitalism is a dramatic illustration of the friction-free economy. Perhaps I can tighten this up somewhat, too.

As Stephen Fleming of Alliance Technology Ventures says, the friction-free economy has "infinite shelf space, and zero marginal cost." Fleming has put his finger on the pulse of the new economy, but what does he mean? Any system that has infinite capacity and zero cost is a friction-free system. Thus, economic expansion runs wild. In the computer industry, economic expansion is measured in market share—not cash flow. This explains how Apple Computer can be in trouble despite an $8-billion annual revenue stream.

Network capitalism values the mainstreaming of products and services more than it does the prices-to-earnings ratio of a company's stock. Unfortunately, network capitalism loves the technology treadmill. I am talking rapid change: products going obsolete before they wear out, and newer technologies overpowering older technologies. We can express this rapid rise and fall in adoption as the market share, M of a product at time t given by

$$M = \frac{1}{\left(1 + \left(P(0) \cdot B^t\right)\right)}$$

where P(0) is a constant proportional to price, and B is the learning parameter I referred to earlier. Typically, B is less than 1 and P is greater than 2. But then, it all depends on the market space.

Add these laws together, and you have the making of a technology treadmill. This treadmill has tripped up a number of companies in Wired World. We'll take a look at one such company. But first, a little more theory.

Five Equations That Changed the World

If you subscribe to Andreessen's theory, then you accept these five equations as governing the new economy and all the products and services in it. They are like Newton's Laws, or perhaps Einstein's $E = mc^2$. They have transformed the world from the classical industrial age through the neoclassical post-industrial age, and very soon now into the age of the friction-free economy. This last is a dramatic step, because it spells death to everything you were taught in the MBA program at Stanford, MIT, Sloan, or Wharton. It's heady stuff. But does it compute?

Suppose we apply a Moore-ism to network capitalism. Moore's Law gives values for P and B in the network capitalism rule: B = 0.5, and P(0) is anything you want it to be. For example, let P(0) = 10, which models the time it takes processor prices to erode by a factor of 10, and see what happens. In other words, we can see how long it will take Intel to mainstream a new processor, squeeze maximum profits from it, and then throw it away because no profit remains in the market. Since Intel likes to take 90 percent of the market, we set the network capitalism market share to 0.90 and solve 0.90 = 1/{1 + 10 [0.5]^t} for t. This gives you the life cycle of an Intel processor.

Figure 8.1 shows a typical microprocessor life cycle for this set of parameters. Of course, you can change the value of P(0)—and perhaps discover a way to out-monopolize the Intel monopoly.

This technique can be applied to some of the other rules in Andreessen's set of laws. Because it is so insightful, let's try the technique on another segment: bandwidth.

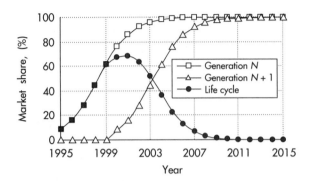

Figure 8.1 *A typical product life cycle for a microprocessor in the friction-free economy. As generation N + 1 ramps up, it takes market share away from generation N.*

Horrendous Bandwidth

To make the wired economy really hum, we need horrendous bandwidth. If Sidgemore is going to be kept in a constant state of glee, bandwidth-ism must be obeyed. Because $(1/2)^4 = 0.063$, we know that $B = 0.063$ in the network capitalism equation. But Internet router companies like Cisco Systems and Bay Networks make switches from semiconductors, so Moore's Law must also be obeyed. A more realistic value is $B = 0.25$. We also know that nobody gets excited unless bandwidth increases by at least a factor of 10. For example, 10-Mbps Ethernet is moving up to 100-Mbps 100BaseT, and eventually to 1 Gbps. So, $P = 10$.

Finally, because Cisco is not the monopoly Intel is, it must settle for a market share of 50–60 percent before innovating. After all, Andreessen did not consider Davidow's Law. If we put all of these assumptions into the model, the product life cycle for 10-fold jumps in bandwidth turns out to look like Figure 8.2.

The Roller Coaster Ride

Dick Eyestone, vice president of US sales, had an office perched atop Building 3 of the Bay Networks headquarters in San Jose, California, where I visited him in mid-1996. Eyestone's office overlooked the Great American Park roller coaster—a ride not unlike the one Bay has been on since it was born from the merger of SynOptics and Wellfleet, two early upstarts in the new industry created by the horrendous demand for bandwidth. At the time Eyestone was in the middle of a bitter business-as-war battle over who was to become the Microsoft of networking. (Note: Dick has now retired to North Car-

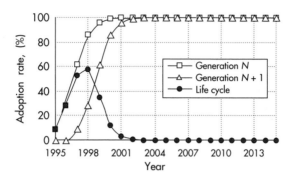

Figure 8.2 *Network switch generational life cycles for B = 0.25, P = 10, and market share of 50 percent.*

olina, where he considers the technology treadmill a spectator sport rather than a contact sport.)

Bay Networks' goal was to own the information superhighway by the end of the century. But it had a problem. It was losing the battle of the technology treadmill. "Customers are becoming tired of rapid change in technology—they want to get off of the technology treadmill," said Eyestone, as he gazed out over the roller coaster. "They want a stable network platform that allows them to plug and play boxes from any vendor. They want to invest in a standard infrastructure that will still be around three years from now."

According to Eyestone, Bay Networks' strategy was to define the universal network platform and then drive that standard platform ahead of its main rival, Cisco Systems. If Bay Networks could establish an end-to-end standard for all networking needs, it could gain the upper hand, and like Netscape Communications did in the browser market, accelerate past Cisco Systems.

But when I talked to him, things were not going so well. Why? Because Bay didn't understand Andreessen's Laws. It didn't realize it was living in Internet time. Until it does, it won't be able to compete. Instead of trying to stop the treadmill, Bay and companies like it must understand the learning curves that govern the industry. It's the technology treadmill that keeps companies profitable.

2005: Network Valley

Bay Networks' revenues grew like a computer virus during the formative years of the network industry, circa 1991 through 1995. In fact, the market value of the top four networking companies in Silicon Valley—Cisco Systems, Bay Networks, 3COM, and Madge Networks—grew an astounding 2,710 percent from 1991 to 1995.

While the Dow average increased by 12.7 percent during this period, networking companies' revenues climbed 65.7 percent.

Riding the Learning Curve

In 1995, the combined revenues of the four largest networking companies was $5 billion. Compare this with the $65 billion in combined revenues of the four largest computer companies for the same year.

Network companies are learning at a rate of about 31 percent per year. Compared to a learning rate of 20 percent for computer companies and a rate of 25 percent for the overall semiconductor industry, networking is a fast and furious business. It might take a while, but at this rate, Silicon Valley will be Network Valley by the year 2005 (see Figure 8.3).

However, with an industry-wide price-learning curve of 36 percent, Cisco and Bay Networks must learn how to reduce prices by 64 percent per year! The entire network industry is on a technology treadmill that renders product life cycles like the profile shown in Figure 8.2.

Keeping Up with the Ciscos

In mid-1996, Bay reported a 31-percent growth rate—right on the industry median, but much lower than the 65 percent it reported in 1995. At 31 percent per year, a company like Bay Networks must mainstream its products at a near-chaotic rate. "Worldwide switch shipments will grow by almost 44 percent and revenue by 16 percent between 1996 and 2000," said Bill Miller, analyst with Dataquest, Inc. "Hub shipments will rise only 12 percent . . . router shipments will grow by 33 percent," he

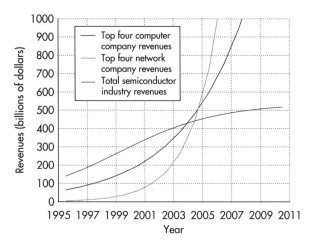

Figure 8.3 *Revenue projections for the top four computer companies, top four networking companies, and the overall semiconductor industry show networking companies outpacing everyone else.*

estimated.[1] Figure 8.3 is a snapshot of the competitors and how they stacked up against one another at one point in time, circa 1995.

Bay's problem was that Cisco Systems grew 93 percent and 3COM jumped 39 percent in the same period. When a business has competitors that grow 93 percent in a year, 31 percent isn't good enough! As a consequence, Bay's share of its high-end router products dropped to 6 percent, its share of the midrange router market dropped to 24 percent from 33 percent a year earlier, and its share of the low-end router market dropped from 9 percent to 7 percent.

Soon after Bay reported these declines, resignation rumors swarmed around President and CEO Andrew Ludwick's office. By the end of 1996, David House—a 22-year veteran of Intel—had taken over as CEO.

Living in Internet Time

Contrast Bay Networks with market leader Cisco Systems, a company that was founded in 1984 by Stanford dropouts. Cisco rode the burgeoning Internet techno rocket to a mainstream position within the network hardware segment. It rode the techno treadmill like a tiger. By 1995 Cisco had become the dominant Internet hardware company, achieving a 75-percent share of the world market for routers. "Cisco Systems is known more for setting industry trends than for bucking them," says analyst Jim Duffy.[2] Cisco has nothing less than Wired World dominance on its mind. Like Microsoft, Cisco intends to lock in the whole enchilada of networking through its operating system software.

Confronted with a problem similar to Dick Eyestone's at rival Bay Networks, Cisco's CEO John Chambers looked for a way to lock customers into Cisco's product line. "We went for market share in each segment, and now we are trying the products in each segment together with software," says Chambers.[3] "What we learned from HP is that you survive only by breaking the market into segments, and then being the leader in each."

In other words, target, target, target.

The Dog with the Biggest Bite

Rather than compete with new upstarts, Cisco simply bought them! In 1993 it bought Crescendo; in 1994 it bought Newport Systems, Kalpana, and LightStream. By 1995 it was earning $2 billion and setting the industry learning rate. In 1995 Cisco bought Internet Junction, Grand Junction, and Network Translation. In 1996, it bought TGV Software, Granite, and two of Paul Baran's companies: Stratacom and Telebit. By 1996 Cisco had spent $5.5 billion to buy the product space, and was earning $4.5 billion from its divisions.

Within two thirds of the time it took Microsoft to exceed $4 billion in sales, Cisco had become the dog with the biggest bite in Wired World.

"This [buying everyone] is part of a global strategy by Cisco for the IOS [Internet Operating System] technologies to touch every single network device over time," says Jeanne Dunn, director of OEM channels at Cisco.[4] No wonder Bay Networks was worried. If only Dick Eyestone and the planners at Bay Networks had known about Andreessen's Laws a few years sooner. But it is not too late for your company.

What's the learning rate for your industry?

References

1. J. T. Mulqueen, "Bay's Earnings Slide Continues," *Comm. Week,* July 29, 1996, p. 71.

2. J. Duffy, "Cisco Enjoys Healthy Route," *Network World,* Dec. 25, 1995, p. 22.

3. M. Janah, "The Rules According to Cisco," *Information Week,* Sept. 16, 1996, p. 18.

4. M. Janah, "Cisco Buys Again," *Information Week,* July 29, 1996. p. 72.

URLs for This Column

3COM • www.3com.com/

Alliance Technology Ventures • www.atv.com/

Bay Networks • www.baynetworks.com/

Cisco Systems • www.cisco.com/

Dataquest, Inc. • www.dataquest.com/

Granite • www.granite.com/

Kalpana • www.kmj.com/

LightStream • www.lightstream.net/

Madge Networks • www.madge.com/

Network Translation • www.jma.com/

Newport Systems • www.newport-sys.com/

Stratacom • www.strata.com/

Telebit • www.telebit.com/

TGV • www.ipo-network.com/members/ipos/TGV_Software.html

UUNET • www.uunet.com/

CHAPTER NINE

The Rise of Strategy

Once a system can be understood and modeled with the mathematical precision of Andreessen's Laws, it is inevitable that the system will be gamed. That is, smart people will do clever things to the system. This is exactly what began to emerge in the computer industry by late 1996 and continues to this day. The gaming of hi-tech has become a high-stakes game of strategy.

Of course the number one strategy of Silicon Valley market leaders is Davidow's Law, which says that companies must obsolesce their own products before competitors do. This is not always easy to do, because it sometimes means killing the goose that lays the golden eggs. For example, why should a company put itself out of business by rendering its own product useless? In the friction-free economy, a company must re-create itself every 12–18 months or else risk losing its leadership position to the Next Big Thing. Davidow's Law makes everyone paranoid.

By late 1997 it became obvious that the PC industry could not go on forever selling desktop PCs to businesses and consumers. The exceptionally long run of prosperity enjoyed by Wintel had to give out sooner or later. This presented two questions of critical importance to Silicon Valley companies: When would the PC run out of time, and What would replace it? The NC had failed, and Netscape's challenge to Microsoft had fizzled. Sun Microsystems' proposed Java alternative was cut off at the pass by Microsoft's dilution of "pure Java." Microsoft and Intel had successfully applied the second major strategy of every market leader: absorb-and-extend.

The strategy of the strong hi-tech competitor is called absorb-and-extend. Whenever a competitor gets ahead of you, perhaps by jumping on the Next Big Thing bandwagon before you, a market leader will first absorb and then extend the competitor's technology, product, or service. For example, Microsoft reversed Netscape's fortunes by building a browser that looked and worked just like Navigator. Then, Microsoft's Internet Explorer went beyond Navigator by incorporating non-standard features that only Microsoft controlled. Within 3 years, Netscape's 85 percent market share of the browser market dropped to less than 50 percent. In another three years, nobody will remember the Netscape product.

When Sun Microsystems beat Microsoft to the punch with Java, it threatened to render obsolete Microsoft's languages before Microsoft could. Once again, Microsoft applied the strategy of absorb-and-extend. It licensed Java from Sun (absorb), and then modified it (extend) so that it worked only on Microsoft Windows. This way, Microsoft put itself in the Java driver's seat. Sun took Microsoft to court, but the damage had been done. While the court case was working its way to judgement day, Java technologies virtually disappeared from the desktop. By 1998 only the server side of Java had survived Microsoft's absorb-and-extend strategy. And at this writing, Microsoft was working on absorbing the entire server side with its as-yet-unreleased Windows NT with COM +, and a new language called COOL Adios Java. Absorb-and-extend is a strategy of the strong. It doesn't work as well for weak players. Take the AMD versus Intel struggle, for example. AMD tried to absorb the Intel x86 instruction set with its clone, the K-6 processor chip. The K-6 was faster and cheaper than the Pentium from Intel. Yet, AMD was not able to effectively compete against Intel. While AMD made small gains against Intel, the reality is that AMD is too weak to apply the absorb-and-extend strategy. After several years of trying, AMD's market share is still less than 7 percent of the overall processor market. Meanwhile, Intel has made aggressive moves into the low-end, low-cost processor segment. It was only a matter of time before AMD's challenge was blunted.

The chip wars subsided. The software wars subsided. By 1997 the computer industry had calcified: Intel and Microsoft had successfully thwarted all attempts by all challengers. The only avenue left to weaker competitors was a legal one: They started taking Microsoft and Intel to court. But, lawsuits are delaying tactics at best. Innovation is the only true remedy. What was needed was a revolutionary shift away from the PC.

What revolution might come along to upset the Wintel monopoly? This was the main question in late 1997 when I visited Ted Selker at the IBM laboratory in Almaden, California, in search of the Next Big Thing. Selker, like so many innovators at that time, was working on wearable computers, network appliances, and other embedded computers. He was convinced that small, ubiquitous, and specialized computers would ultimately replace general purpose, bulky, and hard-to-use PCs.

The idea of embedded computers spread through Silicon Valley like a brush fire in 1997. Once again, the Valley was energized by the thought of overthrowing Microsoft and Intel. Would it become reality or not? In the following essay, I suggest that the really big Next Big Thing isn't smaller and faster at all. Rather, the Next Big Thing in computing is very conspicuous because it is tangible. Tangible computing will drive the computer industry in the early years of the next century.

The question remains, however: Is the concept of a Next Big Thing an application of Davidow's Law, or simply an extension of the absorb-and-extend strategy? What is more important—technology treadmill or strategy? In hindsight, I lean toward the theory that it is a matter of strategy, not technology.

Article by Ted Lewis, Computer, September 1997

Digitopolis Meets Encalming Technology

Digitopolis—the city-like ecosystem of the computer industry—has to keep expanding its installed base or it will go into a major depression. This is dictated by Moore's Second Law: The cost of building semiconductor fabrication plants will increase exponentially. To stay vibrant, Digitopolis requires a rapidly expanding market for computerized gadgets. Think of it this way: For a 20 percent annual return on investment on a $1 billion fab, Intel must make a profit of, say, $10 each on 172.8 million parts over the fab's three-year life. Given the ever-shorter life cycles for hi-tech products, this is becoming increasingly difficult—unless the units shipped or profit margins go up dramatically.

The answer: Expand beyond the Wintel monopoly. Build network appliances, automobiles, telephones, games, and wallet computers as fast as consumers will adopt them. Thus, the next big thing will be gadgets—lots and lots of gadgets. Figure 9.1 summarizes the worldwide shipment rates of several obvious gadgets. Their future designs will almost certainly contain bigger and more powerful hardware and software systems. Both graphs project modest growth in annual shipments for the usual devices, such as copiers. The really big numbers are associated with devices that support e-mail and PCS (personal communication system) telephony. Yet even these numbers may not be big enough to keep Silicon Valley fully employed.

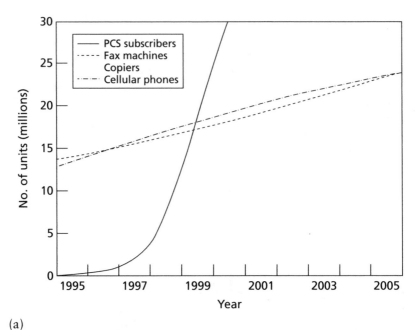

(a)

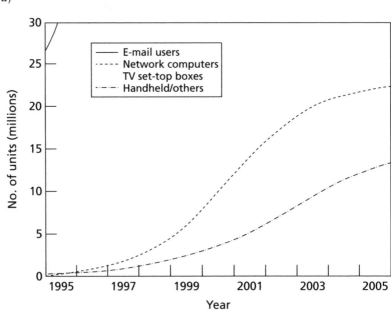

(b)

Figure 9.1 *(a) Network appliance devices: number of units shipped. I project these numbers based on data from Paul Kagan and Associates, Carmel, Calif. (Aug. 1996) and Zona Research Inc., Redwood City, Calif. (Dec. 1996). (b) Common office devices containing some kind of computer: number of units shipped. This graph is based on projections made by GIGA Information Group, Cambridge, Mass.*

Let's look at two scenarios of what might happen in the industry's network appliance segment. In the first scenario, the network appliance is all user interface. In the second, the network appliance is invisible; it disappears. Which is the future?

Scenario 1: Going Tangible

Ted Selker's ideas spill out of his head and end up as toys for adults. The desk in his IBM office in the Almaden foothills is littered with black boxes, wearable computers, and other unusual computing devices. Selker invented the track point—the little joy stick sprouting out of IBM portable-computer keyboards. "TrackPoint II is better than a mouse," says Selker, "because you don't have to take your hands away from the keyboard." It is not just the motion that kills productivity; it is the cognitive shift from "keyboard-like:" to "pointer-like" thinking that does the harm. Selker took eight years to perfect the track point, and another two years of persistence to get it into products. "That is not so bad; most innovations take 17 years to reach the product stage," he explains.

To Selker, computing is all about user interface, and the next big thing in computing makes the user interface more real. Computing's future lies in the concrete, not the abstract. "People respond viscerally to physical things . . . the stuff people are crazy about is all this physical stuff," according to Selker. In other words, computing is going tangible. Thus, the network appliance is user interface—malleable devices that humans can use with little training and even less knowledge of the "Intel inside." And I'm not talking about better track points or color monitors. Instead, the network appliance that will stimulate sales must be much better than a PC, personal digital assistant, or VCR. It must be a consumer electronics device like none other. But what types of devices are these?

Gadget Mania

If we believe the current wisdom, those devices are products for consumer electronics. Consumers love their gadgets, and computer companies are ramping up to meet the demand. Companies like Diba (which was just acquired by Sun Micro-systems) are targeting markets dominated by major consumer platforms: TV, telephone, and cars. This is where tangible computing will prove itself or die trying.

The road ahead looks like it will be littered with "devices as user interface." These devices will be simple: with no disk storage, little memory, and an inexpensive processor. Designers will discard anything that makes the device expensive to build or difficult to use. These devices will off-load serious computing and storage chores to a server and focus on handling the user. The money-making idea is to build lots of different types of devices, each with extensive communication capabilities and extremely intuitive, easy-to-use, special-purpose interfaces. Such slimmed-down, user interface devices can be cheap and simple, two of the most important ingredients in a consumer product.

The New Empire Builders

The next big idea ought to be worth an entirely new industry or at least a major segment of the existing one. It should transform Silicon Valley into Interface Gulch. Indeed, a few companies have already embraced the opportunity. Navio, for example, spun out of Netscape to move Netscape technology into the consumer space. Netscape was supposed to do business software, and Navio was supposed to do consumer software.

Things have not quite worked out the way that Wei Yen, Navio cofounder, expected. Yen was the point man for taking the device-as-user-interface to the mainstream. The first time I met Yen, he burst into Navio's conference room like a gangster toting a talking machine gun. Among his claims: Wired World will have 1 billion netizens by 2000, according to Nicholas Negroponte; everyone will use some sort of network device; and the PC standard will die. He machine-gunned down my objections— especially the ones about couch potatoes leaning backward instead of forward, and the fact that most people cannot read a newspaper, let alone operate a device as user interface. A year later, Yen's Navio was quietly absorbed into Oracle's skunkworks for building the Oracle NC.

So Where Are the Gadget-Makers?

Only one high-profile gadget-maker remains: Diba. Based on the Motorola PowerPC processor and Diba's own realtime, multitasking operating system and browser technology, Diba gadgets work in the kitchen, living room, and home office. The Diba set-top box will compete with WebTV, and their browser-based telephone will be an alternative to Cidco's e-mail telephone. They have other household appliances in the works. But after talking to Diba vice president John Busch, I got the nagging feeling that tangible computing was already in trouble. Where are all of the gadget-makers? Why does Diba seem like the only company with its eye on tangible computing as the next big thing?

Cloaking the Klingons

Tangible computing has one big problem: It has very few users. Various estimates place the non-PC, embedded-systems market at 1,000 times bigger than the huge PC industry. According to Tom Portante of Ernst and Young, over 2 *billion* chips and microcontrollers were sold worldwide in 1994 in contrast to 10 million personal computers. Most of these embedded systems and sensors are in cars. A new car from General Motors contains $675 of steel and $2,500 of electronics, which includes computers in the air-bag and antilock braking systems. Electric shavers contain 2 Kbytes of software, and color TVs contain 500 Kbytes. As global PC sales reach 100 million, embedded systems will expand to at least 1,000 times as many units. Therefore, the business of "sense and communicate" is already many times larger than "compute and store."

This huge market is changing the computer industry. Instead of making computing more visceral, embedded systems prevent people from seeing the computer. In other words, computing is going invisible—not tangible. Maybe the Klingons were on to something.

Scenario II: Encalming Devices

Portante says, "We're searching for the next big idea that allows us to make sense of a lot of seemingly unrelated research. We think we're closing in on it—the idea that circles around the need to develop *encalming technology*." Portante is a disciple of Mark Weiser and John Seeley Brown at Xerox PARC. They claim ubiquitous computing will once again place PARC at the forefront of computer research.

The next big idea in Weiser's head is invisible computing—computers that fade into the background. Invisible computers don't have user interfaces as we know them. Like a good butler, these electronic servants lurk in the shadows and rescue you only when needed. Like Jeeves, they anticipate your every need. The future PC will become part of a room's walls, the carton you throw away after drinking the milk, and the clothes you wear. when you enter a room, computers controlling hidden cameras recognize who you are, fetch your e-mail, and display it on your TV when they determine that you are ready to view it. To delve deeper into this idea, take a peak at http://www.ubiq.com/hypertext/weiser/UbiHome.html.

Is the next big thing really zillions of devices as user interfaces or encalming devices embedded into everything from walls to shoes? Will such a paradigm shift leave Microsoft and Intel out in the cold? I think not. Navio's first product will run inside of Oracle's network computer, a business device not unlike a PC. Diba's products will be privately labeled as someone else's, eliminating Diba from the list of threats to Wintel's dominance. It will be some time before the device as user interface reaches the masses and even longer before the computer becomes invisible. In the meantime, Andy Grove and Bill Gates will have time to figure out another way to earn their 20 percent return on investment.

CHAPTER TEN

The End of the Dream

In the next three essays I present both sides of the argument for and against Microsoft rising. The first essay defends Microsoft on libertarian grounds, and states the case for Microsoft's right to compete. It claims competition still exists in the industry, and blames Microsoft's success on consumer's willingness to buy Microsoft products.

The second article appeared in *Scientific American,* and delves into the meaning of increasing returns, again. It is a more technical analysis of what competition means in the friction-free economy. It explores the fundamental question of whether Microsoft can (and should) be declared a "natural monopoly," as earlier companies have been. The conclusion: probably not!

The third article by John Charles details how Microsoft plays hardball with its competitors. It could be thought of as the case against Microsoft, if you interpret Microsoft tactics as anti-competitive. Charles tries to present a balanced view by quoting company leaders who are perfectly happy coexisting with the elephant. But most of the article details how Microsoft eliminates its smaller competitors.

The reality of 1999 is that Microsoft and Intel have cast a pall on the industry. Wintel's domination signifies the end of two decades of dreaming by entrepreneurs whose ambitions were to become the next King of the Valley. Microsoft and Intel single-handedly defined the PC industry in their own image. This means the freewheeling days of innovation and creation are gone. It is time to move on to the next generation. What that will be, exactly, remains the province of the next group of inventors, entrepreneurs, and moneymen. It is possible that the next event will not even happen in Silicon Valley. In fact, the next major event may occur in biotech instead of technology. There is no guarantee that hi-tech will survive—in its present form—as the dominant knowledge industry. If this is the future, then concern for Wintel will fade as the action shifts to genetic engineering.

Before Silicon Valley logs off, however, it is instructive to study how the game might end. I suggest that Microsoft and Intel are headed toward the fate that befell big oil, big railroad, big auto, and big telephone companies. Just as the industrial age had its robber barons, antitrust litigation, and breakups, so will the information age have its barons, breakups, and calcified age of maturity. Silicon Valley has yet to live through its smokestack era decline. The only questions that remain are: When will it happen, and who will end up on top? Somehow I get the feeling it will be just another stage of Microsoft rising.

Article by Ted Lewis, Computer, January 1998

Who's Afraid of Wintel?

A pple has been defeated. Novell has nothing left but the inertia of its (huge) installed base. Sun Microsystems and other workstation vendors are living on borrowed time. IBM, HP, Unisys, and DEC never really mattered. The Apple/IBM/Motorola challenge has fizzled and retreated to the relative backwoods of embedded systems. AMD cannot make enough K6 chips to be a threat, and everyone else is looking for a niche. Meanwhile, Wintel gets stronger every day. Is competition dead in the computer industry?

The Wintel Cartel

D etractors look forward to the day when the US Department of Justice halts Wintel's further advances. But so far, DOJ has mostly kept its hands off. For example, in their first major encounter, Microsoft got DOJ to back off in exchange for an end to price-fixing in the form of operating system license fees on every PC sold, regardless of whether it shipped with MS DOS. The 1995 consent decree allowed Microsoft to monopolize the desktop OS market, but prevented it from strong-arming vendors into buying other Microsoft applications to keep their Windows licenses. Microsoft got what it wanted in 1995—free rein over the OS market in exchange for a slap on the wrist. This decree will be important in the legal browser wars that will take place in 1998.

This is nothing new. DOJ is constantly investigating Microsoft. In a lower profile investigation, DOJ looked into Microsoft's efforts to

Company	Cash Assets (Billions of Dollars)
Microsoft	9.0
Intel	8.1
HP	2.8
Seagate Technologies	2.3
Oracle	1.5
Cisco Systems	1.3
Apple Computer	1.2
Sun Microsystems	1.1
Applied Materials	1.1
3COM	1.0
LSI Logic	0.74
Total	30.1

Table 10.1   Cash assets of IT companies.

"buy control of the Internet." The Redmond red-meat-eaters bought, invested in, or partnered with more than 20 Internet-related companies. Microsoft spent $2 billion in partnerships and acquisitions over the past three years—a drop in its $9 billion cash-assets bucket. I've compiled Table 10.1, which shows what other computer-related firms have to spend.

The Microsoft acquisitions suggest an Internet domination pattern: Microsoft bought Vermeer for FrontPage; Eshop to get a storefront server for e-commerce; Interse for its Web traffic analyzer; WebTV to control standards; and VXTreme for video-streaming technology. It's entered into joint ventures with First Data Corp., which handles electronic payment (MSFDC), and with GE and NBC to provide Web-linked TV news (MSNBC). It also has a stake in VDOnet (video streaming), Progressive Networks (Real Audio), UUNet (an Internet service backbone), and ComCast (cable TV).

This Goliath of a software company hasn't stopped its buying spree, and revenues keep adding to its cash reserves. Figure 10.1 shows IBM as the richest software company, posting 1996 revenues of over $13 billion—its income that year was greater than Microsoft and Oracle combined! But Figure 10.1 also illustrates what scares people. By the end of the decade, my projections show that Microsoft will become the 800-pound gorilla of software. In short, the American public is worried that Microsoft is too rich and powerful to be a fair competitor.

And what about the other half of Wintel? DOJ has investigated Intel twice in the past decade, once between 1991 and 1993, and again in

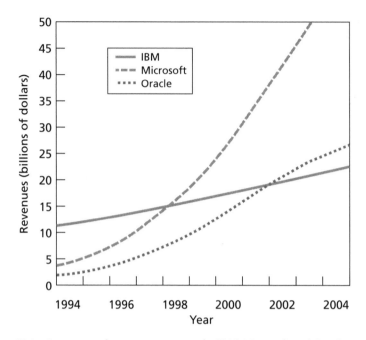

Figure 10.1 *Revenues and revenue projections for IBM, Microsoft, and Oracle.*

1997. The current investigations' focus is that "Intel monopolizes or attempts to monopolize or otherwise restrict price or nonprice competition in the development or sale of microprocessor or other computer components or related intellectual property," according to a subpoena.

Although Intel revenues ($20 billion) are far less than those of IBM, GM, or GE, it has 85 percent of the global micro-processor market. Its dominance allows Intel to mount a $1.4 billion advertising campaign, which involves up to a 6 percent discount on orders for companies using the "Intel Inside" logo. Competitors claim they can't match this deal.

Competitors are also fuming about an Intel design change that could force them out of the market. Rather than a set of pins, new Pentium II chips will plug into boards using a slot configuration. At this time, Intel seems to have no intention of licensing its Slot I and slot II interconnect designs. This means the x86 chips of other vendors won't be interchangeable with newer Intel chips. OEMs would either have to support two interconnect configurations or choose a single supplier. (We can all predict the likely outcome.)

Intel, like any good competitor, is also trying to vertically integrate the entire PC industry. It designs and sells glue chips surrounding the microprocessor, motherboards, disk drive circuit boards, modems, and networking cards. Recently, Intel raised eyebrows by tendering an offer for Chips & Technologies (a graphics chips manufacturer). Partnerships with networking companies and expansion into the lithographic machinery and software segments suggests that the dominant chip maker will expand its influence over the entire industry.

Microsoft is rich, and Intel's market share is a near-monopoly of the chip business. Together, they form a cartel that some say is unbeatable. Shouldn't this be stopped?

The Ida Tarbell Camp

Netscape and Sun Microsystems have positioned themselves as the Ida Tarbells of software. You remember Ida—the journalist who brought down Standard Oil at the turn of the century. Her series of articles described how the company's monopolistic price-fixing crushed competitors. Eventually, these articles led to the breakup of Standard.

These latter-day Tarbells see hope in regulation, and history again points the way: In 1887, the Interstate Commerce Commission was formed to protect farmers against greedy railroad companies. The ICC micromanaged railroad shipping and rates down to the smallest detail. Could this type of regulation help again?

Many in the computer industry see an analogy: Wintel is like the railroads of the 1880s because it controls the transportation system of desktop computing. Wintel, its detractors say, can control prices and the distribution of products to consumers. Some even claim that Wintel crushes innovation by either stifling it with heavy marketing campaigns or buying up the small guys before they have a chance to flourish. This behavior has prompted Netscape to take legal action against Microsoft in the browser war, Sun to launch the Java standardization war, and AMD to declare a "slot war" against Intel.

Case in point: Last year, Netscape filed papers with DOJ to halt Microsoft's alleged predatory pricing and bundling practices. Gary Reback, Netscape's counsel, charged that Microsoft offered clandestine payments, discounts, and other financial favors to companies to stop selling Navigator and start selling Explorer. He said, "Microsoft tactics include manipulating the disclosure of APIs, and the bundling of products such as FrontPage, Internet Explorer, and Microsoft's Internet Server with Microsoft's monopoly operating systems."

In October, Ralph Nader's Consumer Project Technology entered the fray, asking DOJ to take action against Microsoft. Nader's Raiders claim Microsoft should not be allowed to bundle Internet Explorer with its operating system in ways that are unavailable to other firms. Specifically, says Nader, Explorer should not "own a place of prominence" on the screen to the detriment of other products.

As this goes to press, DOJ has forced Microsoft to back away from bundling Explorer with Windows 95. Since the 1995 decree permits

Microsoft to add any capability to its OS, by the end of 1998 the industry could be back where it is now—under Wintel domination. The full story will unfold in this year.

Fair Isn't Free

Let's get real: American free enterprise is not really free. Rather, it tries to emulate a fair-enterprise system in which the government mediates disputes among capitalists, environmentalists, socialists, and college professors like me. The difference between *free* and *fair* is subtle. In a fair-enterprise system, government regulation levels the playing field; it equalizes advantages of size, market share, resources, and sheer wit. Government's role is to balance things.

The question is, does Wintel need balancing? The Ida Tarbells may have reason to fear and loathe Microsoft and Intel, but they *do not* have a case for litigation. Wintel may be one tough competitor, but in general it is not playing on a tilted playing field. Remember, fair-trade laws protect consumers, not competitors. As long as consumers have cost-effective alternatives to Wintel, DOJ won't do much. Before you send hate e-mail, let me explain.

Microsoft Has Competitors

To argue for a breakup, DOJ must prove that competition is dead or dying because its rules give Wintel an unfair advantage. With few exceptions—most of which have now been addressed—the rules have been fair to the ABM (Anything But Microsoft) forces.

For instance, ABMs complain that Microsoft stifles competition because it competes in too many industry segments. Specifically, it has an unfair advantage in the market because Microsoft makes both an operating system and applications. ABMs argue that it should, therefore, be split into at least two companies, one for each product. The key word here is "unfair," and the argument eventually leads back to Microsoft's large market share.

This argument is flawed because Microsoft's dominance doesn't limit consumer choices. Consumers have had a choice of operating systems since the original IBM PC shipped with three operating system options: Microsoft DOS, the University of California at San Diego p-System, and Digital CP/M-86. Even today, consumers can opt for IBM OS/2, SCO Unix, or Sun Solaris on a Intel box.

On the applications side, nearly every Microsoft application has a competitor. Corel, Lotus, and Novell provide alternatives to MS Office. Netscape, of course, fields browsers and servers. Lotus probably has the best groupware, its Notes/ Domino server. In the tools arena, Borland, Symantec, and IBM provide alternatives. And let's be frank—perhaps the best development environments in several important categories belong to companies other than

Microsoft: VisualAge for C++ (IBM), Delphi for client-server (Borland), Visual Cafe for Java (Symantec), and CodeWarrior for cross-platform development (Metrowerks). So it's difficult to claim that Microsoft has no competition. If you think Microsoft is too big, stop buying its products!

Intel Does, Too

I f consumers do not want to be locked into an Intel platform, machines based on the Apple PowerPC, SGI Mips, or AMD K6 offer a choice. Incidentally, Gartner Group research shows that Macintoshes proved a total cost of ownership much less than that of Wintel boxes. So it's no use complaining that this alternative is more costly—it isn't.

Microprocessor competition still thrives, especially in the embedded systems market. Motorola may not make many PC processors, but it dominates the cellular phone, automotive, and other microprocessor-based businesses.

The Telling Difference

A case against the US toy-store chain Toys 'R' Us stands in sharp contrast to Wintel's use of its huge market share. In 1997, the US Federal Trade Commission busted the nation's dominant toy retailer for restricting sales of Mr. Potato Head and Barbie to its competitors. By pressuring suppliers to withhold best-selling merchandise from other retailers, Toys 'R' Us was able to charge 10 to 20 percent more.

Like Microsoft, Toys 'R' Us used its large market share to bully suppliers. But, unlike Microsoft, Toys 'R' Us got into trouble because its actions raised prices and limited consumer options. This is the subtle difference: Microsoft's actions *lower* prices. Microsoft does not prevent competitors from selling their wares—it only makes it more difficult. In short, Microsoft makes competitors compete on price, quality, and volume, not availability. And as long as competitors exist, consumers have a choice. In this case, choice is what makes the market fair. In addition, many of these alternative products come from companies that are as big and powerful as Microsoft, like IBM.

A final argument in favor of a breakup claims that Wintel kills innovation even before it starts. Like Stac electronics (file compression) and WebTV (Internet TV), many startups either get smothered by Microsoft or bought out in their early stages. This is one area where DOJ may need to change the rules: If companies can prove that Microsoft prevented them from bringing innovative technology to market, litigation may be warranted. DOJ, though, must be convinced that these products would ultimately benefit consumers—not merely the companies selling them.

This is where the case for breaking up Microsoft starts to unravel. Suppose DOJ did break up Microsoft. According to economists Robert Heilbroner and Lester Thurow, an industry with one or two giant firms and a tail of smaller ones does not operate very differently—if at all—from one with five or six leading companies. Breaking up monopolies does little to benefit consumers: Local telephone calls, for instance, are more costly today than before the breakup of Ma Bell, and innovation in the telephone business certainly has not accelerated.

Reliance on Key Products

In a couple of areas, Microsoft and Intel will have to look over their corporate shoulders as much as the next company.

A careful examination of Microsoft's revenues reveals its vulnerability: It is a two-product company. Without its upgrade business from MS Office and Windows 95, Microsoft would be a mere shadow of itself. According to venture capitalist Roger McNamee, Microsoft cannot sustain a $6 to $10 billion enterprise on revenues derived from a saturated market for office suites and operating systems. "The ability of Microsoft and Intel to dominate the agenda of our industry may be peaking," says McNamee, a partner in Interval Capital Partners.

To grow, Microsoft must enter some other market. The only one big enough to generate $6 to $10 billion are the Internet and intranets. Microsoft must compete on these battlefields, and this results in its Internet company buying spree.

Like Microsoft, Intel's future is not guaranteed. It is a single-product company, it must deal with technological sea changes, and it depends almost entirely on Microsoft products and their corresponding lock-in to keep its fabrication plants running. Indeed, its fabs could either destroy or save the company. On the one hand, Intel must strive to keep its fabs working at capacity to remain profitable. On the other hand, it takes billions of dollars to ramp up the next-generation fab, and not many competitors can afford to drop a billion or two on a new fab. Intel's large cash position gives it a distinct advantage, but its x86 instruction set won't last forever. What will Intel do after x86?

Clearly, the paranoid forces at Intel seek other sources of business, casting about in networking, software, and flash memories. The Merced partnership with HP—which will not bear fruit until 1999—will depart significantly from the x86 instruction set. One misstep during this transition could end Intel.

The Global Gig

At the turn of the twentieth century, Standard Oil's practices in dominating the US market established it as a monopoly. At the horizon of the twenty-first century, we must reconsider what monopolistic practices are because of one overriding fact: Intel, Microsoft, Motorola, AT&T, and nearly all other US corporations are playing a global gig. The competition is no longer within a single country; it's all over the map. Microsoft and Intel may look ominous when viewed from a provincial US vantage point, but they are not so big when compared with other global giants, companies like Daimler-Benz, Alcatel, Hitachi, and Samsung. Take the situation developing between Motorola, Nokia, and Ericsson: Motorola is in a run for its cellular-telephone life against these giant competitors from outside the US. Should we consider a 95 percent share of the US market alone a monopoly?

Natural Monopolies

More than 100 years ago, the US government created the Sherman Anti-Trust law and ICC regulations. These laws did not prevent monopolies. In fact, they created the so-called "natural" monopolies. Economist Richard Posner defines a natural monopoly as a situation in which (consumer) demand may be most economically and efficiently satisfied by a single producer. In addition, the law allowed natural monopolies where competition resulted in wasted investment and increased prices to consumers.

In today's friction-free economy, economies of scale, efficiency, and wasted investment have been replaced by the momentum of increasing returns. Today, consumer lock-in is more important than lower prices. In her insightful analysis of the telephone industry, Amy Friedlander says " . . . the utility of a given technology increases as more people select that technology . . . the initial selection may be a matter of historical accident, rather than the result of economic efficiencies or technological superiority . . . as increasing returns tend to create a positive feedback that magnifies otherwise random variation, the process of adopting technology will tend to converge on a standard." (*Natural Monopoly and Universal Service,* Corp. for National Research Initiatives, http://www.cnri.reston.va.us/series.html).

Microsoft and Intel have successfully ridden the increasing-returns wave to their monopoly positions. If we want to prevent them from gaining more wealth and power, we must do so by kicking them off the increasing-returns wave. If DOJ wants to solve the Wintel "problem" it must understand the theory of increasing returns, and Congress must legislate against the positive-feedback mechanisms that lock consumers into a single platform.

My guess is that Microsoft and Intel are guaranteed a long and prosperous future with little intervention from DOJ. Then, about the year 2017, Wintel will look as out-of-date and unimportant as Standard Oil is today.

Article by Ted Lewis, Scientific American, February 1998

Is Microsoft
a Natural Monopoly?

The concept of a "natural monopoly" was defined in 1974 by Richard Posner, an economist who studied regulated monopolies, such as water, power, telephone and cable television companies. The government tolerated monopolies as long as it could regulate them, and justifying them as natural somehow made them acceptable in a free-enterprise system. A natural monopoly is allowed when demand is most economically and efficiently satisfied by a single producer and where competition results in duplication and wasted investment and thus fails to operate as a regulatory mechanism.

Big words, but what do they mean? How can they be applied in the modern, digital economy where dominant-market-share companies such as Intel and Microsoft are replacing the old natural monopolies such as Standard Oil and AT&T? The Department of Justice must answer these questions in the next several months as it addresses the lawsuits against Microsoft.

In the old, prewired economy, the argument in favor of a natural monopoly stood on two pillars.

1. Consumers get a better deal (price) because the natural monopoly firm reduces overhead—economies of scale derive from elimination of competition and, often, with government help. the Rural Electrification Administration is an example. Power companies were given a franchise in exchange for spreading power lines to farms and countrysides.

2. Capitalists get a better deal (lower investment, higher return) because competition has been removed. Zero competition is in a sense a way to subsidize industry so it can invest in infrastructure instead of marketing and sales. Covering the U.S. with power lines, cable TV wire and telephone exchanges costs billions. It is difficult to achieve economies of scale until the entire infrastructure is in place—hence the need to protect the risk takers with a monopoly.

From the point of view of an 1880s legislator, water, power, telephone and railway systems seemed "natural" because they provided benefits for everyone. They were for the common good.

Now the rules have changed, producing what I call a friction-free economy. Here economies of physical scale are no longer as important as market share. (That leads to the law of increasing returns, whereby value goes up as the number of customers increases.) Reducing the amount of technological duplication and other "wasted" investment is contrary to chaos in a friction-free economy, because chaos generates innovation and opportunity. Emergent behavior drives new businesses and makes possible rapid progress. So although duplicate investment may seem like a waste, it is really a necessary evil.

Our two pillars begin to crumble under the rules of the new economy. Instead of justifying the common good, a natural monopoly hinders its growth. Here is the friction-free-economy interpretation of the two pillars:

1. Consumers get a better deal (price) because diversity and duplication of products relentlessly reduce prices and improve quality. For example, mass customization and greater personalization are possible because of competition in an unregulated environment. This creates consumer value. Microsoft has to keep its prices low because, regardless of its size, a new innovation or competition from much bigger companies such as IBM could suddenly reverse its fortunes. If it wasn't worried about competition from Netscape, it wouldn't be playing rough in the browser war.

2. Capitalists get a better deal (lower investment, higher return) because competition is the engine that creates huge value. Stock value in regulated monopolies, such as the old AT&T, never went anywhere. Stocks of the new regional telecommunications companies, for instance, have made capitalists ever richer. In short, capitalism loves the chaos of emergent behavior. Accordingly, chaos is attracting more investment in the friction-free economy than ever generated by the old economy that created regulated monopolies. while some win and some lose, the friction-free economy rewards "unnatural risk" via investments in innovative start-ups and fast competitors. Thus, the need to protect the risk takers with a monopoly has been replaced by the need to caution overzealous investors who believe the Nasdaq will rise forever. That's a problem most societies would gladly embrace.

One can argue that Microsoft has an unnatural monopoly because of its huge installed base, which it obtained by grabbing market share. But that base can also rapidly reduce the firm to rubble. Supplanting railroads, water systems and telephone infrastructure in the industrial age was difficult, but replacing customer loyalty and an installed base is not so costly in the friction-free economy. Netscape demonstrated this proposition by giving away its browser and rapidly ascending as a "competitor" to Microsoft in one arena.

Instead of continuing to innovate and beating Microsoft to the punch, however, Netscape has fallen back on industrial-age techniques of litigation and complaining to the government. Microsoft must be forced to correct some of its more egregious acts of persuasion, but in the long run, litigation won't work. Instead Netscape needs to return to its original strategy—that is, to innovate.

The friction-free economy is replacing the traditional economy of supply and demand, and increasing returns stemming from positive feedback are supplanting the concept of a natural monopoly. Microsoft is just a recent example of a positive-feedback monopoly. Until the Department of Justice rules against such monopolies, the government should keep its hands off Microsoft and let Intel, Sun, Netscape and Microsoft battle it out to the bitter end. The department must make sure everyone plays by the rules. But as long as the rules are followed, increasing returns are just as valid a reason for allowing a monopoly as the concept of a natural monopoly was 100 years ago.

Article by John Charles, IEEE Software,
January–February 1998

Indecent Proposal? Doing Business with Microsoft

North America is home to more than 20,000 independent software vendors. These companies produce software for every task and market niche imaginable, from desktop utilities to enterprise-level applications. Many ISVs have little in common beyond falling under the same generic rubric. However, one thing nearly all ISVs share is relationship with Microsoft—be it partner or vendor, customer or competitor. The last of these relationships is easily the least desirable, especially when the mere rumor that Microsoft is eyeing a market can send stalwart venture capitalists running.

Yet, there are those in the software industry who insist you must say "no" to Microsoft, that to do otherwise would be corporate suicide. Quite a few more argue the opposite.

The headlines are full of suits and countersuits concerning Microsoft, many of which may determine the shape of the software industry for decades to come. As important as these legal battles are, they are no substitute for a business strategy; ISVs still have to decide if it's worth the risk to "dance with the elephant."

It's like a Jungle Sometimes

For many ISVs, the central issue in deciding their relationship to Microsoft is Microsoft's own business strategy. Richard Smith, president of Phar Lap, a tools development company for real-time operating systems, says the key question ISVs must ask is "Will I have to compete with Microsoft or not?" To answer that question, you first must understand how Microsoft operates. Smith describes Microsoft's established *modus operandi* as follows. Redmond constantly monitors the marketplace for new technologies; when a promising technology emerges, Microsoft invests in or partners with one or two of the technology's leading vendors. Once the technology becomes popular and establishes a customer base, Smith says, Microsoft approaches the top three of four vendors and offers them a choice: "either you're with us or you're going to be out of business." The latter part of that equation is a recognition that once the technology becomes a standard feature of Windows it is basically free to the consumer—it has been "commoditized." In most cases, a commoditized product means a dried-up market.

After this grim forecast, Microsoft then asks what Smith calls *the question:* "Will you phase out your technology?" This "phasing out" process takes different forms.

* *Acquisition.* Potentially the most lucrative possibility, and the explicit goal of countless startups. When Microsoft took an interest in the Web authoring tool FrontPage, Vermeer Technologies happily sold the farm for a cool $130 million.

* *Licensing.* This scenario Smith can tell you about from experience. Microsoft offers to license your technology and pays you either in cash, consulting, cross-marketing, or all of the above. According to Smith, Microsoft's pitch for cross-marketing goes like this: "If your jump on the bandwagon there's other things you can do to make money [such as add-ons]. Because you already know this business, you can understand what the market opportunities are and go after them." Smith took the bait and is happy with the results. "We did a bunch of horse trading. They were unwilling to spend cash, but they were willing to spend time and effort. We licensed software to them and they gave us a variety of marketing opportunities. We benefited from the association." But what if

you stood to make a lot more money than what Microsoft offered? Cheer up, it could be worse.

+ *Competition.* Microsoft develops its own version of your product internally, offers you no compensation, and competes with you directly. The word processing program WordStar and the spreadsheet application Lotus 1-2-3 offer the most compelling examples. These products, early on so important to the PC platform's widespread acceptance, slowly but surely faded after being replaced by Word for Windows and Excel. Smaller companies with fewer resources are even more susceptible to being put out in the cold, or, as some might say, run over.

Just Say Java

There are many in industry who still agree with former Apple exec Jean Louis Gassée's description of doing a deal with Microsoft, "partnering with Microsoft is like picking up dimes in front of a steam-roller." You pick up a little change in the short term, but you're going to get squashed sooner than later. So what's an ISV to do? How can you say no? The most popular option these days is Java.

Caldera president Bryan Sparks believes that "the only alternative is the Java environment. It's the only way you can write an application and not be 100 percent reliant on Microsoft's operating system. "Sparks, whose company produces the Open Linux operating system, insists that if your product is interesting enough, "it will disappear, one way or another. The only chance is to go on a more neutral environment." While willing to concede that Java is no panacea, Sparks still believes that "it's good enough and getting better, and at least it gives you some portabil-ity on other platforms."

Even if Java were flawless its proponents would still face a Her-culean task in converting a significant number of Windows devotees. Given that Windows has over 90 percent of the market share on the desktop, it's a hard sell to ask an ISV to double or triple its development costs for the remaining fraction of the market. Sparks response is, "don't stop your Windows development, but hedge your bets." If you are using Java, Sparks suggests, when Microsoft takes the top spot in your market "you can be a number one on another platform and help them grow instead of just acquiescing and doing something else."

Tim Sloan, industry analyst for the Aberdeen Group, also sees opportunity hidden in the shadows cast by Windows' bulk. He points out that because many ISVs are "locked in" with Windows, "that leaves the market for 100 percent Java solutions up for grabs to some company who will go out and do it. . . . It's nice opportunity for a company that doesn't have a large installed base at Microsoft."

Mark Coggins, director of developer relations at Netscape, says his company's Java-friendly stance gives ISVs more flexibility and autonomy, "Microsoft is very proprietary and closed, and essentially they say you need to write to the Windows standards, requirements, and APIs." In contrast, Coggins says, Netscape supports a platform built on open standards. "We're not asking our ISVs to do unnatural acts to partner with us, we're only asking them to do things the marketplace would ask them to do anyway."

But what if Java's not your cup of tea? Andrew Schulman, author of *Unauthorized Windows 95,* offers what seems to be an even more unlikely avenue for an end run around Microsoft—HTML. "The promise has been fulfilled already on the Web with HTML. You can pull it up using any browser, all the stuff is being done on the server via CGI. Ship pure, 100 percent HTML." Despite its simplicity and limitations, Schulman says, it is a well-tested industry standard and is used much more widely on the Web than either Java or Active X.

Another way to resist Microsoft's gravitation pull is to go into a niche market, far, far away from the company's core competency. Of course that competency appears to change almost daily—witness Microsoft's ventures into such seemingly unrelated areas as online investment banking, the gaming industry, proprietary networks, and cable television. Schulman says the only area he can think of safe from Microsoft's grasp is pornography: "You're left with the dregs."

Saying Yes

In the face of all this doom and gloom are many ISVs who don't find the Microsoft embrace a life-sapping bear hug. On the contrary.

Take Microsoft's official entry into the video streaming market this summer. The Justice Department began yet another antitrust investigation of Microsoft and most folks began writing epitaphs for the small companies that populated this relatively new market. However, Peter Zaballos of Vivo Software had already grown impatient waiting for a heavy hitter to hammer the market down. Zaballo's company specializes in tools for creating video content on networks. Now that Microsoft is going to integrate the video server into the OS's server suite, there will be a common platform and file format. In Zaballos's estimation, the more stable the environment, the more willing developers will be to create applications and content for the platform. "Everything that Microsoft has done so far has only increased the opportunity for us and increased choice for the consumer. This market was on its way to overheating and stalling because no large company was entering and homogenizing things."

Critics are quick to point out, though, that Microsoft rarely stops with "homogenizing" the platform, and that instead of applauding Microsoft, eager vendors should keep their hands on their wallets. Synon vice president Bill Yeack says its misleading to single out Microsoft as the predator. "It's not Microsoft—big, bad, evil empire—it's the industry. . . . I have more comfort giving my technology to Redmond than anyone else in the industry." He says Microsoft is always very articulate about where they intend to compete," and in 15 years they've never broken a single promise." For Yeack, what distinguishes Microsoft from competitors like Oracle is that "Microsoft wants to control the community, they do not want to own it. They put in more effort than any other vendor in the industry to make your partnership effective."

Indeed, Microsoft has gone out of its way to combat its image as a ruthless predator. For example, Microsoft recently dropped the entrance requirements for joining the Microsoft Developer's Network. "Fill out a form," says Tod Nielsen, general manager of developer relations, "give us your name and address and you then have access to all of the documentation and services." Earlier this year Microsoft also formed the Application Developers Customers Unit, a 600-person group dedicated to providing technical and marketing support for ISVs creating line-of-business applications. "It's pure partnership play," say ISV relations manager Joe Bennett, adding that it is in Microsoft's best interest to have as many strong applications running on Windows as possible. "We build [the ISVs'] selling and implementation channels so they can reach a larger share of the market." Bennett says, "They know for a fact that we're not going to compete with their channel, and we're not going to compete with their applications."

Wide Awake

"I anticipate the worst, so I'm never surprised," admits Brent Frei of Onyx Software. Frei is an ex-Microsoft employee who left Bill's kingdom to fill a niche in customer management software for Windows NT. "At some point I do expect them to get into my market. At that point I need to be able to either leverage what they do, compete with what they do, or change my strategic direction." Frei reminds us that Microsoft isn't the only company out there hungry for Onyx's market share: "If not Microsoft, it's going to be someone else. I could just as easily be taken out by someone smaller who has a lot smarter development staff and smarter marketing folks than I do."

Raxco's Brad Bradley, Director of Products Operations and Services, says his company has readied itself for any number of possibilities. One of Raxco's star products is a defragmentation device, a prime candidate for absorption into an OS. While he hopes his product won't vanish, he would rather his defragger get absorbed over a competitor's. "If that opportunity came up we would say, 'Fine, take it.'" Bradley points out that the "absorber" will then distribute a "light" version of your product for you electronically, which saves packaging costs; if users want extra functionality, it will cost them.

Moreover, Bradley asserts that Raxco would survive commoditization because it has "differentiated" itself with a variety of products and services. "We do so much more than just defrag. We went into this market with our eyes wide open."

Just in case, Raxco has one last line of defense: a patent. While few developers put much stock in the efficacy of patents, Stac Electronics did take home $110 million from Microsoft for patent infringement on its disc compression software.

Money Isn't Everything

Most people in industry would see Diba as one more casualty of the Microsoft machine. Microsoft approached Diba founder Farzad Dibachi last year, expressing an interest in his information appliance software. After being turned away, Microsoft purchased Web TV, Diba's main rival, for $425 million. In August, Dibachi took the best offer left— a bid from Sun Microsystems for under a $100 million.

It looks as though Dibachi lost big for saying no. He disagrees. "We didn't start Diba to maximize profit the first day. Maybe I made a couple of million dollars less. So what? The numbers are absurd," Dibachi explains, "My decision was based on the fact that [I wanted] the product to see the marketplace. That was more important. Still is." Dibachi never intended to get bought out, he says; he purposely avoided backing from venture capitalists to preserve an uncompromised decision-making authority on his product's fate, "our attitude was, we're going to make this on our own."

When he eventually did see a need for support from what he calls "big brother," he wanted to partner with a company "that was more like us. Sun was more like us." Despite his decision to go with Sun, Dibachi is no less determined for his product to make it to market. He says he'll do it, with or without Sun.

As Dibachi's experience suggests, your experience with megacorporations like Microsoft (or Sun) may depend on what you were after in the first place. Should you says yes or no to Microsoft? Unless you have a fortune teller on your marketing team, the best all-purpose answer might be a definite maybe.

PART TWO

The Rise
of the Internet

CHAPTER ELEVEN

The Latest Dance Craze: Browsing

Tim Berners-Lee, the father of the World Wide Web, or Web for short, learned about the ARPANet, a.k.a. Internet, while fiddling around with computers at CERN—the famous European research center. By 1989 the rudiments of communicating by way of the Internet had already evolved, but no one thought to standardize documents. So Berners-Lee proposed a hypertext-like format for pushing documents to scientists and engineers working throughout the world. He combined Ted Nelson's hypertext with Internet standards like File Transport Protocol (FTP), Gopher, and WAIS and borrowed the format from SGML (Standard Graphical Markup Language) to come up with HTML (HyperText Markup Language). HTML soon became the lingua franca of the Internet.

Standardization of all Internet documents opened the floodgates of innovation. HTML would render traditional printing presses obsolete, and cut down on the time it usually took to get a paper circulated to the scientists who wanted to keep up with progress in physics. Serendipitously, Berners-Lee defined publishing for everyone on the Internet.

His concept of a World Wide Web was simple, but elegant. Hypertext systems linked phrases and words of one document to other documents. When implemented on a computer, a hyperlink might expand a word into an entire paragraph by simply clicking on the word. A bibliographic reference might be linked to the document it describes via another hypertext link. A simple click on the reference causes the hypertext system to fetch the entire document.

Berners-Lee thought this idea made a wonderful way to compose scientific papers. What if the papers referenced other papers located miles away? The ARPANet made it rather easy to fetch reports and other documents from anywhere in the world, using FTP, for example. But the user had to know the address of the document, and keeping track of locations and addresses was too cumbersome. Why not embed the addresses—Universal Resource Locators (URL)—in the documents, themselves? Now, whenever a user selected a reference in one paper, the hypertext system would automatically fetch the referenced paper and display it on the user's screen.

Links could point to any document, anywhere in the world. This transparency instantly shrunk the world to the size of a desktop computer. Distance no longer mattered. Millions of documents, linked by Berners-Lee's hyperlinks, spun a web that circled the world—the World Wide Web. It worked like magic.

Berners-Lee figured that the best way to get something working quickly, was to leverage existing technologies. The NeXT workstation was a natural because its operating system integrated easily with the Internet, and its GUI Builder tool made rapid application development, well, rapid. The first version of Berners-Lee's hypertext system was written in Objective C for the NeXTStep operating system. A colleague of Berners-Lee, Nicola Pellow, built a command line interface version of the hypertext browser and demonstrated that such a system could work in 1990. The code was posted on the Internet in 1991 so that others could build on the original.

Emergent behavior began to take over as momentum built up around this freeware. Contributors such as Pei Wei, Tony Johnson, and Marc Andreessen enhanced and promoted GUI browsers based on the original CERN freeware. These second-generation browsers were much easier to use, and accelerated the spread of browsers, as we know them today. In addition, GUI browsers began to proliferate on a variety of other platforms by 1993. Students at the NCSA (National Center for Supercomputer Applications), University of Illinois, enthusiastically built browsers for Unix, Macintosh, and Windows, adding steam to the building pressure behind browsers.

By the end of 1993 http servers grew in number from about 50 to over 200. The idea had arrived. Robert Cailliau was given the go-ahead to organize the First International WWW Conference at CERN that year. Between 1993 and 1996—three short years—the number of http servers on the Internet jumped to over one million. This was Internet rising.

In 1994 I was Editor-in-Chief of *Computer* magazine, the premier publication of the IEEE Computer Society. My readers were the elite of the computing professional community. Most had grown up on the Internet, going way back to 1969. A few were pioneers who had developed the Internet Protocol, packet switching, routers, and switches—all the fundamental technology needed to make the Internet work. They had no difficulty taking browsers in their stride. It was no big deal.

The fact that the Internet might become a commercial success was a big deal to my readers, however. In 1994 the Internet community was not very comfortable with the evolution of the Internet towards commercialization. In fact, there was a small backlash movement, led mostly by the hackers and engineers who had come to think of the Internet as their private plaything. But it was too late to oppose the concept of a commercial Internet. It had already become a fashion, as indicated by this next essay.

In 1994 the average person on the street didn't quite know what the Internet was, but they knew they had to be on it. Getting and staying wired became a topic of discussion in the most fashionable social settings. Mainstreaming of the Internet presented a second problem: how does one go about actually getting on the Internet? As incredible as it may seem, today most people in the general population didn't have the slightest idea how to get wired. In the next two essays I make fun of the radical idea that the Internet was for everyone. Then, by April 1995, even I was beginning to believe that the Internet was rising. So, in 6 months, I was turned on to the Web just like millions of non-techies who would soon make their living in cyberspace.

Article by Ted Lewis, Computer, September 1994

Making the Connection

The Internet-savvy party animal has arrived at most country club cocktail receptions. No longer shunned by the Beautiful People, he or she is in demand as a conversationalist: "Oh, last night on Mosaic I saw the funniest show. . . ." or ". . . it happened to me while I was gophering around the Internet." Everyone wants to get connected. But how does one become a citizen of Cyberville?

Plunking down $8.95 each month to use the miniature virtual reality of eWorld—or a bit more for access to the macho services of Prodigy, Compuserve, or America Online (AOL)—merely gives you gateway access to the Internet. This is not the same as being connected to the Internet, because you are held at bay by the eWorld or AOL server. Still, it is something to talk about at the country club klatch.

To make really impressive conversation at, say, the next fashion show, you need direct access to the Internet. Now you enter a higher level of society, where Mosaic can be used directly. Having all of the world's electronic information at your fingertips is power, and having power is the reason you paid $2,000 for a supercomputer in a box. So the challenge facing the middle class is not taxes or divorce, but how to get connected!

Lifeline to the Workplace

The same story holds for the workaholic who needs access to the office LAN at all hours of the day or night. The terminal emulator and Unix login will not do for you. Only an extension of the LAN into your bedroom will satisfy your need to be connected. This is called remote access. Taken to the next step, remote access becomes remote control. In a remote control system, you can take over the controls of a remote computer without being there. It's a kind of telepresence.

The telephone companies and the modem manufacturers have been hard on the heels of the remote access and remote control trendsetters. Toiling away diligently in their Silicon Valley workshops, they have devised ways for us to dial up from home or road and get on the Internet through our office LAN. The trick is to make it look like you never left work, and to extend the LAN to the telephone line.

For a quick solution to the LAN extension problem, purchase pcAnywhere from Symantec Corp. or Apple Remote Access from Apple Computer. These products allow you to dial up any voice-grade line and connect to a remote access server that is usually part of your LAN. With Apple Remote Access, the disks and printers connected to your office LAN appear as icons on the desktop (or in the Chooser) just as they would from a machine actually connected to the LAN. To a DOS clone, a disk on the remote system looks like drive E:, F:, or Z:. Thus, you are connected. No terminal emulator, no Unix command . . . look Ma, no hands!

Wired to the Max

But remote access through a voice-grade line is for weenies. Real road-ies need more bandwidth. Suppose you want the entire Infobahn to pass right through your bedroom. You can order ISDN services from Pacific Bell telephone for a measly $22.50 per month plus time charges. This will boost your 14.4-kilobit-per-second modem speed by an order of magnitude to 112 Kbps. The ISDN line is actually two lines, each running at 64 Kbps (sometimes called $p \times 64$, where $p = 2$). Allowing for over-head, this gives you an effective speed of 56 Kbps on each pair of wires. Combining them, you get 112 Kbps. (Some manufacturers are planning inverse multiplexing equipment that combines more than one ISDN line into a "fat ISDN" line to multiply these speeds even further, going to 384 Kbps or more. This is $p \times 64$, where $p = 24$ for TI service).

Using a \$995 ISDN bridge from Combinet, for example, you can save charges and still be on the office LAN from home. The bridge automatically dials your LAN server and makes the connection when needed: after a period of inactivity, it hangs up to save money. But this configuration is pricey because you need a terminal adapter, a bridge, and an Ethernet card in series.

Still, this is the future of modem makers. Combining the functionality of remote access from your roving computer is the ultimate modem dream. Making it work over variable $p \times 64$ lines is the goal. Automatically adapting to voice grade, ISDN, or T1 ($p \times 64$) lines renders the connection to the Infobahn seamless.

Article by Ted Lewis, Computer, April 1995

Infobusiness Meets Neuromancer

nfobahn is many things, not all of them evident to Net cruisers who shuttle up and down the Web. Infobahn is social lubricant to the verbose, heir-apparent to TV's wasteland, and magnet to intellectuals in hot pursuit of the world's "knowledge at my fingertips." Infobahn is the new shopping mall in multimedia colors, venture capitalist dance craze of the '90s, political mantra of the ultra left, right, and middle-of-the-road. It is home of the techno-elite yet socially inept, roamed by cyberpunk cowboys and, yes, most carefully defined by the clan of Gates, McCaw, Case, and House of TCI.

Being a webhead cowboy myself, I never believed in the 500-channel network concept of the Infobahn, replete with couch-potatoisms and QVC-on-speed consumerism. Humans are more social than mechanical and, as much as we malign them, I doubt very much that Cyber Bill will shoot his TV and buy a Blockbuster Video vending machine. The stampede to the Internet is an entirely new phenomenon that cannot be compared with existing technology. Little could anyone imagine the internal combustion engine's impact on the livery stable. (Did *you* ever hear of anyone riding horseback to the mall?) Likewise, we cannot predict how the modem will affect home, school, and office.

Nonetheless, I disagree with those who say that FutureBusiness on the Infobahn is all hype. On the contrary, I believe fortunes are waiting to be made. University of Michigan Business Professor Gupta (www.umich.edu/sgupta/hermes.htm) reports that 18 percent of web-heads spent more than $50 on line over the past six months, which doesn't seem like much at first. His sample was under 1,000 users, but if the 7.6 million serious Internet users are considered, we're talking a burgeoning $11 million per month. This study, by the way, was conducted during a period when the straights said FutureBusiness is bad business.

Trilateral Support

The FutureBusiness model is based on interactivity, specialty, and empowerment. Take Xband (Catapult, Cupertino, Calif.) as an example of interactivity. The Xband multiple-user device connects game-playing machines located anywhere in the world together via ordinary telephone lines in a kind of spontaneous Regional Bell Operating Company special-interest group. Catapult's MUD server matches opposing players based on comparable skills and keeps "league ratings" so that a world champion can be crowned some day.

Interactivity Is Key

Another example of interactivity (not to mention instant gratification) is a virtual reseller that began Net operations last summer. "We are looking to expand the pie, not simply rearrange the pieces," said Bill McKiernan, president of Cybersource, which offers 6,500 software titles to program-mers and is logging 1,000 different users per day (*Computer Reseller News*, Jan. 30, 1995, p. 27). A key selling point is instant gratification in the form of downloading juicy software on the spot. You can't match the interactivity and instant gratification with a static mail-order catalog.

Now here's an example of specialty: Dave Asprey owns West Amer-ican T-shirt Co., a cyberspace pushcart that hawks T-shirts to coffee bean freaks (*Home Office Computing*, Feb. 95, p 64). Not old enough to drive a car, he nevertheless earns $2,000 a month toward a Land Rover from these caffeine guzzlers.

Empowerment Is Also Key

Empowerment is the third key to the FutureBusiness model. The Internet has unleashed a flood of creativity not seen since Wolfe's Electric Kool-Aid Acid Test. Eavesdrop on the comic book forum in America Online, for example. Here you'll find comic book artists publishing phenomenally interesting comic books in an interactive marketplace. Gauging audience response on a daily basis, then revising and republishing gives these artists an unprecedented, close-to-your-customer advantage over print cartoonists. Empowerment means that a little guy can look like General Motors, for all practical purposes. In fact, FutureBusiness is probably synonymous with small business.

Specialization Is Where It's At

The net is already too big, so unless you're earning a PhD in WireHead, who needs access to all the knowledge in the universe? In fact, Richard Jennings complains in *Byte* (Jan. 1995, p. 296), "Who needs the Internet?", asserting that it has become plebeian. Too much generality can hurt rather than help. Real fun is cruising with like-minded Jetsons; FutureBusiness is selling to these specialized groups.

Still skeptical? Then listen to Larry Ellison (CEO of Oracle, being interviewed in *Upside,* Sept. 1994, p. 22) when asked whether there is FutureBusiness on the Net: "It's the most bizarre question I've heard in my life. Everything will be digital, everything will be intelligent, but we will have smart TVs, computers, telephones, burglar alarms, and light bulbs. A variety of different smart devices will be attached to the information superhighway."

Free Advice
(and Worth Every Penny)

Now for making a fool of myself with some predictions: Over one third of American homes have some kind of computer right now. Multimedia and compression technology on a PC are improving much faster than HDTV, so my guess is that the Infobahn kiosk will soon resemble today's networked personal computer rather than today's cable TV set-top box. More digital convergence is needed, but the early outlines of FutureBusiness can be found in products like Xband and Netscape/GIF browsers. Don't get me wrong, I'm not picking winners and losers yet—the gasoline engine powers many different vehicles, so we needn't worry about everyone cruising the Net in a white four-door sedan. But we do have to wait for defining applications. Although *Wired* magazine (Feb. 1995, p. 48) claims to know what the killer apps are, including dating and gambling, I personally think the issue goes much deeper.

If you want to get rich from the interactive bonanza, think of a really specialized group activity like chow-chow ranching out west. Organize it as a SIG, open a home page, make up electronic business cards, then sell out to America Online. Read Gary Welz's "New Dimensions" article in

Internet World (March 1995, p. 30–36) for lists of special-interest URLs and ideas on how to cash in. Also check *PC Computing* (March 1995), which lists some of the many cyberspace business addresses out there.

My guess is that the VisiCalc of the Infobahn is still in some teenager's bedroom, but when it gets out on the Net, FutureBusiness will make WWW malls look like street corner lemonade stands. If you think FutureBusiness is going to die on the Internet, then you're living with last week's press release. Get with it!

CHAPTER TWELVE

Rumble in Telecommunications

The Telecommunications Act of 1934 had stood the test of time pretty well, until the Internet came along. Then, strange things started to happen. Emergent behavior was creating opportunities to bypass the regulated telephone monopolies. In fact, the 1934 Act was about to tumble. But nobody could have predicted such a landmark change back in the spring of 1995.

Perhaps I was overly impressed by the telephone applications I saw running at Cypress Research's booth in San Francisco (*MacWorld,* January 1995) when I wrote this next article. I predicted the demise of the PBX, and suggested the rise of "voice on Internet Protocol" (VoIP). My first prediction never came true, but my second one has become a megatrend. Within a few years of early experimentation with voice digitization and transmission over the Internet, VoIP had become a threat to analog telephony. Within another three years, it will revolutionize the long-distance telephone industry.

The impact of the 1996 Telecommunications Act was slow to develop, but the passage of the Act was clearly a direct result of Internet rising. Even today we cannot predict the long-term consequences. But one thing is certain: the rise of IP (Internet Protocol) hasn't been fully felt, yet. When it spreads to analog telephony, the world will not be the same. Indeed, telephone companies are becoming passé.

Article by Ted Lewis, Computer, May 1995

Are Telephone Companies Passé?

Remember what happened to centralized MIS departments during the PC revolution of the 1980s? Well, the offspring of the Philistines responsible for that are now at the gates of the centralized-PBX manufacturers and soon will be storming the walls of major telecommunications providers. If you're a Microsoftian (rhymes with Martian), think TAPI (telephony API). If you live in a Novellian (rhymes with Orwellian) world, the watchword is TSAPI. But if you're one of those rare individuals who think a standard should be made by a standards group instead of a market-muscle company, call it the dash to SCSA (signal computing system architecture). We call it CTI (computer telephone integration). Regardless of name, the movement toward desktop telephony is afoot, and desktop telephony will do to the telephone equipment manufacturers what Gorbachev did to the FSU (former Soviet Union).

It Gets Personal

Like many Info Age technologies, CTI wrests control from the big guys (PBX, Centrex, and handset suppliers) and gives it to you and your PC. CTI replaces the centrally managed and monopolized telephone bureaucracy with a flexible, end-user-controlled telephone-system-in-a-computer.

This shift is not surprising, since it's part of the grand picture: Centralized mainframes dissolve into personal computers, libraries fade as gophers gallop across the Internet, and network television melts down as DirecTV and video tape players saturate the home market. So it is with PBX makers and Regional Bell Operating Company service providers as they face the desktop hordes riding the Internet wave. In a survey by *Communications Week* (Feb. 27, 1995, p. 98), 56 percent of the people interviewed said they think distributed telephony applications on PC servers are a good idea. The only remaining question: What form are they going to take? Knowing the answer to this quiz could also ferret out the next billionaire.

Now for some illustrations. Mediatrends (Concord, Mass.) is selling a TAPI-compliant application that lets network administrators control Centrex and PBX features through any modem or telephone connection via their Windows PC. (There goes your craving to buy a costly Centrex machine.) Cypress Research of San Jose sells a $600 visual programming tool for writing your own Centrex, fax, messaging, and voice-mail management system on a $2,000 Macintosh. (There goes your craving to order services from the affable account manager at your local telephone company.)

I'm talking about features that can be programmed into your desktop without your being held hostage by aliens from planet Bell. I'm talking trivial bunk like disabling call-waiting so it doesn't disrupt your fax transmission (where you have to dial 1170 before dialing your destination number) and dialing *-9 to launch a conference call. (Watch out: PBX technology is still in its mainframe generation where each peddler uses a proprietary code: AT&T, NEC, or Northern Telecom PBXs may interpret *-9 as either a command to initiate a conference call or a command to transfer an incoming call to another number.)

But this is kid stuff. The heavy hitters are small companies like Wildfire Communications (Lexington, Massachusetts), hawking a voice-activated tin-man assistant that totally bypasses a PBX or Centrex system *and* eliminates the desktop computer! Wildfire is a software agent that intervenes during a telephone call to screen, route, announce call-waiting, and in general respond to spoken commands during any telephone call. Wildfire integrates the messaging, fax, e-mail, pager, and call-management features of a big-time telephone Centrex without big-time telephone company impediments.

You can voice-dial a call by speaking the destination person's name as well as program other features without pushing buttons, reading a manual, or sheepishly asking your secretary how to place straightforward conference calls.

Telephone Call to the Future

Bill Warner of Wildfire Communications called me out of the blue to demonstrate Wildfire (don't take my word for it, call 800-WILD-FIRE to hear it yourself). Wildfire seemed to be eavesdropping on our conversation. For example, when Bill wanted some information, he would call on Wildfire, and "she" would join in. But when Bill spoke to me, Wildfire would butt out and remain silent.

Bill: Hi, Ted, I want to show you something.
Ted: Uhh, hi. OK.
Bill: Wildfire.
    Here I am.
Bill: Find.
    What's the name?
Bill: Ted Lewis.

Contact named Ted Lewis.
Bill: Describe it.
Ted Lewis is a person. Work phone number is . . .
Bill: Never mind. Ted, that was my telephone assistant. Actually,
*   Wildfire isn't human . . .*
Ted: That's cool. I'm kinda busy, Bill.

Here's a portion of a conversation (from *Forbes,* Nov. 7, 1994) that shows how you might activate Wildfire to check on your messages while speeding down the freeway, cellular phone in one hand and Big Mac in the other:

Wildfire.
*   What can I do for you?*
Find.
*   Find what?*
New messages.
*   There is one.*
From whom?
*   Mike Richards.*
Play it.

Wildfire is still a tad expensive for home use or small businesses. It starts at $2,000 per user and requires a $900-a-month T-1 line to support up to 72 users (20 at the same time). On the other hand, it does away with the PBX and Centrex. Still, if you think the price is irksome, try Internet telephony.

Long Distance
without the Charges

Wildfire is but one kind of ambush lying in wait for portly telephone companies. What happens to the RBOCs if the Internet replaces telephony altogether? The possibility of replacing telephones with Internet is the motivation behind Windows-based VocalTec (Northvale, New Jersey), Macintosh-based Maven, and Unix-based vat. These products let desktop microphoners place telephone calls to anyone on the Net for the cost of a local call. For example, I can place a long-distance telephone call to my friends in China without using my AT&T calling card. For the cost involved, my friends could as easily be in Carmel as in China. Think of this as an audio surrogate for the bandwidth-intensive MBone (video and audio). Maven et al. might lack the sophistication of Wildfire, but the price is surely right.

Chicken Little and the (Blue) Sky

The sky is not falling in on telephone companies just yet, largely because the Internet *is* the telephone company, but video and audio technology is advancing so rapidly that no company can afford to rest on its patents. I recall how safe and secure IBM was before PCs came along, almost immune to challenges. (No longer!) Are today's dominant telecommunications companies likewise susceptible?

With the action shifting from computing to communicating, telecommunication pacesetters will need to watch their flanks. Could their ruin lie with these next-generation upstarts who will soon offer consumers a personal PBX/Centrex box connected via locally provided wireless services, totally bypassing the phone company? After all, telephone companies are essentially wires and switches—do away with the wiring and replace the switches with PCs, and you do away with the need for telephone companies altogether. Capabilities like those found in Wildfire, services like Ardis that do away with wires, and aggressive pricing from providers like Netcom may yet have telephone company executives ducking for cover.

CHAPTER THIRTEEN

NetGain or NetLoss?

By 1996 the Internet was the equivalent of California during the Gold Rush of 1849. Everyone was going into networking—from building electronic malls to selling Internet connections. But the Internet still had skeptics, and I was one of them. The number one questions was "How can you make money from the Web?" Not everyone was convinced that the Web was ready for business.

One thing was for sure: the number of people logging on to the Web was growing faster than presidential campaign promises (1996 was an election year in the U.S.). This magnet pulled in venture capitalists and technologists by the thousands. Once again, Silicon Valley's unique mixture of greed and clever people worked its economic magic. Web businesses blossomed. But how many were breaking even?

Everyone got wired in 1996, but hardly anyone had a business model that explained how to make money from the exploding population of Netheads. Therefore, 1996 was the year of the business model. In simple terms, money followed eyeballs. The Web site that attracted the most eyeballs, won. Like radio, TV, magazines, and telephones, the Web simply validated the theory of increasing returns. In friction-free terms, the Web provided infinite shelf space, zero marginal costs, and global distribution. The more people tuned in, the more valuable was the Web site. This was known as "NetGain."

This marriage of economics with technology was perfect. In hindsight, the marriage fueled an economic boom that lasted for several years. Stock market valuations for startups like Yahoo!, Excite, Lycos, Amazon.com, and America Online would soon reach unreasonable heights. The general economy performed better than anyone could remember. This was due mostly to the Web.

In this essay, I give one of the first explanations for the friction-free economy and how it is different from classical economics. I then apply friction-free economics to the Web. One of the more disturbing aspects of increasing returns is that it leads to a monopoly, if applied as brilliantly as Microsoft has applied it. Mediocrity is another negative aspect. Because most Internet business successes are based on the number of eyeballs a site can generate, the Web tends to be like TV, a vast wasteland. In fact, pornography has proven to be one of the most successful businesses to transition to the Internet. And at a less prurient level, Web entertainment, news, and information tend to be of much lower quality than print or broadcast media quality. I call this "NetLoss."

The question that lingers after reading this essay is, "Will the Web be good for us, or just another dumping ground for bad taste, crass commercialism, and lowest-common-denominator entertainment?" Will the Internet add up to a NetGain, or a NetLoss?

Article by Ted Lewis, Computer, July 1996

Alice in Wired World: Wonderland or Wasteland?

Like Alice in Wonderland, the almost-21st-century Nethead is plunging headlong down a rabbit hole toward Wired World. But will he emerge in a digital nirvana, or in a bland, mediocre landscape that will strike TV channel surfers as déjà vu?

When television began to rapidly penetrate the mainstream, many industry insiders wondered where the content would come from. Who was going to fill the airwaves with programming? Now we know: The government-regulated airwaves became a toxic dumping ground for B movies, mediocre stage shows, advertisements, and lowest-common-denominator sitcoms.

There was much more air time than creativity. This led to a "mediocrity spiral": The number of Joe Lunchbucket viewers went up as the quality of programming went down. Declining quality led to more Lunchbuckets, which led to more consumerism, which led to a greater decline in quality. About the only thing that improved was the sophistication of advertising. Will this happen to business on the Internet?

As the global consumer continues to pour money into PC- and Internet-based businesses at the speed of an expanding supernova, content providers are quickly falling behind in providing good programming. There are very few creative, interesting, or innovative Web pages on the Internet and even fewer clever uses of intranetworked computers. Things seem to be degrading to the level of TV. Is there a mediocrity spiral operating in Wired World? (See T. Matthew Ciolek's article on the specter of multimedia mediocrity, *Computer,* Jan. 1996, pp. 106–108).

Seeking a Wired World Business Model

Nobody has yet figured out how to sustain an economy purely on the Internet. That is, nobody has a working business model. Sure, there are many companies with home pages, and there are even companies selling things over the Net. In addition, several companies are trying to become Internet bankers: CyberCash, DigiCash, and First Virtual Holding, for example. But none of these firms have a workable business model the rest of us can follow. Right now, these companies are burning up venture capital faster than they are signing up subscribers.

Here is one of the fundamental problems. Joe Lunchbucket is not going to plunk down $30,000 for a car via the Internet. In fact, he probably won't buy software electronically—or even play Internet Arcade—until the First National Bank of Wired World can handle microcash. The average cost of electronically processing a financial transaction is at least several dollars, and this will have to come down before mass consumption goes up. How can you make a profit selling penny cups of Kool-Aid when it costs two dollars to cash the check?

Another fundamental problem is the security paradox. Transactions must be secure, but security is a barrier to selling. PGP (Pretty Good Privacy) is a good example. Setting up PGP passwords and exchanging public keys with everyone on the Internet is a hassle. It's even worse than trying to make Windows 95 Plug-and-Play. Even my nerdy computer science friends don't use PGP to hide their e-mail messages from prying eyes. How will the digitally uninitiated cope?

There are many other problems I could dwell on, but you get my drift. There is simply no good business model.

Out of the Box

When confronted with insurmountable problems, humans do unusual things. One of them is called "changing the rules." This is one of those times when we have to think "out of the box."

The first step is to discard everything you ever learned in school about market economics. Specifically, you must throw away Keynesian economics, the modern theory of Industrial Age economics. If Adam

Smith can be credited with "inventing" the law of the jungle, John Maynard Keynes can be credited with inventing the concept of supply and demand. Keynesian economics is now like gravity—nobody questions it any longer; it has achieved the status of immutable law. And herein lies our difficulty.

In case you haven't noticed, a software economy is distinctly nonlinear, non-Newtonian (what goes up doesn't always come down), and particularly non-Keynesian (supply has little to do with demand, and vice versa).

FutureBusinesses that subscribe to the non-Keynesian theory quickly rise to positions of leadership within their market segments. Netscape's Navigator freeware propelled the company to an 84 percent market share. Eudora, Qualcomm's e-mail client, is arguably the most popular freeware package in existence. Within microseconds, companies will be giving away Java compilers and Java components. Even Microsoft, the symbol of digital greed, is handing out free copies of its Web server.

Not only is this strategy out of the box, but some people think these guys are out of their heads. However, the reality is that these are the FutureBusinesses that really understand software economics.

Mainstreaming (achieving market share) is the goal of these giveaways, but what are the practical consequences? Simplified diagrams of Keynesian versus non-Keynesian models, shown in Figure 13.1, attempt to answer this question.

In essence, Keynesian economics has production dogging demand—the manufacturer waits for demand to rise or fall before adjusting production. This delay introduces cycles and uncertainty into old-style markets, illustrated in Figure 13.2.

In contrast, the FutureBusiness model reverses this order—demand effortlessly follows production. This leads to a radically different result. A company either mainstreams or dies—there is little in between. (Everything is fast in the Info Age, remember?)

In classical economics, the demand-price equation is solved by initially estimating demand, setting a price, and then producing the product or service. Later (steps 1, 2, . . . in Figure 13.1a) market feedback is used to adjust demand estimates, and production is cranked up or down. If the warehouse is overstocked, the perception is that demand has diminished, so the price is lowered to clear out the inventory; production is curtailed, leading to less supply. Conversely, if demand is great, manufacturing and prices are pushed up to balance supply with demand. This takes time; hence, a delay is introduced, which leads to oscillations.

For example, when the semiconductor industry book-to-bill ratio drops below 1.0 (fewer orders being received than fulfilled), manufacturers decrease supply. When the ratio exceeds 1.0, supply is increased—and sometimes prices are, too (especially in the DRAM marketplace). The adjustments and their corresponding delays have produced up-and-down

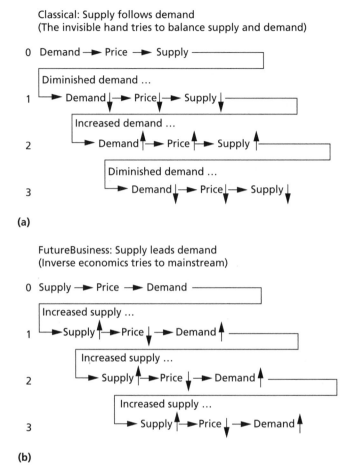

Figure 13.1 *Keynesian versus non-Keynesian (or classical versus FutureBusiness) economies. In (a) the classical model, fluctuations in demand and price result in oscillation, or business cycles. In (b) the FutureBusiness model, supply and price follow a learning curve that drives prices to a commodity level, accelerating both demand and production.*

cycles, as shown in Figure 13.2. This keeps captains of the semiconductor industry up at night, so they've adopted a rule that partially moderates cycles: Adjustments are kept within plus or minus 20 percent per year.

Software Economics

A FutureBusiness optimistically applies the rule "production is boosted so that the supply can double," thereby lowering price according to learning-curve theory. When prices are lowered, demand also goes up

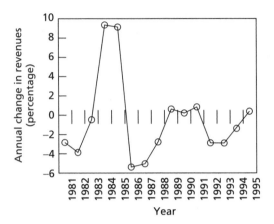

Figure 13.2 *Business cycles in the semiconductor industry illustrates classical "supply follows demand" theory as it applies to chip manufacturing.*

(assuming demand varies inversely with price). Lowered prices stimulating more demand constitutes the positive feedback mechanism of frictionless capitalism. There is no looking back: Production is constantly forced upward until market saturation and mainstreaming are achieved.

Figure 13.1 illustrates the fundamental difference between classical and FutureBusiness models: Demand and price work together in the old model, but they move in opposite directions in the new model. This is inverse economics—a principle of the Info Age. The goal is to apply inverse economics as fast as you can, produce as cheap as you can, and mainstream by winning or buying market share at light speed.

When a Toyota Is as Good as a Mercedes-Benz

One consequence of inverse economics and the positive feedback of the new software economics is that premium-priced products will find it tougher to survive. (A premium market is the so-called high-priced market, while the commodity market is the so-called cheap stuff.)

The key question is, when does a commodity-priced product equal the quality of a premium-priced product? Answer: When the volume-learning curve raises the quality of the commodity-priced product to the level of the premium-priced product. A 1996 Toyota Camry is probably a higher quality product than a 1976 Mercedes-Benz. The technology of 1996 permits Toyota to build a high-quality car—one that is as good as a premium-priced car of 20 years earlier—at a commodity price. This is the consequence of inverse economics.

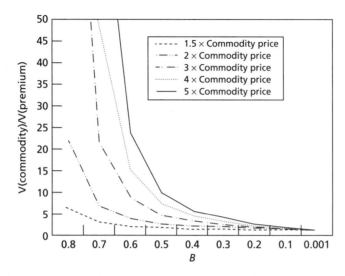

Figure 13.3   *Ratio of volume production of commodity-priced product to volume production of premium-priced product versus the learning rate parameter B. Small values of B represent high learning rates, and high values represent low learning rates: 0 < B < 1.*

Inverse Econ. 101

Here's how the non-Keynesian model works. Classical learning curves predict price declines (or quality increases) as the volume of produced goods doubles. This is the so-called theory of diminishing returns. But in the new software economy the opposite is true: Volume production leads to increasing returns, according to New Age economists such as W. Brian Arthur ("The Theory that Made Microsoft," *Fortune,* April 29, 1996, pp. 65–66). I call it the theory of inverse economics; classical economists call it the theory of increasing returns.

Here's how it works. Assuming true pricing (the price you pay is equivalent to the quality you get), the learning-curve model predicts that the commodity-priced product will eventually overtake the premium-priced product simply because of higher production volumes. This is nonintuitive, because it says that if Toyota makes enough cars, eventually Toyotas will be both better and cheaper than Mercedes-Benz cars.

Figure 13.3 illustrates the effect of inverse economics on premium- and commodity-market segments. For example, suppose a commodity producer manufactures 20 times as much product as a premium producer. This is indicated as a 20 on the vertical axis of Figure 13.3. If both manufacturers learn (denoted *B*) at the same industry rate (say *B* = 0.5), then (0.5, 20) represents the point at which both products are of equal quality. If the premium product initially sells for five times the price of a commodity product, it will eventually be no better in quality than a commodity product that sells 10 times as many units. The commodity product eventually catches up with the premium product.

In a way, volume production lets the commodity product accelerate the learning curve needed to make a better and cheaper product. Mediocrity triumphs over elitism.

Vast Wasteland of Cyberspace

This principle has enormous implications. First, think of the premium Macintosh market versus the commodity Wintel market. Simply by selling 10 times as many boxes, Wintel has roared past Macintosh. Consumers can buy a commodity Wintel box that is just as good as a Macintosh but costs less.

What about the vast Internet wasteland? Given the power of the Internet to "manufacture" products in extremely high volumes, might inverse economics eventually produce extremely cheap yet high-quality content?

We have assumed that selling price is a true reflection of product quality. This is not always the case, of course, but at least the volume producer has the opportunity to increase quality and reduce price. The premium-market producer must work much more diligently to keep up, and in most cases will fall behind.

Will the Internet follow the TV model, or will high-volume production lead to higher quality products? The answer could be as close as your own keyboard and mouse.

CHAPTER FOURTEEN

A Bad Dream

■ had traveled a long way to see Bob Metcalfe eat his words—literally. In front of a live audience of somewhat crazed nerds and publicists, the inventor of the Ethernet carefully blended a copy of his *Info Week* column, and swallowed it whole (stirred, not shaken). The crowd roared.

Metcalfe had articulated what many people were thinking. Growth of the Internet, in terms of new users, was unsustainable. It simply could not go on because bandwidth was not growing fast enough to keep pace. Vinton Cerf, one of the fathers of the Internet, predicted an installed base of 300 million users by 2000. Even if his prediction erred by 100 million, the Internet wasn't big enough to support so many, so fast.

The Internet would soon crash and burn by the end of 1996, according to Metcalfe, or else he would eat his words. Like a bad dream, the Internet would crash; put businesses out of business, and scare away the eyeballs that made the Internet valuable. The Internet era would end, or at least simmer down.

Well, 1996 came and went, and the Internet was still in business. Sure, AOL had its outage, and software problems caused a few ISPs (Internet Service Providers) to black out for a few hours. But the Internet was solid. Metcalfe would have to eat his words. True to his pledge, he went on stage, and swallowing hard, partook of his own pulp fiction.

In the following essay I use mathematics to show how it is possible to black out the Internet like some kind of power outage. The math is convincing, but the reality is that capitalism simply wouldn't let it happen. By 1997 the moneymen had poured so much money into expansion of Internet bandwidth that Metcalfe was resoundingly put down. Once again, greed and clever people made the system work.

Article by Ted Lewis, Computer, November 1996

Netstorms: The Crash of '96

Bob Metcalfe, inventor of Ethernet, founder of 3Com, and now a journalist for *Infoworld*, has added to his reputation by predicting doom in cyberspace. He went public with predictions of an Internet disaster some months ago, and now there are even conferences on the subject. He claims that too many people are riding the Internet and it simply cannot carry them all.

Metcalfe has plenty of empirical evidence to support his dire prediction: Power grids in the Northeast have a history of failure, America Online went down for 19 hours during a change in software, and the bandwidth problems that many Net surfers experience all point to weak links in Wired World. Recently, Metcalfe suggested that there are too many domain names, and this too will contribute to the crash of '96.

If the Net *doesn't* crash by the end of the year, Metcalfe will have pâté on his face, but he's already made his mark, so why worry? On the other hand, if the Net comes to a crashing halt on or before December 31, 1996, Metcalfe will be applauded as some kind of Wired World guru. I might even turn my stock portfolio over to this soothsayer.

Free Enterprise May Intercede

Clearly, the Net does not have infinite capacity, but Bob Lewis (no relation), also writing for *Infoworld*, says there is no way the Net will come to a crashing end, because capitalism won't let it. I guess he has more faith in free enterprise than I do, but it's not the first time capitalism has been called upon to save the world.

I am more analytical than political, so I asked myself, "Is it possible for the Net to overload and blow a fuse?" My answer is "probably."

The Infinite Bus

Probably no single person knows the entire Internet, but a few simple approximations of the Net might yield some insight as to whether a network of interconnected computers can do themselves in by overloading. My first attempt is to view the Internet as an infinite bus. This is a very simple model that treats the Internet as one long daisy-chained bus.

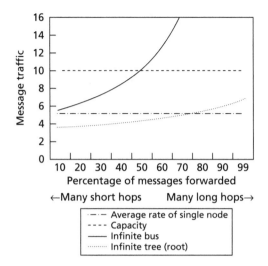

Figure 14.1 *Message traffic comparisons for an infinite bus network versus an infinite tree network at its root.*

Computers are connected to this bus through a left and a right port. They communicate by sending and receiving messages through either port.

Suppose we assume that this bus extends forever in both directions. Let's also assume that each computer on the Net forwards messages some of the time and keeps them some of the time. Let Q represent the percentage of messages that are forwarded. Then $(1 - Q)$ messages are kept by each typical computer. If one half of the forwarded messages go out one port and the other half go out the other port, we get a global average traffic density of $T/(1 - Q)$, where T is the average number of messages per second transmitted by a typical computer in the infinite bus network. I'm assuming that each computer in the Net creates T messages per second in addition to forwarding other messages.

Figure 14.1 shows how traffic builds up as the percentage of messages forwarded increases to 100 percent. After about 50 percent forwarding, the infinite bus network blows up. I did a similar analysis for an infinite binary-tree-structured network. The traffic density at the root of the tree network is shown for comparison. Obviously, trees behave more like logs (pardon the pun).

Thump Theory

My analysis assumes steady-state behavior. In reality, the Net is more likely to experience surges of demand, causing uneven flow. I'll call these *thumps*, indicating that the Net receives a big thump on the head

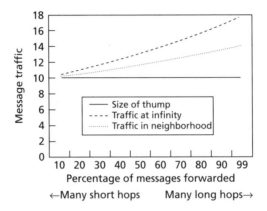

Figure 14.2 *Growth of message traffic in a mesh network.*

whenever a surge occurs. In this souped-up model, the Net is idle until a thump occurs somewhere near an epicenter. If you live in California or Japan, you can appreciate the significance of such thumps.

Thump theory explains possible Netstorms—traffic congestion that can get out of hand. The idea is simple: If a thump propagates to adjacent computers that in turn pass the heavy flow on to other computers, then might these waves of traffic merge? Because the Internet is connected in a convoluted manner, thumps may come back as a knockout punch. The merger of two waves makes a bigger wave. Keep this merger activity up and you cause a major load on the Net.

Netstorms in Meshes

Figure 14.2 shows what might happen in a mesh. I use a mesh to model the Internet because infinite loops are unrealistic, and trees kill off Netstorms because they do not have cyclic connections. Of course, this is a very poor approximation. I leave the harder analysis for some PhD student.

Suppose a thump occurs in the middle of an infinite mesh. Each computer in the mesh is connected to four adjacent computers: one each to the north, south, east, and west. Traffic flows either way across all four connections. The analysis assumes that 25 percent of the messages at each node flow in each direction, and that once again the percentage of messages forwarded equals Q.

The formula for message propagation in an infinite mesh is $T/(1 - Q/4)^2$, for those of you who dabble in such things. This gross approximation assumes both uniformity in all parameters and Netstorm propagation in all directions simultaneously.

Figure 14.2 indicates an overload in the mesh as the percentage of forwarded messages increases. In other words, the thump gets worse as it radiates away from its epicenter. Why? The mesh has many alternate paths from the epicenter computer to all other computers; hence, the load at some distant computer is the sum of the messages forwarded to it via all alternate paths. These alternate-route messages add up. The Netstorm gains force as it spreads.

Figure 14.2 shows the message density for a nearby computer (neighborhood) as well as the asymptote for computers at a far point (infinity). Even the worst-case scenario is within 100 percent of the thump magnitude (18 versus 10).

Doomsday? Stay Tuned

Can the Net crash? Sure. Will it crash? Maybe, but I don't think the vested interests will let it happen. I have to agree with Bob (related or not, we Lewises stick together). However, a question I have not been able to answer is this: How much bandwidth increase do we need to keep the level of service constant as more and more people log on to the Internet?

CHAPTER FIFTEEN

Revolution in Telecommunications

The Internet couldn't crash and burn because greed wouldn't let it. In fact, the Telecommunications Act of 1996 was partially designed to accelerate the growth of the Internet, not slow it down. The growing power of the Internet in 1996 seduced even politicians, who passed one of the most revolutionary laws of the twentieth century. The 1996 Act changed how global telecommunications would be regulated throughout the world. Deregulation of telecommunications would sweep around the world in much the same way that free enterprise had defeated communism as it swept around the globe. Soon after the United States passed its law, Europeans followed suit. Germany deregulated in 1998, for example. Latin American countries would be next. Singapore and China had more trouble with deregulation, but for all practical purposes, it was the Wired West all over again. Telecommunications reform had become a major factor in global change. It started a revolution that might be considered more significant looking back from 2096 than the invention of the Web itself.

But what does it all mean? Many consumers were not aware of how tight the grip of monopoly had held telecommunications in check for decades. For example, prior to the new law, it was illegal for anyone but a cable TV operator to connect devices to household cable. Consumers were required to use the set-top box provided by TCI, Time-Warner, Com-Cast, and others. Similarly, the telephone companies controlled everything to do with voice and data transmission. This made it illegal to transmit digitized voice across the oceans via the Internet. Everyone did it, but the telephone companies could have shut you down, if they had a way to detect that you were bypassing long distance charges in this manner.

The Telecommunications Act of 1996 was revolutionary; it was also controversial. Several years after its enactment, critics complained that the Act had not changed anything because competition had not automatically increased. Rather, big companies got bigger as they consolidated. MCI, Worldcom, and Sprint for example, merged into one big player. Smaller players merged in response. As bigger fish swallowed smaller fish, there seemed to be less competition instead of more. Unleashing previously regulated companies resulted in fewer bigger "monopolies." This was not the intent of the Act.

In defense of mergers, it is clear that the telecommunications industry is a global business. It isn't for regional or local companies. Rather, it will take billions and billions of dollars to build-out the global infrastructure needed to stretch the Internet to all corners of the world. In fact, most people living today have not made their first telephone call! Telephone companies have to be big in order to solve big problems.

The race to own cyberspace is underway. And it will be a defining struggle as the global telecommunications industry reshapes itself in the image of the Internet. It is not clear who will come out on top. It is only clear that it will take big players.

In this next essay I explore the struggle between two groups: the telephone companies versus the cable TV operators. As of 1999, unregulated AT&T was making a play for CABLE, while AOL and its telephone company partners were leveraging xDSL (Digital Subscriber Line) technology in the competition for consumer eyeballs. AT&T's strategy was to bypass the local exchange carriers. AOL's strategy was to go right through them. After all, home is where the paychecks are.

AT&T placed a $4,500 price tag on each American home when it began its siege against the local Bells. While this may seem far too much, the average home consumes $161 a month in telecommunications services. If AT&T gets it all, the break even point is about 28 months. After that, it is all gravy.

Who will own the "last 100 yards" to the consumer? The answer to this question will go a long way toward defining ultimate ownership of the Internet. With stakes about as high as can be imagined, the winner will become one of the monopolies to be feared in the twenty-first century. Along with Internet rising, we will have to deal with an "Internet Monopoly" come the year 2025.

Article by Ted Lewis, IEEE Internet Computing,
May–June 1997

The Software Economy: Greed Is Good

Bigger Than Elvis

Yes, the Internet is bigger than Elvis, which may explain the fundamental shift we see occurring in the economy, namely, the sudden outbreak of greed in Wired Wired World.

Wired World is more than routers, wires, and computers. It is an entirely new product space, an entirely new market space. Companies like Cisco Systems, that realize the value of providing infrastructure and bandwidth to this new market, can make plenty of money. In fact, some say that Cisco is rapidly becoming the third monopoly, after Intel and Microsoft.

But wait a minute. What about the telcos? What about the small Silicon Valley entrepreneurs who yearn to become as rich and famous as Elvis was, too?

A Giant

The 1934 Communications Act gave telephone companies monopolistic rights to your ear, made AT&T the largest corporation in the galaxy, and held back competition in the computer business during the 1970s and 1980s. The original law was weakened in the 1960s and 1970s when IBM battled AT&T for supremacy of the electromagnetic waves, but in general the law stood the test of time.

Until 1996. The 1996 edition threw out the entire 62-year-old law and opened the flood gates to freewheeling competition (see Table 15.1).

The Telecommunications Act of 1996 is arguably the most significant legislation of the century. It is certainly the most radical legislation in the history of hi-tech, and it will profoundly impact the future of the Internet—shop at home, work at home, learn at home, and stay at home. The trouble is, most people understand neither the law nor what it means.

The 1996 Telecommunications Act introduced chaos into Wired World. Entrepreneurs love chaos. Herein lies an opportunity for capitalism.

Who Is Affected	What the Act Does
Cable TV Companies	✦ Deregulates rates for operators serving fewer than 50,000 subscribers. ✦ Deregulates rates for all others by March 1999 or sooner if there is competition by a telephone company. ✦ Lets phone companies deliver video to homes or businesses. ✦ Lets subscribers buy their own set-top boxes.
RBOCs (Regional Bell Operating Companies, the "Baby Bells")	✦ Allows anyone—CATV, telephone, power companies, gas companies— to offer local telephone service. ✦ Allows RBOCs into the long distance telephone business after they satisfy local service requirements mandated by the PFC.
TV Broadcasting Companies	✦ Gives TV stations a chunk of the spectrum so that they can deliver digital TV signals—but they may have to pay big bucks for it. ✦ Requires TV manufacturers to build in the V-chip for blocking porn. ✦ Allows TV broadcasting companies to own up to 35% of TV viewer share in a region. ✦ Allows TV broadcasting companies to own radio stations and CATV operators in same market.
Long-Haul Carriers (AT&T, MCI, GTE)	✦ Permits RBOCs to move into the long-distance market, creating additional competition for the long-haul carriers. ✦ Prohibits the changing of consumers' phone number or service without the consumers' consent.

Table 15.1   High points of the 1996 Telecom Act.

Chaos in Wired World

Because of government interference, Cable Television (CATV) operators and Regional Bell Operating Companies (RBOCs) have tightly controlled the communications market for the past few decades. For example, for years it was illegal to hook anything but a CATV operator's set-top box to the cable in your living room. Think about it. What if AT&T prohibited you from connecting a modem to your telephone line? This selfish rule kept Apple, IBM, Compaq, Packard-Bell, and others from building a PC with a built-in cable modem, leaving the PC-as-set-top-box and free enterprise out in the cold. Without the new Telecommunications Act, there would be no WebTV today.

Before the Act, using the Internet to place long distance calls (*InternetPhone*) was a no-no, even though we all did it. Now Internet telephony is legal, and, according to AT&T, in two years it will be all the rage in Europe. But the telcos have yet to figure out how to charge for it. By the time they do, maybe they will figure out even more ways to make money from consumers.

The Telecom Act also opened up competition to solve the number one problem of Wired World—bandwidth— by releasing the power of something even bigger than the Internet—greed.

Greed . . . at 21 MBPS

Capitalism abhors a vacuum, and the commercialization of the Internet that began in 1991 has taken off now that the Telecommunications Act is securely in place. Companies like WorldCom, Quest, and others have been as busy as worker-bees rebuilding the Internet as a collection of privately owned backbones and LANs that span the world. A private TCP/IP global network called The Grid, for example, is slowly moving in on parts of the public Internet.

In fact, capitalists with more money than common sense have been falling all over one another in an attempt to "own the Internet business." RBOC Nynex bought a $1 billion chunk of MTV parent Viacom thinking the Internet was some new kind of TV channel. US West sunk $2.5 billion into cable company Time Warner. MCI Telecommunications squandered $2 billion on News Corp., and Sprint Corp. linked up with the number one cable company, TCI. Six major TV stations own direct satellite broadcast company Primestar, and NBC joined with Microsoft to run a new cable news channel. Time Warner bought Turner Broadcasting. (Time Warner, in turn, is partly owned by Seagrams, part owner of record and movie production company MCA, which is also partly owned by Matsushita Electric Industrial.) As I write this MCI is being merged with British Telecom.

Why these intermarriages? No one knows what the Telecom Act will bring, so why not hedge all bets? With greed as propellant, the lack of bandwidth will soon be overcome, and the chaos will spread. One thing we do know: sooner or later, all roads in cyberspace will be toll roads.

The Bandwidth Cliff

"I think this communications cliff will be overcome in the next couple of years with cable modems," George Gilder states in a *Red Herring* interview. Perhaps, but it is going to require the telephone companies to cooperate with the CATV operators. Herein lies the struggle among powerful companies such as Viacom, Time Warner, TCI, AT&T, and the RBOCs. Will the Internet become the private property of the telephone companies, CATV operators, or direct broadcast satellite upstarts?

Technology	Maximum Speed (Bits per Second)	Wiring
Analog modem	33,000	Dialup telephone
ISDN	128,000	Dialup telephone
SDSL	1,544,000	Copper—RBOC
ADSL	6,312,000	Copper—RBOC
Ethernet LAN	10,000,000	Coaxial—CATV
Superethernet	100,000,000	Optical fiber—Long-haul telcos

Table 15.2   Home delivery technologies and their capacity.

Piecing Together the Bandwidth Puzzle

Because the telephone companies own the long-haul lines that connect cities and countries, it may seem that they are the only ones to benefit from the new Act. After all, for every long-distance phone call placed, a telephone company collects a toll. However, while CATV operators are small potatoes compared with the long-haul carriers such as AT&T and MCI, significant CATV infrastructure will most likely be in place before the telephone companies can rewire their entire universe with high-speed lines. The local loop delivery mechanism already belongs to CATV.

CATV operators will need the long-haulers to interconnect themselves with high-speed fiber (see Table 15.2). This mixture of technologies will eventually provide high-speed home-to-home connectivity: CATV companies and local telephone outfits for local access, and a variety of long haulers for national and international connectivity. The market will be divided into segments, with each segment providing only one piece of the overall wiring puzzle.

CATV operators have an infrastructure problem of their own. The CATV physical plant lacks the switching capacity of the telephone company. It also lacks the upstream or return-loop facilities of a two-way telephone system. Many CATV physical plants are too old to support two-way broadcasts. And to complicate matters, many CATV operators lack the money to upgrade their physical plants.

The Last 100 Yards

After Paul Baran invented packet-switching for the Internet, he started many successful companies in Silicon Valley. He co-founded

Stratacom, Telebit, and Metricom—all innovators in networking. Metricom, for example, hangs wireless transceivers on buildings and telephone poles to propagate TCP/IP over unlicensed radio waves. Stratacom makes high-speed switches, and Telebit, in addition to networking products, makes lots of money.

One of Baran's newer companies is COM21—a company designed to plug the hole left by the CATV companies as they muscle their way onto the Internet. Bill Gallagher, COM21's vice president of marketing, described the company's plans to solve the bandwidth problem. Gallagher's goal is to put 100,000 cable modems into homes across the United States by 1998. COM21's ATM switch-based CATV solution will provide four levels of guaranteed bandwidth throughout a CATV plant, and a TCP/IP hose right to your doorstep.

URLs for This Column

AT&T • www.att.com/
British Telecom • www.bt.com/
COM21 • www.com21.com/
The Grid • www.gridnet.com/
MCA • www.mca.com/
MCI Telecommunications • www.mci.com/
Matsushita Electric Industrial • www.mei.co.jp
Metricom • www.metricom.com/
Microsoft • www.microsoft.com/
NBC • www.nbc.com/
Nynex • www.nynex.com/
Primestar • www.primestar.com/
Qwest • www.qwest.com/
Sprint Corp • www.sprint.com/index.html
Stratacom • www.strata.com/
TCI • www.tci.com/
Telebit • www.telebit.com/
Time Warner • pathfinder.com/Corp/
Turner Broadcasting • www.turner.com/
US West • www.uswest.com/
Viacom • www.viacom.com/
WilTel • www.wiltel.net/
WorldCom • www.wcom.com/

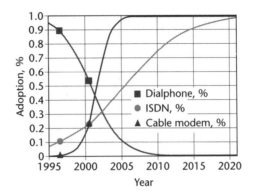

Figure 15.1 *Application traffic distribution.*

The Death of Dialup

Figure 15.1 illustrates the bandwidth problem game plan in the form of adoption rates. At first, CATV companies will install cable modems in homes and locate the back-office servers, the *headends,* in their local offices. The modems will initially operate at digital TV speeds (one million bits per second), eventually increasing to 30 million bits per second. To provide this level of service, however, CATV operators will have to revise their physical plant facilities. Sending a movie from the CATV office to homes is easy, but it is not so easy for information to make the return trip.

As cable modems begin to mainstream around the turn of the century, cable modem companies will take advantage of the projected 67 percent per year dive in production costs and begin selling boxes directly to consumers. Most of the 25 million TV sets and 40 million computers sold each year in the United States will need a fast connection, creating an anticipated market of somewhere between 25 and 40 million units.

Wired World, 1999

Once the bandwidth problem is solved, everyone will have an address in Wired World, and the Internet will prosper and live long. This will create a demand for products and services that far exceeds anything of the past. Bill Gallagher at COM21 has seen the future, and it is capitalism at the rate of a million bits per second. Gallagher has also seen the future of networking, and it is populated by many, many cable modems running the ATM protocol.

The King lives (and the Internet is King).

CHAPTER SIXTEEN

Everything Is Going IP

It reminded me of early radio. Instead of crackling static, however, the words were sometimes cut short and there were long pauses. Quality would be a problem, but price certainly wouldn't. It was my first experience with VoIP—voice on Internet Protocol. I was in San Francisco, and the person I was talking to was in New Jersey. Most importantly, the call was free!

VoIP uses the Internet packet-switching protocol to send and receive telephone calls. In other words, VoIP is telephone over the Internet. Because the Internet uses flat pricing—one monthly service fee for unlimited use and unlimited connectivity to anywhere in the world—VoIP is an attractive alternative to analog telephony. In fact, it is such an attractive alternative that it is killing off analog altogether. Everything, including telephony, is going IP.

VoIP is just one example of how the Telecommunications Act of 1996 is radically changing the industry, and the world. More important, VoIP, and technologies like it, are changing the balance of power within the telecommunications industry. This shift is creating opportunity, and wreaking havoc in traditional businesses.

Silicon Valley loves chaos, because it brings opportunity with it. Thus, the chaos wrought by VoIP has attracted the usual moneymen, entrepreneurs, and clever engineers to Internet rising. Even Microsoft has joined the pitched battle. Will this change who owns the Internet? You bet it will!

In the next essay I explain VoIP, and describe its possible impact on the industry over the next 20 years. Like all other revolutionary technologies, VoIP will take 2 decades to diffuse through society and alter everything in its path. In fact, by the time you read this, you may already be connected to a VoIP backbone service through one of the new VoIP companies like Qwest. And by the time your first born goes to college, everything will have gone IP.

Article by Ted Lewis, IEEE Internet Computing,
November–December 1997

VoIP: Killer App
for the Internet?

With voice on IP, consumers can look forward to cheap phone calls regardless of distance or duration. Are the telcos worried? You bet.

About 16 years ago a high school basketball coach turned small-town motel operator named Bernie Ebbers started leasing long-distance telephone lines from AT&T and reselling them to businesses. His Jackson, Mississippi, company—Long Distance Discount Service—treated customers better than AT&T did and charged them less. And it worked so well the Ebbers kept buying and merging until he had built an empire called WorldCom.

When WorldCom pitched $30 billion for MCI this October, it became clear that Ebbers and company wanted to own the highways and byways of Wired World.

Who Owns the Internet?

By 1995, Ebbers was running the fourth largest long-haul carrier in the U.S. In 1996, one of his deals (the acquisition of MFS Communications) landed UUNet Technologies as a bonus. At first, Ebbers thought about selling off the tier-one Internet service provider. Why would a telco man want a computer network company?

Ebbers had no technical background and even today doesn't use a computer. But he understood how to use a phone. He believed the big bucks were in long-distance telephone calls—not something called the Web. "Mr. Ebbers admits that WorldCom was so focused on acquiring . . . that it didn't realize how important the Internet piece would be," according to Brian Taptich ("Brave New WorldCom," *The Red Herring,* Nov. 1997, p. 86).

After acquiring MFS/UUNet, WorldCom also became the world's largest ISP. UUNet's CEO John Sidgmore, now second in command at WorldCom, scurried to convince Ebbers that his ISP could position WorldCom as the Microsoft of the Information Superhighway. He persuaded Ebbers not only to hold on to UUNet, but also to grab even more of the Internet business. When WorldCom, America Online, and

CompuServe merged in September 1997, Sidgmore's influence was obvious: WorldCom ended up running everyone's ISP operations and was well on its way to owning the Internet.

But why would it want to do that?

Everything Is Going IP

Telcos have been asleep for a century, so we can forgive their tardiness in realizing that everything is going packet-switched IP. Entrepreneurial companies like WorldCom have had an easy time competing with lethargic giants AT&T, MCI, and Sprint. But even WorldCom may have underestimated the potential for IP to turn it into a global megacorporation. None of these companies is quite sure what the Internet killer app is, but they know it has something to do with IP.

There are so many ramifications of transitioning to IP that nobody really knows what the Internet will look like in 10 or 20 years. But we can guess what one of the first killer apps will be: VoIP, or voice on IP.

Overtaking E-mail

Zona Research says Internet messaging was a $30-billion business in 1997 and will rise to $65 billion by 2000. Wilkovsky Gruen Associates says 82.8 million e-mail users will send an aggregate of 6.6 trillion messages in 2000.

But e-mail's era as the killer app for the Internet may soon fade. The Yankee Group values the international long-distance telephone market alone at $90 billion. This is three times the size of e-mail. You can double that to account for long-distance charges just within the U.S., and perhaps double it a few more times to tally similar expenditures throughout the world.

And what if all traffic currently going through telephone switches were diverted onto the Internet? That is, what if everything goes IP? Then the biggest cash cow for Internet infrastructure providers will be not Web browsing, not e-mail, not virtual storefronts, but old-fashioned voice.

Forrester Research and Frost & Sullivan offer different estimates of how fast VoIP will catch on, but both estimates suggest that U.S. VoIP will equal the $90 billion overseas telephone bill in just over 20 years, as shown in Figure 16.1. I emphasize that this number accounts for the U.S. revenue portion only. When the rest of the world catches on, it could easily be several times as much. VoIP could make e-mail look like Apple Computer after the fire sale.

A disclaimer is in order: e-commerce transactions are expected to rise to $225 billion by 2001, so you could argue that e-commerce is the killer app. It may well be, but my argument is restricted to the service

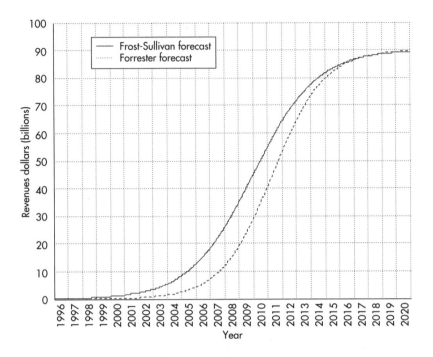

Figure 16.1   *Frost & Sullivan estimates that U.S. VoIP revenues will reach $1.9 billion by the end of 2001. Forrester Research predicts that it will take until 2004 to amount to $2 billion annually.*

infrastructure of the Internet and doesn't include the commodities that travel over it. I'm talking about money earned from collecting tolls rather than the revenue derived from vehicles and cargo that travel on the highway system.

Who Cares?

Why should consumers care about VoIP? That's simple—cheap phone calls. Placing a VoIP telephone call to anywhere in the galaxy will cost the same regardless of where you are, what time you call, or how long you stay on the line. In other words, VoIP is like e-mail—it's charged at a flat rate, so much per month, regardless of usage. (This is bound to change, but even when it does, VoIP technology will be an order of magnitude cheaper than public switched telephone networks, or PSTN.) This has the telcos worried and the venture capitalists drooling.

Enter the WebPhone

H ere's how VoIP works. Consumers replace their analog telephone sets with WebPhones that operate over IP channels provided by an

ISP. The ISP installs an IP gateway from a company like Micom to automatically translate between PSTN signals and VoIP packets. Micom's V/IP gateway, for example, is simply a card and software that install in a personal computer and allow anyone to make telephone or fax calls over standard G.729 lines. VoIP infrastructure is relatively simple, consisting of PSTN, an IP gateway, and WebPhone clients. The difficulty has to do with standards like G.729.

Take some of the products recently introduced at Comdex as examples. The Samsung WebPhone targets TAF (technically advanced family) households initially, but portends the telephone of the future. Based on the ARM 7500 or StrongARM low-cost, low-power RISC processor, ISI's pSOS operating system, and Samsung's own browser software (HTML 3.2), this WebPhone supports Internet mail (POP3, IMAP4, SMTP), Internet audio/video phone (H.323 and G.723.1/729 audio codec), and PSTN video phone (H.324) capabilities, as well as traditional POTS (plain old telephone service). Connected to an IP network, the WebPhone operates like a network device. Connected to POTS, it uses proprietary algorithms to share video, data, and voice simultaneously using high-speed (V.34) modem connections over a single analog (POTS) telephone line. It also specifies interoperability under these conditions, so that video phones based on H.324, for example, will be able to connect and conduct a multimedia session. And of course WebPhones all have address books and simple personal information manager applications like a calendar and a calculator.

The Samsung WebPhone looks like a telephone but has a 5.6-inch LCD touch screen, a CCD camera, and a keyboard. Magnetic and smart-card readers are optional.

Conspicuously absent from most of these devices is anything related to Wintel. No Windows CE, no Intel processor, and no Microsoft applications.

Trouble in River City

But VoIP faces significant technical challenges. The first concerns the public switched telephone network. How will VoIP coexist with PSTN long enough to transition the planet from analog to digital and from circuit-switched to packet-switched IP?

VoIP won't work with PSTN until everyone adheres to standards. The H.323 standard has been established to solve this problem, but not everyone implements H.323 the same way. Lack of rigorous implementations is hampering the VoIP takeoff. H.323 covers compression and control flow. It embraces G.732.1 compression and G711 64-Kbps channels, as well as mediation of multipoint conferences for both audio and video meetings. But H.323 does not fully address IP gate-way translation between PSTN and IP. Henning Schulzrinne of Columbia University

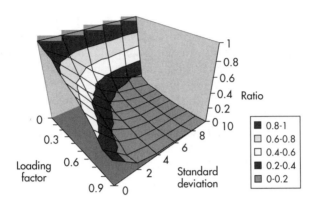

Figure 16.2 *Ratio of effective bandwidth to real bandwidth as a function of utilization (loading factor) and variation in message size (standard deviation).*

(www.cs.columbia.edu) is chairing the Internet Engineering Task Force Committee on Session Initiative Protocol. SIP addresses the PSTN-to-IP problem, but it has not been widely adopted by vendors.

The International Telecommunications Union will vote next month on version 2 of H.323. Version 2 will address gateway issues that arise in WANs—for example, how a gateway should forward a call to a PSTN phone number or another IP gateway. Even so, version 2 does not define how a caller and callee match up. Because IP numbers are often allocated dynamically, they cannot be used in place of telephone numbers. And telephone numbers are attached to devices instead of individual users. Therefore, IP and telephone numbers aren't likely to be used as addresses.

Four11 (www.four11.com) offers a matching service that takes a person's name as input and returns an IP number. It sends a message alerting the callee that someone is trying to call. This is a nontrivial balancing act, because IP numbers and people's locations constantly change, creating synchronization problems that have yet to be solved.

An even bigger problem is VoIP bandwidth. The PSTN system was designed for lots of short bursts of medium-bandwidth activity instead of sustained periods of high-bandwidth activity. A 3-minute phone call on Mother's Day is not like a 30-minute videoconference that pumps movies to a group of conferees.

The effect of increased variation in message size or connection time plus the longer average connection time conspire to sap bandwidth from the Internet. The impact is shown in Figure 16.2, a 3D plot that relates three factors: utilization of bandwidth (loading factor), variance in message size (standard deviation), and ratio of effective bandwidth to real bandwidth. In general, as utilization and variance increase, effective bandwidth decreases.

Figure 16.2 was created by assuming the Internet is one long wire with a sender at one end and a receiver at the other. The sender issues messages of fluctuating duration at random intervals, and the receiver processes them at a constant rate. When the wire is busy, new messages are queued and wait until the wire is idle. Thus, this is a simple M/G/1 (nondeterministic, general discipline single-server) queue with two key parameters: the utility factor, which is the ratio of arrival rate to service rate, and the variance parameter. Using M/G/1 queuing formulas to compute the total time to send a message over the wire, we can compare the statistical results with deterministic results, which assume no waiting-time delays.

The Giants Have Awakened

I may have been unfair to the big telcos, because the giants are beginning to wake up. U.S. West, Bell Atlantic, and Microsoft have invested in VDONet to get their hands on Internet videoconferencing and narrow-casting technology. Deutsche Telekom bought a piece of VocalTec, which provides compression and gateway software. Intel and Netscape have invested in Voxware for tools that embed voice in Web pages. NetSpeak, a developer of gateways and VoIP software, has come under the spell of Motorola, Creative Technology, and ACT Networks. Perhaps these sluggish giants can catch up with WorldCom. But if they don't, the lure of billions and billions of dollars will attract someone who will.

VoIP is on its way whether the giants want it or not, and it will radically alter global communications. Elon Ganor, founder and CEO of VocalTec, says, "It's a serious communications technology that is impacting, in a major way, the entire telecommunications industry" (*The Red Herring,* Nov. 1997, p. 96).

I'd call that an understatement.

CHAPTER SEVENTEEN

Who Owns the Internet?

Nineteen ninety-eight will probably be remembered for the anti-monopoly litigation against Microsoft. It was a year of living dangerously for the company because of lawsuits brought forward by Sun Microsystems, the U.S. Department of Justice, and others. The centerpiece of the complaints brought against Microsoft were claims of "monopolizing" the browser, Java, and operating systems markets. While these were clearly critical markets, I claim that they were not nearly as critical as moves by Microsoft to dominate the telecommunications industry.

Microsoft had come to dominate the software market by 1998, but had its eye on Internet rising for several years. Bill Gates knew that control of infrastructure could lead to control of the entire industry. Thus, control of telecommunications infrastructure would play a key role in his investments. It was not surprising, then, that Bill Gates was a big investor in Teledesic, a cluster of low earth orbit communications satellites that would provide global telephony services in the early years of the twenty-first century. It was also logical to assume that Gates would be heavily involved in telephony—the infrastructure that would support the Internet.

Indeed, a pattern of involvement in all things Internet emerges when examining Bill Gate's investment portfolio, as well as the portfolios of other billionaires. The reason: Ownership of the Internet is up for grabs. In the next essay I examine the question of who owns the Internet. There is no answer at the current time. Furthermore, there is not likely to be an answer for some time. But this essay nominates some companies that have become familiar names in hi-tech.

Article by Ted Lewis, IEEE Internet Computing,
January–February 1998

Who Owns the Internet?

While everyone's attention is fixed on Microsoft versus DOJ, the really important contest is taking place amongst the telco, telecommunications, and software giants. Microsoft's desktop revenues are small potatoes compared with the potential Big Bucks from the Big Network—the Internet.

Because most IP data travels over long-haul lines, the Internet is actually the telephone companies.

The Battle Royal

But who owns the telephone companies? The Telecommunications Act of 1996 actually puts ownership of the Internet up for grabs. Vernon Keenan of Zona Research in Redwood City, California, doesn't mince words: "It's a battle royal between them [Cisco, Bay Networks, Ericsson, etc.] and traditional telephone equipment providers such as Northern Telecom and Lucent for billions of dollars worth of business as service providers and metropolitan areas upgrade their telephone systems."[1] Keenan is quoted in a *San Jose Mercury News* story that describes how network companies like Cisco are positioning themselves for dominance in the new economy. The story concludes that mixing network equipment with traditional telephone switching equipment "will enable Cisco to work with existing telephony switching equipment while it seeks to ultimately replace it."[1]

Cisco isn't the only contender. Microsoft may be getting a lot of media attention because of its predatory pricing practices on the desktop, but the controversial company has something even more diabolical up its sleeve.

The New Robber Barons

The Internet used to be a collection of Unix servers connected via T1 lines to college campuses that served as mini-ISPs. Now it is rapidly being privatized—just as the railroads were in the 1850–90s. No longer dominated by long-haired computer nerds in Levis and t-shirts, the Internet is as three-piece-suit as J. P. Morgan, Edward C. Harriman, James J. Hill, and the Vanderbilts were over 100 years ago. Remember the railroad robber barons?

Enter the new robber barons. Everything is going IP and our rates are going up. But the Internet is undergoing an even more dramatic transformation. The Telecommunications Act of 1996 has put traditional telephone companies in danger of extinction. Upstart companies like **Intel, Cisco, Bay Networks,** and Microsoft are competing against the traditional telecommunications companies like AT&T, Nortel, and Lucent for ownership of the $1 trillion global industry.

The megabillion dollar merger of Worldcom and MCI and similar smaller mergers around the globe don't reveal the fact that AT&T's grip on telephony has slipped from a monopoly to a 52 percent market share. And the slippage is far from over. Within a few decades, AT&T won't exist, or if it does, it will be an entirely different company. Why? In the modern telecommunications industry, either you're a digital networking company or you aren't a player. This implies a rapid rebuilding of the outmoded infrastructure, which in turn implies lots of cash. The old guard doesn't have it. The new guard does.

Companies like Cisco and Microsoft have both the cash and the technology needed to replace analog with digital hardware and software. If they move fast enough, they can put themselves in the catbird's seat. And by the time the Justice department wakes up, Cisco and/or Microsoft may have monopolized the Internet.

One reason to believe the new robber barons will succeed is that we are in a new era—an era of the friction-free economy. The new economy means rapid replacement of outmoded business models. Even the politically liberal governments of Germany and England are capitulating to friction-free capitalism. They, too, are deregulating their telecom monopolies out of fear that the U.S. giants will soon completely dominate the global Internet.

But it may be too late. Powerful U.S. computer companies continue to buy up the main hardware and software lines connecting countries and continents to the emergent private Internet. Most telecom companies throughout the world have reacted too slowly to IP. Their sluggishness will be their ruin. But then, let's not get sidetracked by politics.

My Own Private Net

The global struggle will be waged by big players, but not without assistance. High-profile companies will provide the big bucks, but small companies like **LightSpeed** (bought by Cisco in early 1998), **Starvox,** and **DGM&S** will provide the innovation. The big fish will eat the little fish to accelerate their expansion. Unless they do, they won't be able to expand rapidly enough to beat their competitors.

Who are these small-fry?

Take **TeleHub Communications** of Walnut Creek, California, as an example of how a small hardware infrastructure company is providing the innovation. Tiny two-year-old TeleHub has built a coast-to-coast ATM network for carrying voice IP and providing local number portability as well as other services that should appeal to local markets. TeleHub uses Cisco-Stratacom ATM switches, but operates them over Signaling System 7 services to smoothly integrate their digital IP into existing analog infrastructure. SS7 is the protocol of the traditional telephone electronic switching system (ESS) infrastructure.

TeleHub's strategy is to usurp the ESS system, replacing analog voice with IP voice, and eventually to displace the long-haul carriers altogether! To do so, the company is positioning itself to swoop in and provide access to local exchange carriers (LECs) in place of AT&T, MCI, and Sprint. And because TeleHub runs billing on a Sun Web server system, it can bill in real-time—cheaper, faster, and before the big telcos can react.

Innovative competitors like TeleHub are cropping up all over the Internet. **VIP Calling** recently unveiled its U.S.-to-Hong Kong Internet voice service, which sells to carriers and resellers, including prepaid calling card companies. **Inter-Tel** launched a commercial service in seven U.S. cities in September 1997. **Global Gateway Group** is offering calling services throughout the U.S., Japan, and Europe. **InterNex Information Services** in Santa Clara, California, runs a Sonet network in six U.S. cities and four international cities. **Exodus Communications** is building a national network over ATM and 45-Mbps lines, and runs data centers for major Silicon Valley companies. Internet Systems in Sunnyvale, California, does the same thing for Netscape Communications, Yahoo!, and others.

Little-known backbone provider **GST Internet** is spending $250 million to string fiber across the Pacific Ocean, connecting Hawaii and Asia to the U.S.. GST wants to replace existing voice telephony with IP networking, which will extend high-speed Internet to Asia.

"These companies could ultimately become the data communications equivalent of the competitive LECs," said Gordon Werner, vice president of **NetEdge Systems** in Research Triangle Park, North Carolina. "A lot of these companies did not exist six months ago, but they are a whole new data market."[2]

In other words, Internet hardware infrastructure is being rebuilt by the small-fry, looking for downstream big bucks. They are doing this with computer technology—not traditional telecommunications technology. Their business model is to create a local monopoly in a niche market and then sell out to Cisco, Microsoft, or Intel.

But they aren't the only ones who have heard about the Telecommunications Act of 1996.

Weeding Out the Middle

It is not surprising that massive disintermediation is accompanying the flattening of the established telecommunications industry caused by IP networking. Disintermediation is a polite word for "elimination of the middleman." With companies like **PSINet** "going around the long-lines" and young upstarts re-inventing telephony in the image of Ethernet, the middleman might appear to be doomed.

PSINet, for example, recently announced an aggressive Internet-based telephony strategy to double the company's revenue every year for the next three years through acquisitions and a $310 million investment in its own Internet backbone. PSINet wants to eliminate the middlemen LECs—moving customers directly onto its tier-one super-ISP network. PSINet will acquire ISPs, add 20 POPs (points of presence), spend $100 million on fiber and another $120 million on upgrades.

This kind of integration is reminiscent of AT&T's integration of local exchanges during its buy-up of the telephone network circa 1898—100 years ago. Is history repeating itself? Is the LEC and traditional long-lines telephone company as obsolete as MS-DOS?

The answer is no. The middleman is not being weeded out. Instead, a new middleman is emerging in the form of new intermediaries—integrated ISPs like PSINet and Worldcom, and the rebel cable TV operators like TCI, Time Warner, and Comcast. PSINet is bidding to become a LEC as well as filling its traditional role as an ISP.

In other words, telephone companies and ISPs are merging—both in terms of their technology and business models. And cable operators are making their move into this space, too. TCI, Time Warner, and several smaller operators agreed to buy at least 15 million digital set-top boxes from **NextLevel Systems** (aka General Instruments) between 1999 and 2002. These boxes will feature high-speed IP for Internet access, digital video, e-mail, and games. Microsoft, **Microware Systems, PowerTV,** and **NCI** (Network Computer, Inc.) will compete for the operating systems business.

Does Microsoft's $1 billion investment in Comcast ring a familiar chime? The battle for the middle is already raging.

The New Value Chain

Clearly, Cisco Systems has to be one of the upstarts beginning its rise on DOJ's radar screen. It stands a good chance of dominating the lowest link in the value chain extending from IP router to Web application software. Ten thousand dollars invested in Cisco stock in 1990 would be worth $500,000 today. Its capitalization mushroomed from $4 billion in 1995 to $43 billion in late 1997. Sales were $382 million in 1992; in 1997, they exceeded $6 billion, putting Cisco on a revenue growth ramp that vanquishes the records set by Microsoft and Intel.

"The networking segment of the industry is enjoying the biggest growth rate in the history of high technology," says Selby Wellman, senior vice president of Cisco.[3] Cisco does it by eating its competitors. They would rather buy than fight. Through a series of acquisitions, Cisco has grown from backwater router manufacturer to top dog in the telecommunications game.

A level upward (operating systems) in the new value chain is where it gets interesting. Distracted by Microsoft's bundling of IE with Windows 95, DOJ has missed recent big moves by Microsoft to dominate this new middleman segment. Soon, with help from **Navitel Communications,** Microsoft will start adding Web phone functions to Windows CE. Wireless will follow. Windows NT will get voice response capability and become even more of a threat to Unix as a replacement for carrier switches.

Microsoft's new Telecommunications Solutions unit has two main goals: put Microsoft software on all telephone company switches (eliminates ESS and PBX competitors), and saturate the local loop (LECs) with more Microsoft software. Microsoft is partnering with DGM&S Telecom of Mt. Laurel, New Jersey, to christen Windows NT with SS7 compatibility. Clearly, Microsoft sees a new source of revenue in the highly lucrative middleman value chain. The software powerhouse has its eye on something bigger than the dwindling desktop market (see Figure 17.1). "Anyone that isn't nervous about what Microsoft is doing is crazy," says Scott Wharton, product manager of competitor VocalTec.[4]

Forecasting winners at the next level also gets interesting. No major player is really going after applications, but Sun could position itself here with its Enterprise Computing Platform. Java may be in limbo on the desktop, but Java and JavaBeans with IIOP (Internet Inter-ORB Protocol) could rule the emerging Internet middleman market if Sun, Netscape, or IBM were to become telecommunications savvy like Microsoft.

However, it remains in doubt that they will do so, as they are stuck in a computer industry mindset. Blinded by years of product development on computers instead of telco networks, they may wake to the reality of the telecommunications mega-economy just in time to watch as DOJ goes after Cisco or Microsoft for monopolizing the Internet.

But then, this is what makes the telecommunications industry even more exciting than the computer industry.

URLs for This Column

Bay Networks • www.baynetworks.com

Cisco • www.cisco.com

DGM&S • www.dgms.com/

Exodus • www.exodus.com

Global Gateway Group • www.gcubed.com/

GST Internet • www.gstis.com

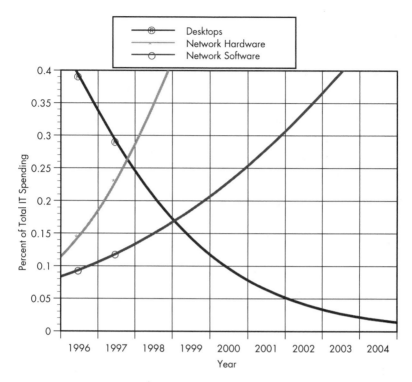

Figure 17.1 *Network spending as a percentage of total information technology (IT) spending. Desktop spending is declining as network hardware and software spending accelerate. (Source data published in* Computer Reseller News, *22 Dec. 1997, p. 151.)*

Intel • www.intel.com
InterNex Information Services • www.internex.com/
Inter-Tel • www.inter-tel.com/
LightSpeed • www.lightspeed.com/
Microware Systems • www.microware.com/
Navitel Communications • www.navitel.com/
NCI • www.nci.com/
NetEdge Systems • www.netedge.com/
NextLevel Systems • www.nlvl.com/
PowerTV • www.powertv.com/
PSINet • www.psinet.com/
StarVox • www.starvox.com/
TeleHub • www.telehub.com/
VIP Calling • www.vipcalling.com/

References

1. T. Quinlan and J. Healey, "Cisco to Gain Ammo in Voice/Data War," *San Jose Mercury News,* 23 Dec. 1997, p. 10C.

2. J. Mulqueen, "Exodus to Network Centers," *Comm. Week,* 21 Apr. 1997, p. 69.

3. B. Nagel, "Routing the Competition," *Red Herring,* Mar. 1997, pp. 82–88.

4. M. Semilof, "Eye on Telco Prize," *Computer Reseller News,* 22 Dec. 1997, pp. 5, 152.

CHAPTER EIGHTEEN

The United Nations of Cyberspace

The question of ownership of the Internet often comes up whenever politics is discussed, because most people think the Internet either belongs to everyone or no one. They rarely think it belongs to a country, company, or single group of people. Maybe they have heard about how the Internet was developed by the U.S. government under the auspices of DARPA (Defense Advanced Research Projects Agency), and then jump to the conclusion that it is similar to the Interstate Highway system. The Internet belongs to the people who use it, perhaps, or it is simply "there." Nothing could be further from the truth. In fact, the U.S. government makes no claim of ownership and is in the process of giving away its last vestiges of ownership.

The Net was opened up for commercialization in 1992 when the National Science Foundation declared it open season on all things Internet. NSF had taken over the day-to-day operation of the Internet from DARPA, and wanted to get out of the business of being a network provider. Therefore, in 1993 NSF *awarded* a 5-year contract to Network Solutions Inc. for domain name management and distribution. Recall that names like www.yahoo.com and www.excite.com are symbolic representations of IP numbers such as 313.32.142.11, etc. These are called *domain names,* and are equivalent to street and city addresses in real space. Because only one business is allowed to use a certain domain name, there is a finite supply of them. Whenever there is a finite supply of something as valuable as a name, we can expect competition. Hence, handing out names becomes an economic and political pressure point.

In September 1998 Network Solution's contract for managing domain names terminated. The U.S. government had to come up with a new way to handle the problem of registering domain names. The solution was radical for a government. In essence, the U.S. government gave up all control, passing the domain name registration responsibility on to a kind of United Nations for Cyberspace.

I consider the Clinton Administration's actions rather generous, given the ultimate value and power that will soon be vested in the Internet. The U.S. taxpayer paid for development of the Internet, and most users of the Net are Americans. In the future, the Web will be host to trillions of dollars worth of e-commerce; it will exert economic and political power in every country that embraces it. Like the railroads, airways, telecommunications easements, broadcast spectrum, and interstate highway systems found in every country, the Internet will become an unparalleled global infrastructure. It is unlikely that another infrastructure like it will come around any time soon. It is incredible that any government would give it away!

In the next essay, I explore the political and legal consequences of domain names. Central to this discussion is the Clinton Administration decision to let go of domain naming authority. While this decision was made entirely in the open, it is as if a secret were being kept. Important policies were adopted with little discussion or fanfare. Nobody objected, and nobody commented. It simply happened.

I believe the ultra-liberal policy adopted by the Clinton Administration will come back to haunt the United States Internet community, and global politics. It may take another decade for the slip-up to be noticed, but it will eventually get noticed. And when it does, it may be looked back on as one of the biggest mistakes of the Internet age. This is one prediction that won't be verified until long after you read this essay. But I ask the reader, "Who should own the Internet?"

Article by Ted Lewis, IEEE Internet Computing, March–April 1998

A Rose by Any Other (Domain) Name

Over 100 years ago the U.S. government accelerated the expansion of the United States into Oklahoma and other western states by offering free land. In the Great Land Rush of the 1880s and 1890s, all anyone had to do was live on the land and raise corn, wheat, cows, pigs, and children. The plan worked, and soon the United States stretched from ocean to ocean.

The Great Cyberspace Rush

Things are different in the Great Cyberspace Rush of the 1990s. People recognize the high value of real estate in cyberspace, and it's in domain names. In fact, domain names are so highly valued that the U.S. government is having trouble keeping poachers under control. The battle for cyberspace properties is more like a range war than a land rush.

In many other countries the reigning government would use force, if necessary, to hang onto their news, communications media, and Internet packet business. But not in the United States. In a radical move, the U.S. government is trying to divest its lingering interest in all things Internet. This radical move is almost as bold as giving away land was in the last century. It is likely to have a similarly big impact on the future of the Internet.

The U.S. government deserves accolades for boldly going where no government has gone before—to a relatively open Internet. However, two obstacles may stand in the way. First, the U.S. government's divestiture plan may be legally challenged. And second, the old-fashioned legal system itself may rise up to create such a fuss that nobody will want to "head West."

Will the Great Cyberspace Rush of the late 20th century come off as smoothly as the Great Land Rush of the 19th century? I don't think so.

Header Wars

In the good old days, the Internet and e-mail were one and the same. But e-mail could not travel across the vast Internet, into a LAN, and end up in the proper desktop computer until about 1984, when **Jon Postel**, of USC's **Information Sciences Institute** (ISI), and two colleagues, Mockapeti and Partridge, created a uniform naming convention for all of the Internet. After a few years of flaming with other Netheads over how it should be done—the so-called "header wars"—Postel succeeded in establishing today's widely accepted format (name@machine.entity.domain). Originally, only seven domains were established: .edu (education), .com (companies), .gov (government), .mil (military), .net (service provider), .org (nonprofit organization), and .int (international treaty organization).

The header wars may have been nasty, but less than a decade later things got worse. In 1992 the U.S. Congress gave the National Science

Foundation legal authority to commercialize its NSFNet, instantly opening up the Internet to anyone who wanted to live on it, grow a business, transact e-commerce, advertise, or download controversial content.

Bold New World

Every computer on the Internet is assigned a unique IP number. Remarkably, this number is dispensed by one human—Postel. This situation is a little like the president handing out social security cards to newborns, although Postel does have help in the form of the Internet Assigned Numbers Authority. DARPA pays ISI (through its IANA role) to allocate IP numbers in big blocks, which are spread throughout the world via IP registry organizations—**ARIN, RIPE,** and **APNIC** (located in North America, Europe, and the Asia/Pacific region, respectively). These registry holders turn around and sell numbers to ISPs, who in turn sell the numbers to consumers.

The whole structure is hierarchical with TLDs (top-level domains) fanning out to secondary levels in a multitiered network. Hence, tier one ISPs, such as MCI, are at the top and smaller ISPs are somewhere at the bottom. National TLDs are administered by their corresponding governments or by private entities with governmental authority. But generic TLDs (gTLDs) such as .com, .edu, and .org cut across national boundaries. These are registered through **Network Solutions Inc.** (NSI) under a five-year agreement with NSF, which ends 30 September 1998. September 1998 is nearly upon us, hence the impending cyberspace rush.

What will happen on 1 October? Will your government let business dictate the Internet's future? The first place likely to see action is the domain naming-service itself. By watching what happens here, we can guess which direction the Internet will take in each country. It should be entertaining to watch this bold new world take shape.

A United Nations for Cyberspace

Let's backtrack a little. On 1 July 1997, the Clinton Administration directed the Secretary of Commerce to "privatize, increase competition in, and promote international participation in the domain name system." A day later, the Department of Commerce issued a request for comment. Over 430 comments were gathered, leading to the development of the following "shared principles":

+ The U.S. government should end its role as a DNS supplier and instead simply promote the stability of the Internet.
+ The Internet should be regulated by market mechanisms (such as consumer choice) that encourage innovation and maximize individual freedom.

+ Technical management should be coordinated by a "private coordinating process" that reflects the traditional "bottom-up governance" of the Internet.
+ Technical management of the Internet should be established "to ensure international input in decision making."

The Department of Commerce used these shared principles in a policy paper written by the National Telecommunications Information Administration (NTIA) and released in February 1998. Informally called the "**green paper,**" the draft outlines how to implement divestiture. It recommends that part of the Internet be given free reign, but that another part be "coordinated." Governments would set policy, but an authorized "nonprofit corporation" would implement these policies within a competitive, market-driven, self-regulating economic system. The nonprofit replacement of IANA would itself be governed by a board of directors from around the world, a United Nations for Cyberspace.

Range Wars

The U.S. government intends to transfer its authority over domain names to this private nonprofit corporation before the end of 1998, and allow only five new top-level names to be added to "Postel's list." The problem is, everyone wants a .com domain name, and there just aren't enough to go around.

As outlined by the proposal, some domains would be siphoned off to the new nonprofit while others would stay within NSI's control. NSI would continue to operate .com, .net, and .org, but would give up .edu. NSI would also have to transition its technical capabilities to the U.S. government (all data, software, licenses, and its "A" root server) so that the government can use them to establish the nonprofit organization. In short, the proposal creates a structure in which private interests will run into public interests, with NSI and the new "private nonprofit" splitting the responsibility of governing cyberspace. The inevitable result is a range war that could cause long-term damage to the Internet.

Legal Flames

In 1995 NSF authorized NSI to charge a domain name registration fee of $100 for the first two years of "rental." Of that amount, 30 percent was to be deposited in a fund for the "preservation and enhancement of the intellectual infrastructure of the Internet (the Intellectual Infrastructure Fund)." More than $46 million has been collected, $23 million of which has been siphoned off by the U.S. Congress to pay for Internet2.

Almost immediately, the Intellectual Infrastructure Fund became the subject of litigation, and the controversy over domain name trademarks has embroiled many cyberians on the range.

Legal flames over intellectual property in cyberspace are likely to escalate as the range war intensifies. According to Randy Barrett ("Domain Name Disputes Continue," *Inter@Active Week*, 2 Feb. 1998, p. 26), "Case law concerning trademark infringement and domain names is growing—with wildly divergent precedents." Barrett cites Brainiac Services Inc. of Rhode Island, which is being legally hounded by DC Comics. DC Comics, a Warner Brothers subsidiary, claims trademarked ownership of the name "Brainiac" and wants the ISP to stop using their cartoon character's name for a domain name!

And then there's Intermatic versus Dennis Toeppen—an example of turbulent waters awaiting the as-yet-unnamed nonprofit registry proposed by the NTIA draft. In 1996, Dennis Toeppen lost his domain name in a trademark infringement suit brought against him by Intermatic Inc., on the grounds of "trademark dilution."

Toeppen had registered the domain name with NSI, and set about selling his software products over the Internet. Later, Intermatic tried to register its name with NSI, found that it was already registered to Toeppen, and filed suit. The judge ruled in favor of Intermatic, reasoning that "Intermatic was famous enough that Toeppen's only motivation was to trade on its reputation." Toeppen had also registered ussteel.com, crateandbarrel.com, and deltaairlines.com, as well as many other big-name corporations, hoping to cash in when these giants woke up to the value of cyberspace real estate. In this case, it seems that the legal system ruled in favor of the big guys—with no more reason than brand name recognition—to the detriment of the small entrepreneur.

The question of who owns the Internet may be settled once the U.S. government divests itself of domain name ownership, but the question of squatter's rights will flame into the next century. A rose by any other name is still a rose, but a domain name like www.rose.com could be something to fight over. (In fact, it's already taken!)

URLs for This Column

APNIC • www.apnic.net/

ARIN • www.arin.net/

ISI • www.isi.edu/

NSI • www.netsol.com/

NTIA "green paper" • www.ntia.doc.gov/

Jon Postel • www.isi.edu/div7/ people/postel.home/

RIPE • www.ripe.net/

CHAPTER NINETEEN

The Year I Shoot My TV

Internet rising means that everything that communicates will do so in packet-switching IP (Internet Protocol). As a technology, packet-switching is overpowering circuit-switching simply because it is more efficient and flexible. A circuit-switched network pays for the entire circuit for the entire duration of a conversation. But a packet-switched network pays only for what it uses. Thus, a packet-switched link can be shared with thousands of others. This makes the IP inevitable as a global communications technology. It is a fundamental shift that will banish everything else in its path. Even television.

Everything is going IP, but it isn't there yet.

The next step in the grand plan is convergence—the process of combining all communication media into one big pipe—the Internet. Convergence is especially aimed at broadcast media like TV and radio. After a 50-year reign of control, TV is about to capitulate to convergence. This shift has big implications for hi-tech, as well as for Hollywood and the other mass media producers. The first signs of convergence around IP are already showing up. It is called Internet TV, WebTV, or some similar phrase.

Convergence will take decades, but you can already see it in action. Messaging went IP with e-mail and the global Internet. Then, telephony began to go IP when the global telephone system adopted VoIP (voice over IP). Now, broadcast media is going IP with the convergence of Internet protocols and television. When the transformation is complete, all of us will shoot our TV. By 2020 most of the world will be watching the Web.

The first commercially successful product to contribute to the coming digital convergence was WebTV by WebTV Networks, Inc. The rise

143

of WebTV in 1997 demonstrated how convergence might unfold. WebTV combines the Web with an ordinary TV, today, and will seamlessly merge the two together, tomorrow. Future TVs will be indistinguishable from Web browsers. At least, this is the idea.

Perhaps the economic model of WebTV is as important as the technology used. In consumerland, the cost of an appliance must be greatly dissipated, because consumers are extremely price sensitive. Thus, a cellular telephone is bundled with a service. It is not sold as a stand-alone device. In fact, the monthly service fee covers most of the cost of the phone. This kind of subsidization is necessary to establish a dominant market share, and drive your competitors out of the market. WebTV, and its set-top box competitors use the same subsidy model.

To get a foothold in the coming digital convergence sweepstakes, every manufacturer of an Internet device must offset the cost of technology by factoring in a service. This is the true meaning of the term, "information society." When selling information—news, weather, TV shows, magazines, books, film, and other intangible goods—becomes the major source of revenue for a business, that business is deep into the Information Age. Therefore, devices like the WebTV simply provide on-ramps to the Internet. The real money is in content.

Internet appliances like WebTV offer hope for the future of Silicon Valley because they expand the market for chips and software. But Silicon Valley isn't the source of content. In reality, there must be a cultural convergence, also. The content providers in New York, Los Angeles, and elsewhere have to become part of the digital culture of hi-tech. This will take longer than most techies in Silicon Valley realize. Yet, WebTV portends a future where there isn't much difference between a TV and a computer.

WebTV is central to "Who owns the Internet?" And guess what? Microsoft bought it shortly after I wrote the following article. Convergence was rising, so Microsoft jumped aboard. Now Microsoft was rising along two fronts of the Internet: computers with browsers, and consumers with TVs.

In 1999 AOL announced an alliance with TV manufacturers to build its own version of Internet TV. Steve Case, CEO of AOL, has always believed the Internet would evolve into a next generation TV. The use of a "channel" metaphor was not a coincidence at AOL. The AOL TV set-top box commissioned by AOL pits AOL against Microsoft in the convergence race. The rise of the Internet is being closely shadowed by the rise of Microsoft, with AOL in hot pursuit.

Article by Ted Lewis, Computer, January 1997

The Year I Shoot My TV

This might be The Year I Shoot My TV. It's beginning to interfere with my Internet viewing. The Internet attack on TV is well under way. But there is a deeper meaning to what is happening in the computer industry. As I see it, three factors have begun to work their way into our thinking and will shape the computer industry in the next few years:

+ The industry's focus is truly shifting from business users to the unwashed masses.

+ As product lines have segmented, producers have responded by figuring out how to make money along the value chain that connects a consumer to a product.

+ The Internet is moving away from a push toward a pull paradigm, to better address the first two trends.

The Fifth Wave

By now many of you have opened Christmas gifts and discovered a $350 Internet set-top box instead of the $3,500 PC you wanted. Did your disappointment turn to excitement when you realized that you had joined the vanguard of the fifth wave of computer consumers? That you had become a member of the next generation of consumers who will define products for the next decade?

The first wave of consumers, of course, bought mainframes. The minicomputer defined the second wave; the PC, the third; and networking the fourth. Now wave number five has crashed ashore, in the form of the appliance, or network, computer.

Network computers, sold by unknown companies like WebTV, Diba, and Navio, as well as established companies like Sony, Philips, Thomson, and Zenith, are changing the way money is made and products are designed in Silicon Valley. The implications of this shift are significant.

Invasion of the Couch Potatoes

Consumerism is transforming our industry, prying it away from its business and academic roots and propelling it toward consumer electronics. Intel, Motorola, MIPS, Sun, and other core computer companies may be influenced more by product managers in the entertainment and consumer market than by hard-core MIS managers.

Consider a sobering fact: Americans watch 250 *billion* hours of TV every year. Even assuming a modest $1 of revenue generated per hour, TV Land represents a business that is roughly twice the size of the entire computer industry. Why should the networks get it all? If Siliwood can combine the Internet and TV, it may be able to milk the combination for a few hundred billion per year. Instead of four major networks (NBC, CBS, ABC, and Fox), the Internet can easily supply content-crazed consumers with 50 million channels of programming! If content is really king, Wired World should rule the world in about a decade.

To make money from Internet TV, add a set-top box to a TV that can dial the Internet, make the Internet look as much as possible like another cable TV channel, and then just sit back and rake in the bucks. This simple plan has attracted the attention of companies like WebTV, ViewCall, Diba, Navio, and Microsoft. Once these pioneers make a profit, it will attract many more companies.

Moore's Second Law, Again

Appliance network computers will segment product lines into niche market spaces, which in turn will influence product design, but in strange ways.

Segmentation, declining price-learning curves, and the consequent inverse economics (which reduce everything to a commodity) all conspire to make profiteering more difficult. Think of it this way: Intel must cope with Moore's second law, which says that the cost of fabrication plants increases as fast as clock rate. A factory that costs $1 billion must sell 1,000 times more processors than a factory that costs $1 million. At some point, Intel must move into more and more market spaces in order to sell more and more product. Thus, the entire market is divided into more and more segments in the hope that each segment will grow to be as big as the original business, the so-called divide and grow strategy.

Tax the Food Chain

But it is difficult to make segmentation work in the computer industry. The reason is that the high end of the business has been saturated for nearly the entire life of the computer industry—everyone wants to sell premium products because the profit margins are better. To segment on the low end, you need very large volumes. A PDA vendor must sell 10 units at a $10 profit to equal one PC sold at a $100 profit. Segmentation at the low end also implies declining prices, which squeeze out profits as products become commodities. That $10 PDA profit margin declines as the product becomes a commodity, which wipes out all profit.

Yet it's the low end where the appliance computer comes in. These products must be low-priced, specialized, consumer-oriented. They must be designed to consume little power and require little training. And they must implement something so compelling that the hordes will be enticed to buy like crazy.

The challenge is to discover how to make money from products that have such a thin profit margin. The answer is to tax the food chain, or what's called the value chain in the consumer electronics market space. In short, the captains of industry are employing novel licensing methods to siphon revenue from the value chain to subsidize their investment in appliance computers.

The phrase I use to summarize this trend is, "Products are disintegrating and markets are integrating." As the computer industry segments, it must integrate a value chain that leads from basic technology vendors to consumers. This idea will shape not only markets, but products as well.

Contrarians at the Gates

The extremely low cost of Internet TV—and other appliances—threatens the very foundation of the Wintel fortress. Products from WebTV, ViewCall, and Welcome-to-the-Future are redefining some very fundamental notions about the computer industry. These contrarians are massing at the gates of Intel, Microsoft, IBM, Dell, Compaq, and Toshiba.

Here is what they believe:

+ Moore's law allows faster and bigger (more RAM) machines to be built at a fixed price. Applied to the fifth wave, Moore's law also allows cheaper, smaller machines to be built at a fixed speed and size.

+ Davidow's law drives Wintel factories into frenzied, six-month product life cycles, creating a technology treadmill. Fifth-wave consumers resent buying products that become obsolete as soon as they are plugged in and will resist cycle times that are less than about five or six years.

+ To meet customers' expectations, products that cost more must do more, which is why we end up with bloated, cumbersome products like Microsoft Office. Low-priced fifth-wave products will be limited to special purposes and will reap higher profits by targeting narrow market segments, requiring less training and support, and reducing development effort.

The Young Turks who hold these beliefs fully intend to redefine the industry and eat Wintel's lunch. But creating a market for appliance computers won't be easy. Consumers in this market space are "lean-back buyers"—they want to lean back in their recliners while they cruise the

Internet. A number of companies are trying, however. The first one to hit the stores was from WebTV Networks, Inc.

WebTV's set-top box contains a 112-MHz MIPS processor, 4 Mbytes of flash RAM, a 33.6-Kbps modem, and a slot for a smart card. It is far thinner than Oracle's Network Computer and is priced at game machine levels. At $350, it rides Moore's law down to rock-bottom consumer prices instead of up to the premium prices demanded of a 300-MHz, 64-Mbyte RAM, and 2-Gbyte disk drive configuration.

WebTV's set-top box is thin: nearly everything is done on the server. The box itself merely renders HTML text, connects you to a telephone, and handles security chores. It is the dumbest of dumb terminals: The first version didn't support Java, smart cards, or audio. It is not Communicator for the masses; it is a TV channel for targeted subscribers. In fact, it will work only with the WebTV Networks. How special-purpose can you get?

The major selling points of WebTV are its price, convenience, ease-of-use, and softness—most functions are implemented in software that can be easily upgraded from the server. By making nearly everything about WebTV soft, consumers can get new functionality without buying a new box. The consumer can finally get off the technology treadmill, at least for a few years.

WebTV and boxes like it demonstrate my point. They are ridiculously cheap, but not powerful. Because they are soft, they are designed to be useful for three to five years. They are not really computers—they are dedicated appliances.

Digital Keiretsu

If products get cheaper and cheaper and the consumer hops off the technology treadmill, how will companies survive? How can Intel continue to make billions once PC prices have dropped from $3,500 to $350 to $3.50 and when consumers don't have to buy a new computer every time Intel releases a faster processor?

The answer lies in how many other markets work. Nintendo, Sega, and Sony lose an average of $150 per game machine. They sell millions of machines, so they must lose hundreds of millions every year! How do they stay in business? By licensing the games. In other words, they give away razors to sell blades. And the result is a $5–10 billion value chain.

Cellular service providers do the same thing. Every new CellularOne customer gets a free phone valued at $200. Thirty million customers sign up annually, so the investment is in excess of $6 billion! But what is $6 billion to an industry that is generating $100 billion a year in connection charges?

As products disintegrate into segments such as game machines, game cartridges, and cellular telephone sets, companies enter into joint ventures

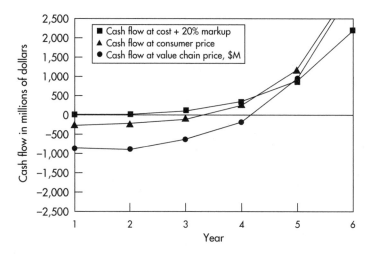

Figure 19.1 *There are three approaches to mainstreaming a consumer product. The value-chain subsidy approach sacrifices instant gratification for global domination. It buys market share by cutting prices to the bone in order to mainstream its products. Once mainstreamed, the product achieves a near-monopoly status and profits are generated for years.*

so that they can live off the same food chain. They form a *keiretsu*—the Japanese word for an informal monopoly—that integrates the food chain into one big feast. Product disintegration makes value chain integration necessary, because the whole must be greater than the sum of the parts.

A cluster of computer companies now live off the same value chain. Each company in these digital keiretsus provides an essential link in the chain, but the partners share revenues derived from part or all of the chain. Nintendo may make only machines, but it derives revenues from licensing the game cartridges. GTE may lose money on telephones, but it makes a bundle every time you use one of them. WebTV may not make money selling set-top boxes under the Sony and Philips label, but it gets a check every time one of the boxes dials its server.

Figure 19.1 compares three methods of generating revenue from a value chain. One curve extrapolates revenue generated when a product sells at true cost plus a 20 percent markup, assuming that true cost starts at $1,000 and declines according to Moore's law. No digital keiretsu is involved in this traditional method. Another curve forecasts revenues from a product that is subsidized by the manufacturer. The price point is artificially low (say $300, regardless of the true manufacturing cost), making it more attractive to buyers. Again, there is no keiretsu involved in this scenario. Obviously, reaping a profit with this method is difficult until inverse economics kicks in and lowers manufacturing costs. The third curve shows what happens if the product is sold at an even greater loss (say $99), but the vendor gets a kickback of $100 per customer. This requires a digital keiretsu. The kickback comes from other links in the value chain. Think of it as a tax on the whole value chain.

Obviously, the more you give away, the longer it takes to make a profit. As Figure 19.1 shows, the value chain curve is more profitable in the long run, but it may take years to break even. So why do it?

The digital keiretsu sacrifices instant gratification for global domination. Profits might appear at a much later date, but market share appears overnight. In a sense, the digital keiretsu buys market share by cutting prices to the bone in order to mainstream its products. Once mainstreamed, the product achieves a near-monopoly status. Monopoly locks in the installed base, which spends real money for years into the future.

The purpose of a digital keiretsu is to control the value chain of an industry segment from inception to death. Once controlled, the value chain can be milked by all members of the chain, hence everyone is guaranteed a profit.

Push Me, Pull You

The Internet is being tossed to-and-fro as the appliance network computer and PC encroach on each other's territory. One of the immediate consequences of this tug-of-war is the transformation of Wired World from a push to a pull model. Fifty million channels are simply too many for anyone to watch, so the next stage of Internet computing will push information to the consumer. This year, Wired World will get in your face.

Every wild-eyed, credit-card-wielding consumer who careens onto the Internet currently uses a browser to pull information from the server to a PC. Netscape's Communicator and Microsoft's Internet Explorer are essentially fishing poles that hook onto things and reel them in. The problem is, not everyone knows how to fish: The pull model won't make it through 1997, because it is too much like the PC model—too general and too sophisticated for couch potatoes.

The push model is different because it lets the merchant push information from the server to the client. Information flows out to the desktop through a channel—through 50 million channels! PointCast is a classic example of push. The PointCast owners, brothers Greg and Chris Hassett, had a brilliant idea. Instead of making people come to a Web page, why not make the Web page go to the people? As Chris put it, "We're not in the off-line business, we're in the broadcast business." ("Young Turks Point The Way Off-line," *Interactive Week*, Oct. 14, 1996, p. 43). Disguising their channel as a screen saver, PointCast invaded desktops everywhere. They gave away the browser and they let consumers tailor the information that automatically streams onto their screen. The PointCast browser does not expect to generate much from cubicle dwellers. In fact, it only expects them to buy something from time to time. Instead, PointCast, like Marimba and BroadVision, is redefining how Wired World operates, a shift that has major implications.

A channel in Wired World is an aggregation of content plus the tribe that subscribes to it. It is the analog of a TV channel because, like TV, an Internet channel pushes information from the broadcast station to the consumer. According to the Hassett brothers, "we are to the Internet what ABC and CBS are to the airwaves. We are building a road between the producers of content and their customers." I think this says it all.

Why is channeling such a big deal? First, it affects product design. Much more functionality is placed on the server, and client devices become much more specialized. The general product is dead, because it costs too much to make and distribute. Besides, why design a general-purpose appliance for use by a narrow tribe?

Second, channeling fits rather nicely into the value chain model. Publishers, movie makers, and TV producers adopted the value chain model long ago. The computer industry is just now starting to borrow these ideas.

CHAPTER TWENTY

From Here to Ubiquity

R eed Hundt was the right guy, in the right place, at the right time in 1994, when the most significant law of the past 60 years began its road to passage. It wasn't an easy road, but it led to radical change in the most fundamental industry underlying the Internet—the telecommunications industry. And Hundt's law would spread to nearly all industrialized nations, as the rest of the world followed in the footsteps of the U.S.A.'s telecommunications deregulation binge.

Hundt's years of experience as a communications lawyer with Latham & Watkins, Washington, D.C., prepared him well to become the chairman of the Federal Communications Commission (FCC) at the very moment in history when the telecommunications industry was prime to undergo massive revision. The new chairman wasted no time making big plans for a new telecommunications industry. He wanted to accelerate technical advancement, bring massive connectivity to every stratum of society, and instigate huge price declines for consumers. His approach as chairman of the FCC would be to deregulate the regulated monopolies, e.g., AT&T, RBOCs (Regional Bell Operating Companies), and Cable. What Reed Hundt set out to do would not be easy. His goal was nothing less than a complete dismantling of the long-standing Telecommunications Act of 1934.

AT&T, Cable TV, and the RBOCs were such powerful regulated monopolies that they dictated every detail of telecommunications life. Only AT&T was allowed to use long-distance lines and only the RBOCs were permitted to use local wires. Only the Cable TV franchises were allowed to connect set-top boxes to the cable in your home. They had the "information superhighway" locked down. They had good reason to resist change.

But like I said, Reed Hundt was in the right place at the right time. The National Science Foundation had set the Internet free only two years earlier, and the nation was adopting computer technology as if it was the hula hoop of the day. Vice President Albert Gore had heightened interest in the Internet by declaring it the "information superhighway." People were signing onto the Web at alarming rates. It seemed like a good time to strike.

So Hundt re-wrote the 1934 Telecommunications Act. Indeed, it was radical. Maybe too radical as it failed in Congress. When asked why the bill failed, he replied, "special interest lobbying." (Eric Nee, "Reed Hundt, Riding High at the FCC", *Upside,* December 1994, pp. 66) The regulated monopolies and other special interest groups were too powerful. Congress handed the FCC chairman his first of two defeats.

Hundt's timing was still good. The Republicans swept the elections in 1994, and because they wanted to deregulate everything, Hundt's ideas merely gained steam. They resonated with the new power in Congress. Besides, the Internet was gaining favor as the Next Big Thing in politics as well as fashion. In 1995 very few legislators wanted to go on record as being against the information superhighway. The special interest groups now had to deal with a Republican Congress bent on change. This time, public opinion and the Congress were on Reed Hundt's side.

The 1995 bill was radical. It would let cable operators enter long distance telephone markets, and RBOCs enter cable and long distance businesses, with some restrictions. It would create a national policy designed purposely to inject competition into previously regulated monopolies. It would open up telecommunications to anyone with the billions needed to compete in the new Wired, Wired, West.

The antagonists were all over the bill. AT&T, the RBOCs, and the cable operators took opposing sides, and when Congress closed shop in 1995, the bill narrowly missed being passed. The forces of the RBOCs and AT&T fought to a draw. Hundt took his second defeat in stride. He was getting closer. The House had passed its version by a vote of 423 to 5. Even though the Senate was unable to match the House's accomplishment before the end of its legislative session in December 1995, the stage was set for passage in 1996.

It took one more Congressional session to pass the Telecommunications Act of 1996 and replace its 32-year-old predecessor. Reed Hundt was victorious! In 1996 *Upside* magazine listed him as the tenth most influential person in the "convergence industry." [Kora McNaughton and Tish Williams, "Upside's Elite 100," December 1996, pp. 33.] Only Bill Gates (Microsoft), Andy Grove (Intel), John Doerr (Kleiner Perkins), Michael Eisner (Disney), Larry Ellison (Oracle), Scott McNealy (Sun), Jim Clark (Netscape), Jim Barksdale (Netscape), and John Chambers (Cisco) ranked higher than Reed Hundt. He was swimming with very good company. The magazine said this about the successful FCC chairman,

"Hundt is no paper pusher, and he's made it clear that fostering competition is his top priority. He managed to muzzle the screeches of the telecom industry's 300-pound gorillas—the RBOCs and the long-distance service providers—and pass the landmark Telecom Reform Act."

It might take another decade or two before the world at large appreciates what Reed Hundt did back in 1994–1996. His new law would have far-reaching implications. After its first year of existence Andrew Madden of *The Red Herring* wrote, "Think of what a telecommunications company offered five years ago and what it will have to offer five years from now. Add it all up, and you'll likely find that telecom as you know it is dead." Reed Hundt, upon retiring from the post as chairman of the FFC said, "One thing is certain, there will be a war between the circuit-switch businesses and the packet-switch businesses. And the outcome will make or break numerous fortune seekers." [Brian Taptich, "The Thrill of the Hundt," *The Red Herring*, November 1997, pp. 103.] Both of these assessments—coming only two years after the passage of the new law—are turning out to be massive understatements! What hath Reed Hundt wrought: nothing less than a revolution?

Article by Reed Hundt, Computer, October 1997

The Internet: From Here to Ubiquity

Reed Hundt, FCC chair, in a speech at the IEEE Computer Society's Hot Chips Symposium August 26, 1997, in Palo Alto, California, gave his analysis of and recommendations for the future of the Internet. This article was excerpted from that speech. Although you may not agree with Hundt's policies and visions for the Internet, I think you will agree that he raises many important issues that will influence the Internet's next generation. Reed Hundt's term as FCC chairman will expire June 30, 1998, but all signs indicate that his views reflect those of the Clinton administration and will be reflected in his successor's policies. As always, Computer *welcomes your feedback. Contact me directly or write to computer@computer.org.*

—Ron Vetter

As a kind of farewell message to Silicon Valley, I want today to talk to you about what no one has yet done, and what needs doing for and by all of us, because none of us can do it acting alone. We need a fully developed Internet to give us competition, deregulation, economic growth, social change, high productivity, and new, record sales of hardware and software. I want to see the Internet grow like kudzu everywhere in this country, with access for poor and rich, seniors and kids, English and non-English speakers alike.

I also want to see the Internet provide a key answer to the problem of competition in the local telephone markets. A year and a half after the opening of California's telephone markets, only about one percent of consumers are taking phone service from anyone but the traditional monopolist. And many major companies are delaying or canceling plans to compete. This is totally unsatisfactory.

What We Need

We need a high-speed, congestion-free, always reliable, friction-free, packet-switched, big-bandwidth, data-friendly network that is universally available, competitively priced, and capable of driving the American economy to new heights. We need a data network that can easily carry voice, instead of what we have today, a voice network struggling to carry data.

We need instant access to the libraries of the world at the fingertips of every child in every classroom in every school in the country. With this step alone we would do more to eliminate inequality in educational opportunity than has ever been done since Horace Mann invented public schools.

We've built new infrastructures before: a hundred years ago our country needed ubiquitous railroad and telephone systems. The stories of the railroad and the telephone are stories of how bottleneck monopolies built the economy but also choked competition, raised prices, created wealth and pockets of poverty, and sparked government intervention to assure some fairness in the balance between citizens and capitalism.

The construction of the 21st century network, our packet-switched Internet, will be equally complicated and challenging. But I believe that we can get this job done better and smarter and fairer than any other major construction project in history. Our successes so far encourage us. But I see major threats to the rapid and successful development of this new world of communication.

Internet Economics

The economics of the Internet at this time are, to use a technical term, wacky. Demand for bandwidth isn't met; reliability is too uncertain;

and prices for many components and services are too high. The principal reason is that the Internet is, for the most part, a legacy of the hybrid of regulated monopoly telcos and the anarchic not-for-profit academic world. This hybrid needs to evolve. But unless efficient and competitive markets drive the growth of the Internet, its successful evolution is threatened.

Already, dangerous signs of congestion appear: the circuit-switched network designed for three-minute calls is far from ready to handle several hours of Internet traffic per household per day. There's only one sure way to solve the congestion problem: open and aggressive and efficient competition.

Just look at some of the congestion points and what's needed to relieve them:

+ *The local loop.* Those wires weren't engineered for digital, packet-switched communications, and they are owned by monopolies that want to dictate their use and their users. We need to free up those loops for high-speed digital communications.

+ *The local switch.* Local switches are what telcos use to route traffic from users to ISPs. These switches are for the most part owned by monopolies. We need to ensure that any new competitor can share their efficiencies or, better yet, route data traffic around them onto packet networks.

+ *T1 circuits.* T1s are the basic data transmission circuits purchased by ISPs. They are usually offered by telco monopolies, and the prices are far higher than they should be. Competition is necessary to lower these prices. In the meantime, the FCC needs the power to lower these prices for both interstate and intrastate T1s.

+ *The Internet addressing system.* We need a new means of managing Internet domain names and other addresses. The current system is not reliable or fair.

+ *Inside and outside wiring.* The connection to the house and the wires inside the house need to be open to competitors. The existing telcos and cable companies have legitimate rights to some of these facilities, but these rights can't be used to exercise their monopoly power and thwart competition.

For our high-bandwidth, packet-switched, Internet-friendly world we need the right rules to guarantee competition at each of these congestion points.

The Role of Legislation

There are continued efforts to write new rules of law to "help" the Internet. So far they aren't being written right. The first example is the U.S. Communications Decency Act, overturned by the Supreme Court, fortunately. A new bill introduced in the Congress last month, called the Internet Protection Act, is another example of a grievous misstep. Though the stated aims of the bill are generally worthy, in practical effect the bill would let telcos overcharge ISPs; would stymie access to their loops; and would fail to cure any of the market failures that cause Internet congestion today.

Even if we have the right rules of law, they can be frustrated and undermined by the rules of lawyers. The 1996 Telcom Act is a right law, but the legal process of implementing it is turning out to be a nightmare of delay and distortion by reviewing courts. So far the monopoly telcos have persuaded judges to believe that the FCC has no power to insist on competition in local telephone markets. We're trying to get this case to the Supreme Court, but the telephone companies are fighting for delay.

Here we have a law that everyone thought empowered the FCC to open all communications markets, and the courts are enjoining us, telling us that the states get to decide these matters. When the states' rights agenda is used to help shrink big government, I admit to some sympathy. But when it's used to bolster monopolies and stifle interstate commerce and create years of litigation-induced delay, I think something's gone grievously wrong with our legal culture.

Barriers to Big Bandwidth

The new data networks and the new services they will carry depend on big bandwidth. No bandwidth, no business. The faster it's made available the faster it will be used. But the pushback against pro-bandwidth spectrum policies has already begun.

In July, Congress nearly passed a law ordering the FCC not to let spectrum licensees have freedom to use their spectrum the way they wanted. That could have stopped us from just getting out of the way, for example, when wireless cable firms decided to use their spectrum for high-speed Internet access.

It's not just Congress. The status quo will also be erecting barriers to Internet growth. Eventually, when the poaching gets rich enough and there's Internet access in every pager, curtain rod, belt buckle, and laptop, the powers of the status quo will mount an army of lobbyists and public relations firms and economists to take on the packet-switched threat. So I suspect.

In my view, within five years in some markets and 10 in most, packet-switched minutes will exceed circuit-switched.

Already this year you have seen the telcos seek from the FCC new charges, called access charges, on the Internet. Their idea was that all Internet traffic would generate about six cents per minute in charges paid to the local phone companies that originate and terminate the call on their local loop, the lines to your house or office. At a couple of hours of usage per day—hardly unusual for Internet folk—that's about $200 a month.

Prominent political forces told the FCC to agree with the phone companies.

We didn't.

If humans can create all the obstacles to rapid, efficient, and private-sector development of America's future networks, then humans can solve them. We do need a new law, a Free the Internet law. It can be blessedly short. Here are its key components.

- ✦ First, the First Amendment to the U.S. Constitution, which guarantees freedom of speech, should clearly protect Internet content from government regulation.
- ✦ Second, the FCC should have the power to order states not to regulate digital packet network services, whether offered by new entrants or by incumbents.
- ✦ Third, the data networks should be free from subsidy. They shouldn't pay into any subsidy pool and they shouldn't take out. Let the markets build them.
- ✦ Fourth, the FCC should have clear authority to impose policies that open any and all communications bottlenecks to competition.
- ✦ Fifth, all judicial review of the essential issues in the telcom world should be a single court of appeals. So far, GTE has sued in 30 federal district courts in 23 states, arguing that the company is entitled to charge competitors for its historic cost of building its networks.

A short and simple law along these lines wouldn't guarantee the Internet's success. Whether we have a ubiquitous high-speed, high-bandwidth, packet-switched digital network really depends on the brilliant entrepreneurs here in Silicon Valley and elsewhere working around the clock to invent the services and products that will drive Internet expansion.

Washington can't make the Internet succeed. But it can be an obstacle to its success. There are plenty of good ideas in Washington. Whether my modest, market-oriented, competition-friendly, deregulatory proposals fall into that category—you be the judge. But I'm confident this nation can get its communications policies right and get the real info highway built fairly and efficiently all across this land.

PART THREE

Street Rumble in Software City

CHAPTER TWENTY-ONE

The Dark Side of Objects

I t was colder and rainier than expected in Silicon Valley one December day in 1994 as I made my way to an industry conference at the Convention Center. There would be many database vendors under the big tent in downtown San Jose. But my interests were on a smaller segment of the market—the component companies. These were the avant garde makers of snippets of pre-compiled code that went into every Visual BASIC application. Because Visual BASIC was used to link desktops to databases, rapid application development was becoming big-time in the corporate environment, hence the connection between databases and components.

In late 1994 nobody knew that the component makers were only a few short years away from extinction at the hands of Microsoft. You see, component technology soon took center stage in the war over who would own corporate computing into the next century. It was to be a galactic war over software. And I would get to witness an early street rumble in Software City as Microsoft began to burrow into corporate information system's departments.

The twenty-year-old object technology that researchers at Xerox PARC dreamt about never really happened, but it did spawn an entire subindustry called the "component makers." These were companies that wrote reusable pieces of code that other programmers could use to quickly put together big applications. Theoretically, a software industry would grow up around component makers similar to the automobile industry that grew up around parts makers. Ford Motor Company doesn't make the steering wheel and air bag. Instead, it buys them as parts and assembles the entire car by combining these parts. Like the parts makers of the auto industry food chain, software component makers are near the bottom of the food chain. Only brand name software publishers like Oracle, Symantec, Inprise, and Microsoft are at the top.

The emerging market for components had gathered steam by 1994, hence the reason I was headed to the Convention Center to check out component makers. Reusable software had seemed like a good idea for decades. Now, a number of small companies were starting to actually build and sell them. It seemed like time to learn more about the component business.

Information system's managers in large companies knew way back in the 1970s that they could increase programmer productivity if only they could get their programmers to buy lots of components and assemble them into whole systems. It works for the automobile industry, so why not for the information technology industry? The answer: components would never become mainstream technology until a standard emerged. After all, if you want a component from one company to work with components from other companies, you need a standard way to plug everything together. As it turned out, component makers could never create a large enough presence in the software industry to force a standard.

But big and powerful companies can turn almost any technology into a standard. That is exactly what IBM and Apple Computer thought in 1994. IBM, Novell, and Apple Computer created a standard called OpenDoc, which defined how components could work across many different systems. Any component maker that obeyed the OpenDoc standard could write code that worked everywhere. This was the theory that captured the imagination of programmers, especially programmers who worked in large organizations.

In 1994 it appeared that the OpenDoc consortium led by IBM, Apple, and Novell would make reuse a reality. It would also assert IBM's control over enterprise computing. Apple was a major player because of its technology, and Novell was a key player in networks. Together, the newly formed CILabs (Component Integration Laboratory) looked unbeatable in 1994. It seemed that nothing could stop this powerful combination of technology, standards, and financial backing.

But, OpenDoc would soon fail under its own weight as IBM and Apple made major mistakes. For example, IBM and Apple formed Taligent—a company created specifically to build cross-platform, component-based, interoperable, enterprise-ready modular applications made from components—hired too many people too fast, and grew the size of its vaporware product even faster. It was crushed under is own weight. Instead of taking the world by storm, Taligent soon went out of the component business and was absorbed by its parent companies.

Meanwhile, strategists at Microsoft closely watched the amusing CILabs episode. The company was slow to catch on to the game, but the huge amount of effort and money that IBM, Apple, and Novell put into

OpenDoc sounded the wake-up alarm. Being the quick learner that it is, Microsoft quickly rallied and struck back. Microsoft's reply to OpenDoc was a very poorly designed and buggy afterthought called OLE (Object Linking and Embedding). It was based on Microsoft's early success with Visual BASIC, but it was far inferior to OpenDoc.

Microsoft had an uphill road ahead of it in 1994. It didn't understand object technology, the theoretical basis for components. It didn't understand interoperability, which it needed in order to work with other people's operating systems (UNIX, OS/2, and VMS). It had few deep thinkers on the payroll, because until now, it didn't need them. Rather, it needed quick and dirty programmers. And yet, component technology— as shown by CILabs—could be used to enter the vast and rich mother lode of enterprise computing.

The stage was set in December 1994 as Microsoft began its run up the component adoption curve. Microsoft would hype its OLE in public and try to derail OpenDoc in private. This would give it time to catch up. If Microsoft only knew that Taligent would crash a year later, perhaps the Redmond, Washington, upstart wouldn't have rushed its poorly designed and implemented technology to market so early. But Davidow's Law had to be obeyed!

Once again, Microsoft was about to impress the computer world with a come-from-behind display of force. In just a few short years it would learn object technology, gain a deep understanding of enterprise computing, and pull ahead with a succession of technologies. OLE would evolve into OLE 2.0, then COM (Component Object Model), ActiveX, and COM+, and so on. Microsoft's enterprise level operating system, Windows 2000, would be heavily warped to fit the component model of software development. Each software release would get closer to the ideal established by OpenDoc. And after each revision, Microsoft would gain more market share. ActiveX and soon-to-be relabeled DNA (Distributed InterNetworking Architecture) would reverse the big company fortunes of the company. That is, until the OpenDoc companies discovered the component powers of Java! But, I get ahead of myself.

In hindsight, the description given in the next essay makes it clear that component technology would have a bigger impact on Microsoft rising than thought in 1994. Microsoft may have misunderstood object technology, but within a few short years, it would dominate it. By 1999 almost all software development within large organizations would be defined by Microsoft component technology. Competitors like CORBA (a warmed over OpenDoc) would have to yield to Microsoft's COM technology in order to get a foot in the door of corporate America. It was yet another sign of Microsoft rising.

Article by Ted Lewis, Computer, December 1994

The Dark Side of Objects

I had planned to meet my Microsoft-employee friends at the airport so we could all go to the OOPSLA conference put on by that other computer society. However, my flight into Portland was late (the reservation system used Microsoft products), so I used my Microsoft Windows laptop-turned-Microsoft telephone to leave a message at my Microsoft-guru-friend's hotel. (Later I would find my friends watching cable TV via their Microsoft set-top box, playing Microsoft Flight Simulator, and banging on a beta release of Microsoft Windows 95.) After a brief conversation about how rich they'd become from Microsoft stock options, I agreed to meet them at the conference next day and headed for my room.

The U.S. Justice Department really showed those Microsoft biggies, I thought, as I smugly used WordPerfect to edit this column that evening. The 140 satellites that Bill Gates wants to put up, the new Microsoft e-mail replacement for the Internet, and the bank encirclement deal with Intuit obviously eluded the Antitrust Division. But the free world is safe from the monopoly because DOS WordPerfect is out there selling like peanuts at a ball game. As I drowsed off, Microsoft sugar daddies danced in my head.

That Old Gang of Mine

Well, WordPerfect, IBM, Novell, Lotus (almost), Apple, and some other "minor league" players have joined forces to upset our comfortable Microsoft world. Those saviors of free enterprise formed Component Integration Laboratories (CILabs). Huddled like orphans in the wind, the CILabs club is plotting Microsoft's downfall. We're talking OpenDoc (compound document technology) to challenge Microsoft's OLE and DSOM (Distributed System Object Model) to wreck Microsoft's COM—Common Object Model. We're talking megabucks and market domination. We're talking OOT. Like plastics in the 1960s, objects are the buzz in the 1990s.

Objects of Affection

OOT is the software industry's next craze. Just look at the names of these companies and products: Object Design (Inc. 500's top growth company in 1994), VisualAge OOP from IBM, Object Studio from Easel Corp., Object Works, and so forth. Not to mention the object-oriented frameworks from Taligent. Next, HP, Apple, and Sun-Soft, and the thousands of object-oriented-software vendors pressing their noses against Windows. The affliction has even spread to noncomputer companies. Mercedes-Benz just paid $5 million for a share of object-oriented-database-maker ONTOS. With a spreadsheet in hand and your cousin Vinny in tow, almost anyone can get the capital to start a company to make object-oriented thingies.

Everything is an object these days; if it doesn't have o-b-j-e-c-t in the name, it won't sell. Everything from everyone but Microsoft, that is, and here's the perceived crack in Microsoft's defense strategy. Everyone but Microsoft is betting that the OOT revolution will catch Microsoft with its shields down, and the megalith's slight hesitation will be the chance of a decade to beat out an old rival. If we run fast enough and program hard enough, we might slip one over on Microsoft, so we think. In 1995, those mindless consumers will buy Warp instead of Windows 95, or System 8 (Copeland for the Macintosh), and on goes the scheming.

Bearer of Bad Tidings

But I feel compelled to tell Taligent, HP, IBM, and Apple (I just love to bring bad news) that there is a dark side to objects: Object technology does not sell computers. Is a consumer going to know whether it's object-oriented or Memorex? Which OOT features allow my application to do tricks that were previously impossible with procedural programming? Yes, I know there have been promises, but where is the hard data? Component programming, reuse, rapid application development, and visual programming are still "ether net" dreams.

Second, OOT is so radically different that we must break and reset programmers' coding hands before they can write object-oriented instead of procedural programs. This is much worse than the structured programming hoopla of the 1970s. If C++ is the answer, I forgot the question. If we convert one Cobol programmer per minute to Smalltalk, we should have a revolution by the time Capt. Kirk and the USS *Enterprise* return from Vulca on impulse power.

Third, OOT has a nasty "fragile base class problem" which means that once a program is designed and implemented as a class hierarchy, it is maximally coupled. Changing one interface specification brings the whole house of cards tumbling down. We were warned against this in 1975 (minimize coupling, maximize cohesion). Coupling is a serious maintenance nightmare that bit Mentor Graphics (Falcon Framework) in the bottom line. How many other software companies are headed for OOT malaise?

Fourth, the good old compatible language bindings of the past are long gone. Smalltalk and C++ are fundamentally incompatible, so we are even further away from interoperability than the Ada creators could imagine. For example. Object Design's object-oriented database must read Smalltalk objects, convert them to C++ objects, process them, and reverse the conversion each time it crosses a language barrier.

Is OOT Moot?

But the darkest of dark sides is a little thing that Microsoft hastily concocted called object linking and embedding. With OLE you can write a desktop application on a Macintosh to be understood by an application on a Windows PC. You can also embed rich types (such as text, sound, or graphics) in a document and have the editing program corresponding to each type instantly available without switching in or out of the application. Once OLE/COM is distributed across a network near you, OLE-enabled applications can talk to each other over miles of cable, wireless, string, and so forth.

OLE is catching on like e-mail at Al Gore's house, but unfortunately it is the deadliest possible blow to OOT—mainly because it isn't object-oriented, it isn't fully specified, it's inferior to OpenDoc, and there is little that anyone can do to stop it. OLE will become synonymous with OOT, yet it is a fraud. Microsoft sidesteps charges of forgery through fancy labeling. Can you say "aggregates" instead of objects (maybe we should call it ALE—aggregate linking and embedding)?

If you are a developer, give OOT more of your time and attention. Although watching the OOT wars rage outside your corporate window is great sport, serious movements are afoot. Your software architectural future is in the ballast. Luckily for Microsoft, it's difficult to see a naked emperor in the dark.

CHAPTER TWENTY-TWO

The Big Software Chill

The new economy is propelled by computer technology, and two things propel computer technology: semiconductors and software. Moore's Law rules learning in semiconductors, but what dictates progress in software? It doesn't take long to discover that software is ruled by Darwinian forces—just like a biological system. In fact, progress in software is as accidental as the mutation of a species in the natural world. And if this reminds you of chaos, welcome to the club!

A big chill descends upon the software industry whenever a big technology like CASE (Computer Aided Software Engineering) fails. CASE was supposed to save the world by making software development projects practical. CASE promised to cure all of the ills of a chaotic science. The so-called "software crisis" would go away if every programmer learned the strict discipline of CASE. This fairy tale never happened. Instead, CASE failed with a thud heard all over Silicon Valley. Its crash cast a pall over an industry. It was the big software chill.

CASE enjoyed a relatively short life, spinning up in 1988 and dying off by 1996. The idea was simple, but its realization impossible. Most software projects fail because programmers are an optimistic lot. They promise more than they can deliver. Programmer estimates of how a system should be created are especially poor in the early stages of development. They find it difficult to glean requirements. They find it even more difficult to make their code work once the (wrong) requirements are determined. Adding these two critical steps together sets the stage for unrealized expectations. In short, software projects fail because they get too big, take longer than expected, and cost more than the boss asked for.

The remedy is to automate what you can, and train programmers to use a strict methodology on the parts that cannot be automated. Automated and methodical development was christened CASE. By 1988 everyone who was anyone in software had jumped on the CASE bandwagon.

That is, everyone except Microsoft. By early 1992 the early adopters were becoming skeptical. By 1996 the bandwagon was empty. CASE wasn't declared dead, exactly, but other things were taking its place.

This essay attempts to generalize on the failure of CASE. But in hindsight, CASE is a special case. Its failure cannot be generalized. Did it fail because it was impossible to achieve? Did it fail because it lacked support from major companies? Perhaps it would have succeeded had Microsoft backed it with its own product.

CASE failed because it couldn't achieve widespread acceptance in the short time that Silicon Valley expects new ideas to gain ground. It was a slow technology in a fast industry. Similarly, other technologies like C++ (programming language of the 1980s) were on their way out, just like CASE. Programming languages are subject to changes of fashion, and C++ was a programming language badly in need of a face-lift.

So this essay reveals the subtle changes taking place in the software industry. Companies that pursued a religious pilgrimage to save the world of software development through CASE have had difficulty saving themselves. Companies that pursued the shifting sands of lowest-common-denominator technologies like C++, followed by Java, followed by COM+, etc. have not only survived, but prospered. Software development is not science or engineering. It is art. Only the brilliant artist knows how to cope with chaos.

Article by Ted Lewis, Computer, March 1996

The Big Software Chill

If a technology (or idea) does not achieve mainstream status quickly enough, it dies. Video on demand (ITV), the information superhighway telco (ISDN), and massively parallel supercomputing are obvious examples. These ideas were okay, but they died for lack of legs. Consumers simply shunned them, illustrating the power of Info Age mainstreaming (see *Computer,* Sept. 1995, pp. 8–10).

A corollary to this law: A technology (or idea) thrives, even if it is a bad technology or idea, as long as it quickly achieves mainstream status. Microsoft Windows, Java, C++, and others illustrate the overwhelming power of mainstreaming. It's what Bill Gates (*The Road Ahead,* Viking) calls "positive feedback." Simply put, the rich get richer, especially when they hold a monopoly. In the Info Age, the definition of wealth includes domination of standards as well as having cash in the bank.

The Quick and the Dead

Of course, there are always in-betweens, technologies that teeter on the verge of failure or success: MacOS, OpenDoc, Corba, and ATM networks, for example. We need more time to find out whether these are next year's hits or misses. But how long must we wait to apply the test? Whether a technology or an idea achieves mainstream status "quickly enough" depends on the age you live in. During the Industrial Age, "quick" took about 50 to 100 years (the telephone, capitalism). In the Post-industrial Age (circa 1945 to 1991), "quick" took 10 to 20 years (television, business PCs). In the Info Age, "quick" takes 5 to 10 years (the VCR, home PCs).

These two rules are invisible hands guiding much of the computer industry today. Take software development technology as an example. It is close to the hearts and minds of computer nerds like us—enough so that the reader might get agitated when I claim that software development technology flunks the mainstreaming law. For developers, programming is experiencing the big chill because none of its tools and techniques are ramping up fast enough to mainstream.

The Rise of High Tech

Figure 22.1a compares the learning curve of VLSI hardware technology (Moore's law, again) with that of software developer productivity as measured by the cost per function point. This software function point performance, obtained from Capers Jones at Software Productivity Research Corp., is an estimate of the rate of decline in programming cost per function point, that is, \$/FP (read my upcoming article "The Next 10000 Years" for more on this topic). The dramatic difference in learning curves is due to the difference in learning rate ($B = 0.675$ for the hardware industry versus $B = 0.955$ for software).

The mainstreaming rule is obtained by plugging the learning curve formula into the mainstreaming or logistics growth curve, that is, $M = 2/(1 + L) - 1$, to get the S-curve that readers of this column have come to adore (see Figure 22.1b). Don't ask why this works, because there is no sound theory behind forecasting.

Now we can restate the mainstreaming rule in terms of the Info Age: If a technology (or idea) does not achieve mainstream status within a decade, it dies. Even a bad technology (or idea) can thrive if it captures the mainstream imagination within 5–10 years. Venture capitalism aside, modern society lives on instant gratification.

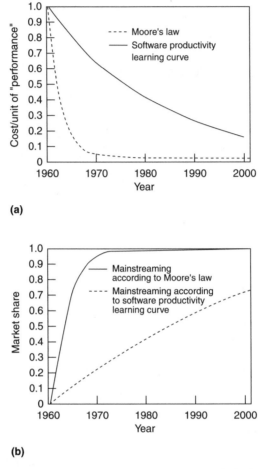

Figure 22.1 *Learning curves (a) versus mainstreaming curves (b) for hardware and software. Learning curves are computed as P = B^t; mainstreaming curves are obtained from M = 2/(1 + P) − 1.*

Government Interference

Objections to these ideas are easy to come up with. What about the Internet? It has been around for 25 years, without "mainstream attention" during most of that time. This seems to violate the rule. However, ARPA and NSF funded the Internet, thereby subverting the rule. Examples of government interference include the artificial economy of supercomputing fostered by ARPA funding, NASA's space program, and other charities. (I am not speaking against these subsidies, but merely pointing them out. After all, my bread, just like that of many of my readers, is buttered by government grants.)

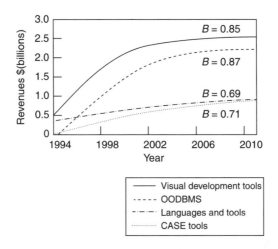

Figure 22.2 *Revenue estimates in billions of dollars for CASE tools, languages, visual development tools, and object-oriented database management systems. Parameter B is the learning curve parameter. (Sources: David Linthicum, "Component Reusability Linked to Tool Domain,"* Application Development Trends, *Jan. 1995, p. 48, and Monica Snell, "A New Visual Attitude,"* LAN Times, *May 8, 1995, p. 47.)*

The problem with software is that we don't get many artificial price supports for software technology development. Unlike the American farmer, software companies don't get paid unless they plant something, nurture it, and reap a profit within the time limit set by the mainstreaming law. Commercial software companies have to hit the big time, or else.

CASE is a Case in Point

The CASE (computer-aided software engineering) tool vendor business has collapsed, contrary to wild claims made over a decade ago. In 1987 I proudly edited one of the first special issues undertaken by a respectable publisher (*IEEE Software*) on the topic of CASE. Since then, CASE has declined, rivaling AI as the most overhyped software technology of the decade. The "decade problem" is an important clue: Had CASE delivered the goods within the 3–5 years required to get beyond the early-adopter stage, it might have mainstreamed, leaving competitive technologies in the dust. (See Figure 22.2.)

The revenue projections of Figure 22.2 hint at the root cause of the software productivity paradox. In all cases, including visual development (a.k.a. Visual Basic, PowerSoft, Pictorius, and related technologies), the learning rates are simply too low. For example, Figure 22.2 learning rates range from $B = 0.69$ to $B = 0.87$. In the Info Age, "quick" means "less than a decade," and CASE has run out of time.

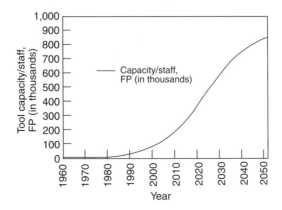

Figure 22.3 *Software tool capacities in leading software-producing enterprises. (Source:* New Directions in Software Management, *Capers Jones, Information Systems Management Group, Carlsbad, Calif.)*

Figure 22.3 holds even less hope that software tools will gain mainstream status. Software tool capacity per staff member, again expressed in terms of function points, will simply rise far too slowly to hit the mark. With a learning rate of approximately 10 percent per year (staff are obtaining "tool power" at a rate of 10 percent per year), tools are improving faster than the software industry in general, but this rate is still far too slow.

An aside: If you read previous columns in the Info Age series, you might wonder if the Lanchester Strategy applies to the CASE segment. Bingo! At the 1995 OOPSLA conference, the leading CASE vendors agreed to merge their competitive designs; OMT and Booch vendors agreed on a single standard. They recognized the folly of splitting a declining market. OMT, with 40 percent, was almost a market leader, and Booch, with 11 percent, was unstable. But together, they plan to push their 51 percent share toward a monopoly, ending the game. This is classic Lanchester Strategy for achieving mainstream dominance. Unfortunately, CASE no longer has a dog in the fight: All CASE vendors are losing ground to people sliding down much steeper learning curves.

The Dismal Science

Software is the dismal science of the 20th century. The problems—including the lack of a methodology, a formal basis, or a trained priesthood—have been exposed by outsiders as well as insiders. *Wired* (June 1995, p. 74) invited notables such as Danny Hillis (Thinking Machines), Scott Brown (Novell), and others to comment on the following embarrassing point:

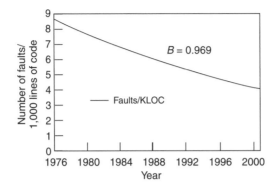

Figure 22.4 *Drop in software error rates per KLOC (thousand lines of code) at NASA Goddard Space Flight Center. (Source: "Turning Software from Black Art into Science,"* Business Week, *special issue, Dec. 1991. Can also be found in* IEEE Software, *May 1995, p. 86.)*

> *Raw computing power is doubling every 18 months, but software is still too high-priced, too difficult to use, and too buggy to trust for many purposes. To compound the problem, only an elite few are able to program useful applications. So computer scientists are developing new paradigms of program design, development, and distribution. But today's highly paid programmers may find the results unwelcomed.*

Most of the *Wired* panelists admitted that the software industry is unlikely to ever produce a provably correct application. However, they agreed that interoperable objects and "evolved" applications are possible— by 2020! But a technology that requires 24 years to reach maturity will fail the mainstreaming test. In effect, the expert panel does not have a clue about how to solve the software crisis.

Take the "provable correct programs" problem as an example of the theory of mainstreaming. Figure 22.4 is the learning curve for error-rate removal in various NASA Goddard Space Flight Center programs. It follows about the same dismal learning curve as software productivity in general—in this case, 3 percent per annum.

No Panacea

D evelopers are grabbing for anything they think will save their development projects. They are grabbing at straws in the wind. Martin Marshall, writing in *Communications Week* (Aug. 7, 1995, p. 12), shows results from a Dataquest survey of MS Windows programmers. From 1993 to 1994, C/C++ use declined 32 percent while Visual Basic and Smalltalk use increased 60 percent and 200 percent, respectively. Even Fortran and Cobol use increased 49 percent and 75 percent,

Tool	Percentage of Companies Using
PowerBuilder	44
Visual Basic	42
Cobol	40
C++	20
Access (DBMS)	18
Oracle (DBMS)	14
Borland Delphi	8

Table 22.1   Responses to the question "What are your top three development tools?" (Source: Forrester Research Inc., Cambridge, Mass.; multiple responses from 50 Fortune 1000 companies.)

respectively, faring better than C/C++. Marshall points out that C++ especially is under siege: "In part, C++ is slowing down because there were a number of early adopters and the momentum has not been sustained." This is killing the once-mainstream momentum of C++. Now, retreaded C++ programmers are rushing to C-like Java to save their jobs—grabbing at whatever the wind blows by.

Frank Hayes, writing in *Computerworld* (Oct. 30, 1995, p. 69), and using a Forrester Research study of Fortune 1000 company developers, shows a trend toward the use of nonprogrammer tools in place of programming languages (see Table 22.1) This once again proves my point Programming languages such as Pascal, C++, and even Smalltalk are doomed to extinction unless they can maintain and improve widespread acceptance. (Fortune 1000 companies, not university computer science programs, are mainstream. Consumers are mainstream, not computer industry programmers or PhD professors who teach C/C++ to the next generation of frustrated application developers.)

Even though the data in Table 22.1 shows a leaning toward visual development, these tools are not the panacea we make them out to be. They are simply gadgetry for dealing with the complexities of windowing systems. We still need a software technology that will put us on a learning curve to compare with that of Moore's law. Until someone discovers or invents a breakthrough software technology that puts us on a faster learning curve, the big software chill will get bigger.

Article by Ted Lewis, Computer, August 1996

Software Architectures: Divine Plan or Digital Darwinism?

When Bellcore guru Robert Lucky described the World Wide Web as "a case study in chaos theory" (*Computerworld*, June 3, 1996, p. 70), I think he raised a much larger issue: Is there a hidden pattern to developments in the computer industry, or are they simply a demonstration of Darwinism?

The fate of software architectures is a good example of digital Darwinism. At best, most of them go awry. At worst, their degeneration is a consequence of natural selection run amok. Moreover, it isn't just designers who are affected; chaotic design practices have seeped into our entire high-tech culture. Having infiltrated the whole computer industry, Darwinism is spreading faster than promises in an election year. And much of this chaos is driven by an old nemesis—requirements creep.

Survival of the Clueless

Let's face it, most of the success enjoyed by Microsoft and other FutureBusinesses has come from surviving the dog-eat-cyberdog jungle rather than from executing a careful plan. This may be obvious to the stock market investor but us geeks tend to think the computer industry is going somewhere in particular.

On the contrary, in the computer industry jungle, you can't see very far ahead. Not only has marketing success been achieved without a clue, but most of the successful technology in use today has also emerged from a clueless industry.

In the case of Darwinian architectures, Microsoft currently hoards the biggest pile of market share. But does the Big Bwana in Redmond have a map? The company's actions suggest otherwise.

Consider Microsoft Money—built to kill Intuit (the whole company). It deflated when pitted against Quicken. Gates could not compete, so he tried to buy the company. When that failed, spin doctors smothered the dismal incident.

There are so many examples of jungle fever that I could write a book. Microsoft hasn't been able to compete in several juicy segments: Where is MS-Cobol and MS-Fortran? How many people use Works? Where was Microsoft when Netscape was scooping up market share? Remember Microsoft's Xenix? I doubt it. What about SQL Server? Sure, it's doing okay, but Oracle is the real database company. Microsoft's brief romance with personal digital assistants went down the tubes with the failed WinPad, which may return for a second try in the form of Pegasus—a crippled version of Windows 95 for PDAs.

The vines grow thick farther south, too. As Robert Cringley put it (*Accidental Empires*, Addison-Wesley, 1992), "The boys of Silicon Valley make their millions, battle foreign competition, and still can't get a date." Indeed, the computer industry is a messy place governed by serendipity, ruined plans, and scattershot targeting—hardly the kind of traits that inspire confidence.

But it's not like this everywhere. Let's look at two contrasting engineering models.

Swiss Army Knives

Charles Elsener, the fourth-generation descendant of the Swiss Army knife inventor, supervises 900 workers who churn out 110,000 knives per day. Except for a change when stainless steel was invented in the 1920s, the company has been replicating the same design since the 1890s.

The Swiss Army knife is based on a simple architecture that permits tools such as can opener, screwdriver, nail file, and toothpick to be easily mixed and matched in 800 different variations of the same design. In short, the Swiss Army knife has a solid architectural basis leading to a solid design that has made millions for the Elseners. The architectural underpinnings were so good that there has been little to change in 100 years. The Swiss Army knife is right on target.

Swiss Cheese (American Style)

Compare this with software products. According to most software engineering textbooks, product development is an orderly process progressing through requirements capture, preliminary design, detailed design, development, and testing—all carefully carried out per the Capability Maturity Model. When completely mastered, software engineering is like churning out Swiss Army knives, with everything tidy, predictable, scalable, and controllable.

Central to this software engineering myth is the idea of a software architecture, a collection of clean interfaces and rules for using them. In the business, these interfaces manifest themselves as APIs (pronounced "apes"). In this fairy tale, every good software product starts with a good solid architecture; every good programmer knows his or her APIs.

This model couldn't be further from reality. The truth is, most software products are designed on the back of envelopes that are lost or thrown away, designers leave companies halfway through projects, or the competition causes product revectoring in midstream. And this happens every day of the product development cycle. As a consequence, few products have what might be called an architecture. APIs are a moving target. The concept of an architecture is a fantasy.

Middleware Mayhem

Now let's look at the hard-fought battle for dominance in distributed computing's "software bus architecture" arena. I'm talking about DDE, DLE, OLE, OLE/COM, OLE/DCOM, and, more recently, Microsoft's ActiveX. Microsoft isn't alone—there are similarly unruly products from the OMG Corba/OpenDoc/SOM camps of IBM, Apple, and Oracle. The problems also apply to the Unix world of DCE, NEO, WebObjects, and JavaObjects. Everyone is guilty.

Perhaps one or more of these "architectures" were truly designed with foresight, but they have nevertheless all succumbed to chaos. At this moment they are being cast aside in favor of even more unruly, poorly devised, ad hoc "plans" for the Web. The Web is simply another place to demonstrate the triumph of chaos over order. We're about to pile up more software-industry victims of Darwinism.

Distantly Related

Microsoft's halting steps toward ActiveX provide a good example of the software chaos theory. ActiveX is the current incarnation of Microsoft's proprietary middleware "glue" that has recently been aimed at Java. ActiveX is too proprietary to beat out Java, just as Money was no match for Quicken, but the next three years will be colorful as Microsoft and the Java Beast grapple for a spot on the food chain.

ActiveX has its roots in the late 1980s with the idea (gleaned from Apple Computer's publish-and-subscribe) of "hot-linking" applications through a technology blandly called DLE (dynamic linking and embedding). A hot link is a pipe for connecting two desktop applications such as Word and Excel so that data can flow seamlessly between the two. Simply linking a graph in Excel to a picture in Word accomplishes the goal of interoperability. A change in an Excel graph is automatically propagated to all documents that reference it.

DLE evolved into OLE (object linking and embedding), which evolved into ActiveX (distributed OLE). The word "evolved" is appropriate. Instead of a plan, there were mutations. Instead of an architecture, there were remodeling jobs piled on top of remodeling jobs. OLE's design and implementation were so chaotic that version 1.0 had little in common with version 2.0—OLE 2.0 was essentially a different product. ActiveX follows the same pattern, merely resembling OLE 2.0.

OLE works through binary DLLs (dynamic link libraries) rather than source-language bindings. This is one major difference between ActiveX and, for example, OpenDoc. A binary interface allows disparate developers to create and sell their components without exposing their source code. It also permits objects to be sewn together at runtime rather than being statically bound at compile time. This flexibility alone explains OLE's fast start in the component world. But the binary approach resulted in unwieldy designs that make it difficult for developers to build applications with the interoperability and portability of, say, Java. More importantly, ActiveX is a hacker's dream, not an example of sound architecture.

Requirements Creep

The main reason architectures go awry is creep—the rate of change in requirements between the time the coders start hacking and the time the product is delivered. Figure 22.5 compares program size in function points to creep rate. (As a very rough approximation, each function point is about 100 C/C++ statements. Therefore, 1,000 function points entail about 100,000 lines of C/C++.) Any software system larger than the maximum size for a given creep rate (above the curve in Figure 22.5) is impossible to build. Let me demonstrate why.

Capers Jones (*Computer,* March 1996, p. 117) says, "Creeping user requirements will grow at an average rate of 1 percent per month over the entire development schedule." In the same article, he says, "Raising the number of function points to the 0.4 power predicts the approximate development schedule in calendar months." In mathematical terms this means

$$R = FP*(1.01)^{(FP^{0.4})}$$

where R = requirements and FP = function points (program size).

When R reaches 100 percent change, we are building the system twice—once according to the original requirements and then a second time according to the new requirements. Set R to $2*FP$ and solve for FP. This will tell you when the requirements have changed 100 percent, rendering the original specification totally wrong.

$$FP = (A/B)^{2.5}$$

where $A = \log(2)$ and $B = \log(1.01)$. This yields FP = 40,500—a pretty large program.

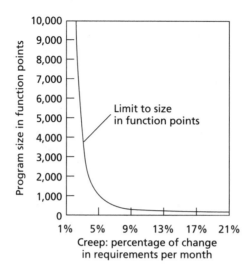

Figure 22.5 *Maximum program size, measured in function points, versus the monthly rate of change in requirements.*

Suppose we let the 1 percent creep rate slide? Then, setting $B = \log(1 + C)$, where C ranges from 1 percent to 20 percent, we get Figure 22.5. This shows that a small deviation from 1 percent, say 5 percent creep, radically lowers the size of a "feasible" software system.

So whether or not a software product can be developed without chaos depends on the creep. As Capers Jones and Figure 22.5 show, extremely small values of creep (5 percent or more) result in chaos. Without a strong architectural basis, creep is inevitable. Without an enduring architectural plan, creep rates are more likely to be 5 percent than 1 percent—and suddenly it's a jungle out there!

The Reset Button

What is the consequence of creep? Does it matter that applications based on pervasive infrastructure software like ActiveX resemble the Denver Airport baggage-handling system rather than a Swiss Army knife? You bet it does.

About once every decade the computer industry collapses under the weight of its own chaos. We even name these collapses: the mainframe era, the minicomputer era, the personal computer era, and now the network era. This catharsis sweeps away the tangled webs of the past, and everyone starts over. The old legacy systems are allowed to fade away; next-generation systems rise up like a phoenix.

Our most recent era is nearly over. The industry has pushed the reset button, and everyone is about to start over again. Soon Windows API, DMI, MIB-II, OLE API, Corba ORBs, OpenDoc, TAPI, TSAPI, CTI, and others will be gone. Like an old copy of Bill Gates' first Basic manual, these systems will be little more than stories we tell our bright-eyed graduate students at boring faculty parties.

In their place will be new systems based on Netscape plug-ins, HTTP/HTML, Perl/CGI, VRML 2.0, Java, JDBC, Beans, and other yet-to-appear pretenders—mutations from today's Internet and WWW fall-out. These, in turn, will be tomorrow's troubling legacy systems. Like their predecessors, they will crawl out of the swamp of chaos, evolve into giants of the industry, and thumb their noses at strong architecture. And the Binary Critic of 2012 won't have a clue as to where the industry is headed. Long live Cobol!

CHAPTER TWENTY-THREE

Tiny Beans

CASE and many other panaceas for solving the software crisis were handed defeat in the 1980s and 1990s. That is until Java hype appeared in 1996. Java was in the right place at the right time. It had the backing of a powerful company (Sun Micro) and was in step with the Internet. Its technology wasn't anything new; in fact, it was as old as computing itself, but it captured the imaginations of thousands of programmers new to the field.

Most people didn't know what Java was in 1996, but they knew it was a panacea. First, it was object-oriented. Then it was simple. Finally, it was Web-enabled. A small Java program called an applet could be attached to a Web page and downloaded into the Web cruiser's PC and instantly run on any machine. Because Java was based on a hypothetical machine called the JVM (Java Virtual Machine), all that anyone needed to run a Java program was a JVM. JVM's interpreted J-code is a universal machine language. JVMs are available for every kind of computer— Intel, PowerPC, HP, Sun, and so on. Like the Pascal system a generation before it, Java ran on everything that had a JVM. It didn't take long for entrepreneurs to offer free JVMs for the asking.

Java is just warmed over C++ with remnants of Pascal copied from the work of Niklaus Wirth (1970). But what became important about Java was its component technology—JavaBeans. This language extension made it possible to build stand-alone programming parts called Beans, and then use them to build full applications. A "Bean factory" turned out the building blocks, and a "Bean assembly line" used the building blocks to build entire applications. Programming would become like building a brick building, one brick at a time. The theory predicts the creation of independent software developers who perfect thousands of Beans, so that other developers can raise their awareness. Application developers could concentrate on the application and ignore low-level programming details. Reuse would overcome the software crisis and everyone but Microsoft would benefit. It was yet another utopian dream.

Would JavaBeans revolutionize software development? Would it overthrow Microsoft? The potential for Java to upset Microsoft's position in the industry had as much to do with Java as its technical merit. In the next three articles, I explain why JavaBeans will continue to be central to the software industry, and why Java-the-language isn't a very bright idea, technologically. Along the way I dispose of more dead end technologies that succumbed to the Darwinian forces of software evolution. Who remembers OpenDoc?

If Java succeeds, will we have overcome the software crisis? No, the software crisis will remain long after the Java hype dies down and programmers build millions of lines of Java legacy code. Like the many panaceas before it, Java won't cure what ills programmers, because Java isn't an improvement over Pascal. And Pascal failed to cure the software crisis. The ultimate cure lies in a galaxy far, far away, years from now, when some bright Ph.D. student discovers how programmers think. In other words, the software crisis is equivalent to the problem of human cognition. And this Holy Grail won't be found for a long time. In the meantime Java will fulfill its goal: to sell more handcrafted software.

Article by Ted Lewis, Computer, September 1996

Will Tiny Beans Conquer the World Again?

Why are Microsoft, IBM, Oracle, Apple, Borland, Sybase, and just about everyone who is anyone looking nervously in the rearview mirror? Because Java, and—more threateningly—its component technology called JavaBeans, is getting closer all the time.

It wouldn't be the first time beans conquered the world. Upon arriving in "New Spain," conquistadors discovered tiny, mysterious beans whose product, chocolate, was used not only for daily nourishment but also in rituals and financial transactions. Until people's palates became more educated, it was slurped down rather than chewed. In fact, the Maya called it *chokola'j*, literally "to drink chocolate together." Now JavaBeans, like chocolate beans, is about to go global.

When It's Hip to Be Square

Will Java honk for the passing lane or just steamroller over the slow starters? With its growing momentum, Java is rapidly becoming an industry. Many moons ago, Stewart Alsop said, "Let's get real, Java will not meet these expectations, [because] your average marketing-dweeb-turned-webmaster isn't going to be mastering Java and its C-like syntax any day soon" (*Infoworld,* Dec. 18, 1995, p. 114). Alsop pointed to Macromedia's Shockwave and Director as the right choice and likely successor to Microsoft's boring Visual Basic. Today, nobody knows what Shockwave is, but everyone is learning Java. I hate to be square, but Java is inevitable.

Forget Paris

The last time anyone set out to design a language and force it down everyone's throat was when the U.S. Department of Defense picked the Green Language out of a hat. Renamed Ada, in honor of Charles Babbage's gambling sidekick, and designed largely in France, this nouveau language resoundingly failed to get anyone's attention. What happened?

Back in the 1970s, the design and success of programming languages depended on the skills of technical people rather than on those of marketing whizzes. But not anymore. Maybe if the DoD had had a bigger PR department—one that understood the software economy . . . well, that would be another story. Forget Ada—forget Paris.

We can also forget that Java has semiautomatic garbage collection, multithread control, semisecurity, just-in-time compilers, and now Microsoft's blessing. Nobody really cares about these things, because Java's real selling point is that it's architecturally neutral. This is polite slang for "it will run on something besides Wintel."

Anti-Microsoftians

Microsoft's rivals will grab anything that might loosen the company's lock-in monopoly of the desktop. These anti-Microsoftians are hoping that Java's neutrality will be just the thing to render Wintel inconsequential.

Microsoft feels the heat. In a classic move to deflect the Java onslaught for a few months while getting its Internet strategy in place, Microsoft licensed Java and elevated it to the same level as its Visual Basic. Still running scared, Microsoft began licensing Basic to third-party developers, hoping to stall Java for a few more months. Next, Microsoft will be dumping corporate ballast into Lake Washington to make itself lighter and faster as it huffs and puffs to catch the Java wave.

Big Wheels in Wired World

Regardless of Java's inadequacies and the hurried patches that Sun keeps throwing at us, Java is not just another language, as some writers have tried to convince us nerds. But so what? Languages are dead anyhow. The battlefront has shifted to middleware standards. Middleware is the next Wired World platform. Why?

Maybe middleware won't generate enough revenue to rescue a floundering software company, but as Figure 23.1 shows, it's the tail that wags the dog. According to Input Research, the U.S. market for software that supports ActiveX, CORBA, OpenDoc, and eventually JavaBeans is $14 billion this year and will burgeon to $25 billion next year.

The name of the computer biz game is "distributed processing," and middleware is the software equivalent of the Internet's routers, switches, and hubs. If you want to be a Big Wheel in Wired World, you have to dominate middleware standards. Microsoft can't push ActiveX ahead of JavaBeans while still riding on training wheels. So Microsoft did a clever thing: It changed the name of OLE to ActiveX, turned up the PR machinery, and absorbed Java.

Chocoholics

Just as chocolate was thought to be a cure for tuberculosis, gout, and ulcers, Java is thought to be a cure for middleware malaise. But it isn't. What are the alternatives?

According to Figure 23.1, third-party ActiveX developers will earn $180 million this year selling 2,500 reusable components to Wintel addicts (Input Inc., *Datamation*, July 1996, p. 62). OpenDoc parts vendors will make $20 million. I'm not sure of the numbers for CORBA vendors, but I'd guess that they're on the verge of filing bankruptcy—or doing other products. Java and JavaBeans probably generated more than $200 million for advertisers alone. Another $500 million in venture capital is probably going up in smoke from investments in silly little JavaSoft spin-offs like Marimba or high-risk money pits like Dimension X.

Don't get me wrong. I agree with Dan Kara of Software Productivity Group, Westboro, Massachusetts, when he says, "OpenDoc is a better solution." In that respect, it's like Ada. OpenDoc parts let developers build middleware for all major platforms, and it works with OLE—oops, I mean ActiveX. If you're going to develop for Wintel, why not use OpenDoc and get its extra benefits? OpenDoc is a better ActiveX than ActiveX. But so what?

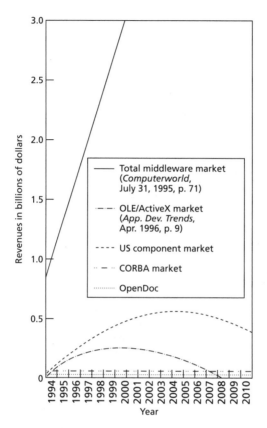

Figure 23.1 *U.S. revenue forecasts for component technology and the leading standards—CORBA, OpenDoc, and ActiveX.*

FUD and Other Means of Persuasion

Of course, I'm being rational, and middleware warfare is not rational. The only things that matter are lock-in, software economics, and FUD (fear, uncertainty, and doubt—the three main reasons why data processing managers buy from Microsoft). OpenDoc will live in IBM's dreams but fade as ActiveX and JavaBeans nuke each other for your IS budget.

Is JavaBeans the next big thing—or the next Ada? It all depends on who has the biggest marketing budget. Anti-Microsoft forces like Beans because it makes middleware work across all desktops. Thus, it has a slight chance against ActiveX. ActiveX compiles into Wintel binaries, while Java compiles into J-code that will run on kerosene if it has to. One is fast, the other is portable.

But Microsoft is about to apply some pressure by flooding the Internet with compelling applications that require users to adopt ActiveX. It will also force developers to make their software interoperate with ActiveX. ActiveX compatibility will be a necessity just like Windows NT compatibility, so why not simply do everything in ActiveX?

In fact, Microsoft is so intent on beating rivals Netscape (HTML/Java), Sun (JavaBeans), and other anti-Microsoftians to the punch that it recently *gave away* ActiveX. On the surface, this move looks like a way for ActiveX to become open, that is, nonproprietary. However, Microsoft is placing ActiveX in an open forum for exactly the same reason Netscape gave away its browser—to kill off competition.

NetMeeting

Microsoft's next big revenue stream will come from corporate intranet software like NetMeeting. Working in harmony with Microsoft's Explorer 3.0 browser, NetMeeting hits all the corporate hot buttons. It does voice and data conferencing and application sharing over the Internet. It uses T-120 and RTP (real-time protocol) for streams. It lets tightwads place free international telephone calls over the Internet. NetMeeting has whiteboard capability, chat, file transfer, and shared clipboards. It makes sharing of any Microsoft application across the Internet just like being there. And guess what? NetMeeting is built on ActiveX. If you want NetMeeting, you have to get ActiveX.

A Mad Dream

Borrowing from the Maya, the anti-Microsoftians might exhort us with a single word—*javala'j* . . . "let us drink Java together." But can *these* Beans conquer the world?

> It sounds like a mad dream, yet these people represent it as we have come to know it. Their lives conjure up all the childlike magic of that sweet stuff.
> From The True History of Chocolate, *Sophie and Michael Coe (Thames & Hudson, 1996)*

Article by Ted Lewis, Computer, March 1997

If Java Is the Answer, What Was the Question?

Within a very few short years, Java, JavaBeans, and everything to do with Java will be pervasive. Java's adoption curve will rival just about everything else in Silicon Valley for living in real time. The technology will burn brightly for a time and then burn itself out. Before that happens, though, Java will be as common as a household mop.

Product hype is as much a part of the computer industry as celebrity is an essential part of Hollywood. Excellence often falls victim to PR. In the case of Java, it is particularly difficult to separate the PR from the reality. Who can you turn to to get the truth about Java?

So your first question might be, is Java really an improvement? Simply put, no. If today's languages are inadequate for today's software engineering challenges, then Java must be inadequate, too. Remember, most of Java is warmed-over C/C++. In spite of its celebrity status, Java lacks many of the features needed to improve the dismal science of software engineering, just like its predecessors. How so, you ask? Here is my analysis—with a minimum of hype—on the pros and cons of Java.

Java as Dial Tone

I wrote my first program on a vacuum tube computer that had a fantastic 32-Kbyte rotating drum storage unit and all the paper tape I wanted. This amazing machine ran 32-bit software—more than you can say for many Win95 applications! I soon graduated to transistors, Algol, Fortran, Pascal, Ada, and C++. I should have been content with such rapid progress. But I was a chronic complainer. I wanted more. I wanted a universal programming language that worked on any computer, any operating system, from anywhere.

A band of nerdy programmers who hung around the computer center shared my dream. In fact, many people did. This popular dream even had a name, the UNCOL (Universal Common Language) Problem. Sound familiar? The term was coined in 1963 when the gleam in everyone's eye was Algol because it promised to solve the UNCOL Problem. It couldn't.

Then Pascal happened. Pascal gained a huge following because PL/I was too big, messy, and unruly (much like C/C++ today). It didn't solve the UNCOL Problem any more than Algol. Then Ada happened. Ada was supposed to be a better Pascal, but the Ada command economy failed because capitalism abhors a monopoly. Then C++ happened. You get my drift. Over the years we have found that software cannot be constructed from a standardized, universal, platform-neutral language.

The more things change, the more they stay the same: Now it's Java that will solve the UNCOL Problem. Java, they say, will become the dial tone of the twenty-first century—not! If past is prologue, Java-as-UNCOL has a highly dubious future.

Hostages of Legacy Code

In the meantime, Java will have its 15 minutes of fame. And then what? The really important question is this: What devastation will Java leave in its wake?

Because of Java's adoption rate and expected life cycle, applications written in Java today will have to be replaced or vastly modified within a decade. As Java ushers in a new era of technology, our responsibility as technologists is to ensure that future applications built with Java are well-behaved legacy systems.

When viewed in this light, the question of Java-as-UNCOL becomes serious. For example, one study has estimated that the U.S. Department of Defense alone will spend $30 billion on the Year 2000 Problem. Maintaining legacy Cobol systems is a major industry today, and holds many organizations hostage to 1970s technology. Legacy software is what keeps IBM, Andersen Consulting, EDS, and many Fortune 500 companies in business. It is the tail wagging the dog. By 2010, Java will be the maintenance tail wagging the software dog, instead of Cobol.

Doomed to Repeat History

Elegant minimalism is one of the goals of Java. It is a simple language, just as Pascal was a simple language—on purpose. But we know from history that minimalism rarely succeeds. Safe, reliable, minimalistic Pascal failed because minimalism is interpreted by the market as "incomplete." Pascal was instantly tagged a toy language.

Java as a general-purpose language is also incomplete: It lacks I/O, intrinsic functions, APIs to an OS, and other features. Because it copied many of Pascal's minimalist attributes (byte codes, strong typing, restricted pointers, and meaningful keywords instead of cryptic symbols), Java has chosen to trod the path blazed by Pascal, the first portable language.

In spite of many pleas for simplicity over the ages, minimalism has failed in the language domain, just as it has in nearly all other segments of the software industry. Java may be virtuous as a better C++, but markets rarely reward "best-of-breed" technologies. Why should it reward Java?

What Was the Question?

Clearly, the software industry needs a new paradigm: Is Java the new paradigm? When applied to Java, the word "paradigm" may be far too strong. Most of Java is watered-down C++, plus some retrofitting of Pascal (strong typing, keywords, packages—from the UCSD P-code version—and portable byte code). Java threads are vast improvements over Unix tasking, but they are certainly nothing new.

About the only thing in Java that comes close to deserving the "new paradigm" label is the tagged applet. Applets and servlets are truly new, but there is no real-world requirement that they have to be written in Java.

Which leads me to wonder: If Java is the answer, what was the question? What problem does Java solve that could not be solved before Java came along? I address this question first with some general comments and then with some specific comments about Java technology versus the alternatives.

Dog Food for Thought

What are some of the problems awaiting future Java programmers? First, Java still retains too many of the error-prone features of C/C++. Syntactic problems abound, but I mention only a few, samples of the dog food being fed to Java programmers.

Consider C's bad habit of increment and decrement. What does

    int i = ++ i–;

mean in Java? In horrible C tradition, Java arrays start from zero, instead of one. How many future programmers will spend hours locating off-by-one errors? What's wrong with the number one?

Java's unruly scope rules add insult to C++ injury. Scope, range, and synchronization constructs are overly complex, sometimes contraditory, and mostly poorly thought-out. There are no fewer than 10 object modifiers in Java (more dog food): public, private, protected, static, final, native, synchronized, abstract, thread-safe, and transient. The sacrosanct public modifier completely breaks down encapsulation in Java. Static, final, and public are contradictory, confusing, and poorly motivated. Native is unforgivable in a language that lays claim to platform neutrality.

Like Pascal, Java eschews I/O. Both Pascal and Java off-load I/O to ill-defined, incomplete libraries. As a consequence, I/O libraries are already starting to flourish, creating a variety of Java dialects. Lack of a standard language is what eventually killed Pascal—Microsoft has pounced on this flaw of Java and is destroying the Java "standard" even as I write this.

Threadbare Java

The designers of threads, Java's most highly touted feature, missed a golden opportunity to make future legacy systems more reliable. They got some things right, but created some deeper problems for future programmers to struggle with.

Java's creators did get lightweight threading right: Lightweight threading in Java is generally an improvement over heavyweight tasking in Unix. It opens up many opportunities—for good and evil. Java reincarnates Donald Knuth's atomic procedures as a mechanism to ensure mutual exclusion. But Java does not go far enough. In fact, Java atomic procedures and lightweight threads can lead programmers down the road to ruin.

For example, suppose a program manipulates data stored in a double buffer, as shown in Figure 23.3a. It creates two threads. The first thread copies data from L2 into L1 and eventually into the first running thread, T1. Another thread does the opposite: It copies data from L1 into L2 and eventually into the second running thread, T2. In Figure 23.3a, T1 and T2 simultaneously access L1 and L2. In fact, the access order is immaterial—the important thing is to avoid race conditions.

In Java, a programmer uses atomic functions to ensure mutual exclusion; for example, using the synchronized modifier. Synchronized functions ensure mutual exclusion by allowing only one thread at a time to be active within a synchronized function. Now, a programmer could innocently declare a synchronized Java function like the (simplified) one below. In this example, a get access function is declared within a list class, and then instantiated twice, once for list L1 and again for list L2.

```
class LIST {
synchronized public
get (List L; char c) {. . .}
. . .
L1 = new LIST(. . .);
L2 = new LIST(. . .);
```

Now suppose thread T1 uses these objects in the following order:

```
get (L1 . . .); get (L2 . . .);
```

and thread T2 inadvertently uses them in the opposite order:

```
get (L2 . . .); get (L1 . . .);
```

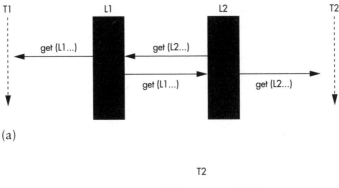

(a)

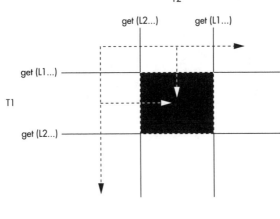

(b)

Figure 23.3   *A sample deadlock created by Java's atomic procedures and lightweight threads. (a) The double-buffer problem and (b) an interleaved matrix showing a deadlocked state.*

The resulting double-threaded program works *most* of the time but *not all* of the time, as the interleave matrix of Figure 23.3b illustrates. Most of the time T1 accesses L1 followed by L2, and T2 accesses L2 followed by L1 (the sequence shown as vertical and horizontal dashed arrows in the figure). Once in awhile, however, and depending on the underlying operating system's time-slice algorithm, T1 is interrupted immediately after it gains exclusive access to L1, and T2 is allowed to gain exclusive access to L2. When the time slice returns control to T1, T1 is blocked by T2. When the time slice returns control to T2, T2 is blocked by T1. The two-thread system is deadlocked!

This is a particularly nasty fault, because it may occur irregularly, almost like a random hardware error. It can neither be predicted nor easily discovered through ordinary debugging techniques. From the programmer's point of view, there's nothing wrong with the code. The fault must lie in the hardware! Thousands of future programmers will spend hundreds of hours trying to locate such errors.

A better solution to thread control in Java would have been to adopt Path Pascal's path expressions. Path expressions have been around for 20 years, just like most of Java's other features. They can be placed in classes' interface portion and therefore used by the compiler to check for synchronization problems. In other words, synchronization should be an interface specification, not a coding mechanism.

A Better Mousetrap

This example illustrates only a few of the problems lurking in Java— problems that will be cursed by future programmers as they maintain the tons of Java legacy code that is expected to accumulate over the next decade.

In fact, Java fails to deliver on a number of nagging problems that will continue to plague software development for years to come. If Java is to become a better mousetrap, it must address the core problems of software development that continue to plague the industry:

+ *Requirements.* Requirements capture and specification has proved to be a "bridge too far." Java does not even attempt to address this problem, and Java hype threatens to hinder what hard-won progress that has been made.

+ *Defect removal.* Over the past 30 years, nearly all the progress made in software development can be attributed to early defect removal. On the positive side, Java does enforce strong typing, restrictions on pointers, and single inheritance. On the negative side, Java is subject to C/C++ syntax problems; nonstandardized APIs; the fragile base class problem, whereby interface changes to abstract classes destroy entire class hierarchies; and the fragile interface problem, whereby one change in an interface specification can propagate to all points in a large program that use the interface, to name just a few. Java takes only a small step toward early defect removal.

+ *Components.* We know that the development cost per function point increases exponentially with application size: It costs more than twice as much to develop twice as much code. JavaBean component technology may be an improvement here. Even so, other technologies like ActiveX, CORBA, and OpenDoc promise similar improvements. There is nothing intrinsically better about Java than alternative solutions.

+ *Cycle time.* Applications must change at the rate of Internet time, approximately every 18 months. This limits a new system's size, its functionality, or both. Java does little to accommodate Internet time. However, when combined with RAD (rapid application development), Java's platform neutrality may allow the construction of some systems within Internet time—systems that may not have been possible without RAD.

+ *Complexity.* Today's applications are vastly more complex than previous applications. Tomorrow's applications will be even more complex and demanding. In general, society's expectations are rising faster than the ability for software technology to deliver. Java does not appear to be a bigger intellectual lever than Ada, Pascal, and siblings. Even worse, Java does not advance the intellectual frontier. Functional, graphical, rehearsal, and other languages may or may not be an improvement, but they have not been given the same opportunity to prove themselves.

Java has some things that should be applauded: its error-handling, single inheritance, and interface specification constructs. In addition, Java has wisely borrowed some beneficial features from pre-C/C++ languages, and innovated the idea of an HTML-tagged applet. So progress has been made, even though it's taken 20 years. This is far too little progress, however, for a grown-up industry. Java simply produces too much disappointment at this early stage of its development. While there is hope that Java will eventually mature, I cannot recommend that we turn our future over to Java, not quite yet!

Article by Ted Lewis, Computer, March 1998

Java Holy War '98

In this corner, we have Scott McNealy of Sun Microsystems fighting for the rebels. "With his boyish face and mouthful of large teeth, McNealy resembled a large chipmunk when he smiled," wrote Jim Carlton in his must-read book, *Apple: The Inside Story of Intrigue, Egomania, and Business Blunders* (Random House, 1997). Looking more like Bullwinkle Moose's friend Rocky the flying squirrel than fictional boxer Rocky Balboa, McNealy has set his sights on the prize—knocking off Bill Gates in the next round of computing.

"Sun," writes Nikki Goth Itoi, "intends to use Java to cash in on the next major shift in the computer industry: the move toward simpler computers and smarter, networkable consumer devices. Sun also wants Java to replace today's dominant enterprise computing platform: Windows" ("Sun Inside," *Red Herring*, Sept. 1997, p. 87).

And in the other corner, we have Bill Gates leading the Empire—I mean, Microsoft (they're equivalent, after all). Microsoft's culture, imprinted on the company by a 15-year-old Gates, persists to this day. "Microsoft's insularity, its focus on hiring stereotypical nerds without an outside life, is what has come back to haunt it. 'Microsoft has never put any effort into figuring out how to schmooze with people,' said Tina Podlodowsky, a Seattle City Council member, who left Microsoft in 1992, 'they simply don't understand why people don't see things the way they see things.' So I guess they're suffering now for being intellectually arrogant and socially inept," writes Timothy Egan ("The Barrage Against Microsoft Appears to be Taking Its Toll," *San Jose Mercury News*, Jan. 17, 1998, pp. 1C, 3C).

Round Three

The conflict is over who will own the computing infrastructure for round three, the post-OS round of the computer industry sweepstakes. Anthony Perkins ("Why Microsoft is Vulnerable," *Red Herring*, Feb. 1998, pp. 12–14) sums it up: "Round 3 for Microsoft is about owning the software that connects computers everywhere. The back end of the worldwide network is the corporate enterprise system. It is in perhaps its biggest battle—the fight with Sun over Java—that Microsoft is most vulnerable." This battle pits the glib hype of a toothy salesman against the grim determination of a super nerd. It's a battle for the pocketbooks of corporate computing—the Great Java War of 1998.

But wait a minute. Java is just a language. Or is it?

Not Your Father's Programming Language

Java is far from just a language to Sun, which sees it as an entree to centralized computing. Sun is betting the company on this concept—the same idea that made IBM ruler of all that computes during the 1970s. Only in 1998, centralized computing means Web servers connected to desktop clients via an Internet, intranet, or virtual private network. Sun's powerful Unix servers will do the heavy lifting, while scaled-down desktop boxes called thin clients will perform most of the lightweight user interface functions. At least this is the theory.

"We are pretty confident that by the second half of '98 we will see volume deployment of thin clients," says Ed Zander, president of Sun Microsystems Computer Co. ("Sun's Vision From Mover and Shaper," *San Jose Mercury News*, Dec. 29, 1997, p. 3E). Zander is confident that Java and the thin-client concept will win out over Microsoft's desktop PC concept, leading to greater riches for the Palo Alto maker of hardware servers and Java software.

But thin isn't the main issue: Middleware is. While much of the attention of the computer industry has been focused on Java the language and the Sun-versus-Microsoft litigation over pure Java, the real stuff lurks below the surface. The Great Java War of 1998 will make history because Java is no longer a language—it is an infrastructure technology designed to reinvent computing in the image of Sun's Enterprise Computing Platform (ECP) architecture.

This is where the plot thickens. Java is not as important as the JVM (Java virtual machine), nor are Java applets on the desktop as important as JavaBeans on the server. If Sun or anyone else can define the API (application programming interface) to some universal middleware, they can rule the world—at least for a short while. Hence the reason for IIOP (Internet InterORB Protocol), which marries CORBA (Common Object Request Broker Architecture) with JavaBeans.

Microsoft, on the other hand, is pushing its Distributed Network Architecture, a collection of technologies for accomplishing the same thing as IIOP. It defines DNA as "the integration of Web and client-server application development models through a common object model." To achieve this integration, "Windows DNA uses a common set of services such as components, dynamic HTML, Web browsers, and servers," according to Microsoft's Web page.

IIOP proponents hope consumers won't want DNA (alias ActiveX) if they can get IIOP, because IIOP is a universal standard that spans all platforms, not just Wintel. Vendor independence leads to greater options down the road, and information technology managers like to increase their options. Table 23.1 compares DNA with Sun's ECP architecture.

The Middleware End-Run Game

The purpose of this technology—besides winning the Great Java War of 1998—is to write an HTML page containing a control script that packages a user's inquiry in a middleware wrapper and sends it to a server. At the server, an SQL query is fired off to the database for answers. The answers eventually retrace their path from database server to Web server to client browser. This round-trip rides on DCOM (Distributed Component Object Model) in Microsoft's world view, and on CORBA/IIOP standards in Sun's view.

Function	Microsoft DNA		Sun ECP Architecture	
	Standard	Product	Standard	Product
User interface	Windows API	MFC (Microsoft Foundation Classes)	AWT	Java AWT
			Swing Set	Swing Set
Server	HTML/XML	Info Server	HTML/XML	Netra
Browser	DHTML+	Internet Explorer	Pure HTML	None
Scripting	Visual Basic Script Java Script	Denali	Java applets	Enterprise Java
Middleware	DCOM	ActiveX	IIOP	CORBA ORBs, XML
Components	ActiveX	ActiveX	IIOP	JavaBeans
Database	ODBC OLE database	SQL Server	IIOP wrappers	None
E-mail	MAPI (Mail/Messaging API)	Exchange	POP3 (Post Office Protocol, version 3)	S/MIME (Secure Multipurpose Internet Mail Extension)
Directory	Windows NT Server	Active Directory	Directory	LDAP (Light Directory Access Protocol)
Security	Secure Sockets Layer	WinSock	Java Sandbox SSL	JVM

Table 23.1 Comparison of Microsoft DNA to Sun ECP architecture.

Microsoft has cobbled together a bunch of products, renamed them, and restarted its marketing machine under the name of DNA. ActiveX may or may not keep its name as Microsoft's marketing machine plays shell games with words. DCOM, Hydra, and the other monikers will appear and disappear like a fireworks display as this PR game unfolds.

Meanwhile, Sun has a different vision of the future: Technology is secondary, PR and vision are primary. The rhetoric to customers goes something like this: First, banish the Wintel desktop using various dialects of Java and the JVM, instead of various incantations of Windows. Replace PCs with thin clients. Of course thin-client software can run everything from wristwatches to laptops and desktops. These devices may use a variety of operating systems, but they all communicate via the "Java dial tone," that is TCP/IP, HTTP, IIOP, and JavaBean components. This is classical absorb and extend.

Next, banish Windows NT at the server level. Customers don't need NT—it's a step backward to weaker, less reliable computing. Sun will tout Unix as an industrial-strength server OS that can scale from desktop to supercomputer. Server applications will run on mainframe iron and use Java frameworks and Java components according to the IIOP/CORBA standard for interoperability. The JavaOS will reach downward from network computer and appliance (set-top boxes and handheld gadgets) to wristwatch and pocketbook (smart cards based on the JavaOS). We won't need Microsoft frameworks and ActiveX components.

So much for theory.

Who Will Bite?

How likely is Sun to win the Great Java War? Litigation aside, the reality is that Sun is struggling to implement its strategy. Right now, Java technology is a mess. Take Sun's recently released Swing Set, advanced APIs for building industrial-strength Java applications—finally. The problem with Swing Set is that it renders code written for Personal Java inoperable! Personal Java uses the AWT (Abstract Windowing Toolkit) instead of Swing Set. Programs written in Swing Set won't work on systems that use AWT and vice versa. Java's main claim to fame is its interoperability and write-once-run-everywhere promise. Swing Set violates Sun's commitment to scalability, which won't play in Peoria.

Sun is considering a Java registry—called JINI—which would contain information about the capabilities of each device that hosts JVM software. Thus, a Java program would read the device registry and adapt to the device by downloading appropriate interface components. Programmers would still have to choose between Personal, embedded, or enterprise Java, an added dilemma. This appears to increase complexity, not decrease it. If Sun doesn't clean up this mess, Java will be too complex for anyone to use.

Most of us complain about Microsoft's monopoly position and then turn around and order its products. IT managers don't want to get locked in to Microsoft products, but they keep buying them by the disk full. The reason is this: DNA looks like a sure thing, and ECP looks like a risk. Most of DNA exists as renamed products. Most of Java exists as marketing hype.

So the question we are being asked is: Do we want genuine competition in the industry badly enough to share the risk with Sun and its ECP supporters? Nobody gets fired for buying Microsoft products, but if Java doesn't work, say good-bye to your career. How many are willing to take that chance? Java looks like a long march to freedom.

The Long March

The Long March began in December, when Sun unveiled the Enterprise JavaBean (EJB) specification, which defines its vision of server-side component-based computing for the next decade. At the same time, Oracle announced its pure-Java product line, Oracle Applications 10.7 NCA—Oracle's entire suite of applications in all-Java packages. Netscape is developing all its internal applications in JavaBean technology. Sybase is shipping its first implementation of embedded Java in Adaptive Server version 11.5. Object database vendor Versant will announce its Java support in ODBMS 5 in early 1998. IBM will expand support for Java in DB2.

Java, JavaBeans, and IIOP are gaining support among customers. "We're building mission-critical applications with Java and it's working," says Mike Anderson, director of application services for Home Depot, the $20 billion chain of hardware stores. (Rich Levin, "Java For the Enterprise," *Information Week,* Dec. 8, 1997, pp. 18–20). Levin claims, "Database vendors are displacing SQL with Java because SQL isn't portable and because object developers cringe at using legacy procedural code in interchangeable component frameworks."

"We're building directly for the Beans API," says Thomas Greer, chief architect at Visa International in San Mateo. "When the EJB tools finally arrive, it's a quick flip, and then we're going to be able to drag-and-drop the enterprise. That's the real power of all this. If we tried to do this application in C++ it would take three or four times as long."

The skirmish in 1998 will be over who owns the right-of-way to middleware—Microsoft's DNA or Sun's JavaBeans with IIOP. This battle will be so important to the eventual domination of the computer industry that we can expect more unusual behavior from the competitors in the coming months. For example, don't be surprised to see companies like Sun jump-start the transformation from Wintel to the JVM by giving away thin-client boxes to consumers who adopt Sun's middleware. Also, expect more mergers and joint ventures among the Nethead Gang. For now, the intellectually arrogant and socially inept shall lead.

CHAPTER TWENTY-FOUR

The Trouble with Programmers

When Roger Pressman, author of the world's best-selling textbooks on software engineering, asked me to participate in a panel on developing Internet applications, I was simultaneously honored and puzzled. Roger is a highly respected member of the software engineering community of experts, a club that I could never belong to, because of my counterrevolutionary ideas. Software development is equivalent to art as far as I am concerned. Engineering isn't. The phrase "software engineering" is an oxymoron because it simultaneously says "this is a rigorous activity, but no, this isn't a rigorous activity." But Roger assured me that his panel had room for naysayers, so I volunteered.

Programming is still an art, and programmers are an unruly bunch as pointed out by Ware Myers in the following article. Ware underscores our weaknesses as human beings and then chants the software engineering chant. One cannot argue against his prescription, but most of us live in the real world where software projects are just as risky in 1999 as they always have been. Indeed, because software development is a human activity, it will always be subject to human frailties. The trouble with programmers is that they are humans.

The next article after the one by Ware Myers is a reality check. In the real world, the more software you make and sell, the more times you get to make and sell software! This circular argument is exactly why Microsoft dominates the software industry. They make lots of software, and because it sells, they get to keep on making it. So what better place is there to ask the question, "What is the trouble with programmers?" If we cannot answer this question by examining the practices of the industry leader, then where can we find answers?

Unfortunately, Microsoft isn't any better at developing software than anyone else. They may be better at selling it, but they don't have any secret weapon. It is simply as difficult for Microsoft to write code as it is for everyone else. Maybe they work harder and longer, but the bottom line is this: software is beaten into submission. In other words, testing is more difficult, costly, and time-consuming than everything else put together. Until we solve the testing problem, we won't know what troubles programmers.

Microsoft software development capability may be near its limits, because Microsoft had great difficulty bringing its largest operating system, Windows 2000, to market. It was simply too big and ugly. Nonetheless, testing was the secret to turning Windows 2000 from junk to product. At one point, Microsoft employed 400 code testers and another 120 usability testers to check the work of 400 programmers. In addition, Microsoft sent out 60,000 copies to beta testers who volunteered their time. In fact, Microsoft has made its customers a big part of its development process. Even with all of this free labor, Microsoft still delivers damaged goods.

Microsoft isn't alone. The entire software industry is riding on the backs of programmers who, because they are human, are error-prone and imperfect. This leads to imperfect software products. As a consequence, the software crisis lives on, and consumers have adapted to the notion that it is acceptable for software to fail. My guess is that this situation won't continue; sometime in the next decade or two, programmers will get into trouble if their programs don't work.

Article by Ware Myers, Computer, April 1998

Why Software Developers Refuse to Improve

Wrote Jane Austen in the opening sentence of *Pride and Prejudice* 200 years ago, "It is a truth universally acknowledged, that a single man in possession of a good fortune, must be in want of a wife." It is a truth less universally acknowledged that a software developer in possession of a good temper must be in want of a more productive environment. In fact, many developers fail to acknowledge that there *are* more productive environments. When a software organization loses a bidding contest, the losers roll their eyes heavenward and tell each other, "Better luck next time."

Well, this is the reality: There are software development organizations that are more productive than others. "Luck" is not the whole story; you need to look for ways to improve.

Vast Range of Productivity

A reality that is not universally acknowledged is that the general capability of software organizations extends over a truly enormous range. The difference between the productivity of individual developers is on the order of 10 to 20 times. The difference between the capability of software development organizations is at least two orders of magnitude greater—100 to 200 times. The reason is that organization capability is also affected by the deftness of management, investment in process improvement, the development process employed, and the tools in use. This difference goes a long way toward explaining why some organizations win contracts and complete projects on schedule, within budget, and at satisfactory quality levels—and others don't.

This vast range is illustrated in Figure 24.1 by the frequency distribution of the process productivity index. This index, a metric devised by Lawrence H. Putnam in the 1970s, measures the capability of a software project organization. He reported it in July 1978 ("A General Empirical Solution to the Macro Software Sizing and Estimating Problem," *IEEE Trans. Software Eng.*, pp. 345–361), and I followed up with an article in *Computer* ("A Statistical Approach to Scheduling Software Development," Dec. 1978, pp. 23–35). Our book *Industrial Strength Software: Effective Management Using Measurement* (IEEE Computer Society Press, 1997) contains perhaps the most accessible explanation.

Measuring Productivity

Putnam calculates process productivity from an equation containing the size of the system, the development time, and effort (in person-years). This relationship is nonlinear, and the nonlinearity's result is that the process productivity values extend over a huge range.

To make the scale more easily understandable, Putnam represented it with the *linear productivity index,* currently extending from 1 to 33, the highest yet reported. This is a useful simplification when estimating projects. When thinking about the productivity range, however, the nonlinear version is more to the point. Thus, the multiple from one index to the next is 1.27. That is, an organization with a capability measured at index n works 1.27 times more effectively than it did last year, say, at index $n - 1$. That means the nonlinear range from index 1 to index 33 is 1.27^{32} or 2,098 times.

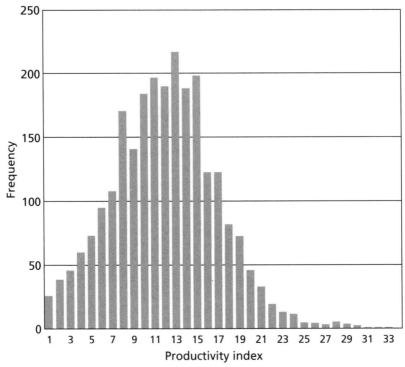

Figure 24.1 *The more than 4,000 systems contained in the QSM database distribute over the range of process productivity index numbers in a pattern close to the statistical normal curve. (Data courtesy of Quantitative Management Systems.)*

There are only a few data points beyond index 25, so it might be more realistic to compute the factor from 1 to 25; it is 310 times. To be still more conservative, we might compute the factor between one standard deviation below the mean and one standard deviation above, since the distribution is approximately normal. For business systems, that factor is 10.6; for engineering systems, 5.9; and for real-time systems, 5.5. In other words, an organization now about five index numbers below the mean can increase its process productivity by a factor of five to 11 times by improving not to the very top, but to five index numbers above average.

The great productivity difference between software development project organizations is also implicit in the five Capability Maturity Model levels developed by the Software Engineering Institute at Carnegie Mellon University. It is implied by ISO 9003. In effect, both say, "If you learn to use better ways, you will reap good things."

What Are the "Better Ways?"

The number of better ways is legion, but here are a few examples. They seem fairly obvious, but many software organizations manage to ignore them.

Establish Feasibility First

A small team should develop the beginnings of an architecture, especially as it relates to novel aspects of the proposed system. These risky aspects should be sufficiently resolved (probably not totally) before the organization tries to proceed to full-scale development. Yet Capers Jones estimates that 65 percent of large systems—more than one million source lines of code—are cancelled before completion (*Asessment and Control of Software Risks*, Prentice Hall, 1993). These large systems are the ones you hear about in the media. For systems exceeding a half million LOC, the cancellation rate is around 50 percent, and above 100,000 LOC, 25 percent. The main reasons Jones gives for this sad state of affairs is that the cancelled projects were "poorly planned, incompetently estimated and tracked."

Establish a Plan

A valid plan is necessarily based on some degree of architecture and some degree of risk reduction. Some call this functional or high-level design. The degree to which the team carries architecture, risk reduction, and planning has to be sufficient to enable the software organization to estimate the cost and time schedule of the main build. The organization must also estimate the level of reliability the product will attain. Apparently only about one-quarter of projects begin with much of a plan in place.

Have a Repeatable Process

You can't carry out a plan within an estimate if your organization can't repeat its process. About two-thirds of organizations evaluated so far rest in CMM level 1—they don't have a repeatable process.

Review, Inspect, Test

It has been established that reviews and inspections along the way are a good idea. Less productive software organizations do few of these things. Test people agree that organizations should start planning tests early; most don't.

What's the Hang Up?

There may be several reasons we don't try better ways:

* *We face many psychological hurdles.* Managers, executives—they all resist change. Moreover, we all like to get to the "meat" and hate

to spend time on the messy preliminaries. We are anxious to get coding.

+ *We just don't know about these better ways.* In spite of the plethora of conferences, courses, books, magazines, and consultants, software developers may not have time to search out new approaches. Here knowledge really is power: Business-system projects, on average, have been gaining 10 percent productivity per year; engineering systems, eight percent; real-time systems, six percent.

+ *We are gun-shy.* A few score of "better ways" have already inundated the software field, and sad to say, many of these highly touted "better ways" are not effective in practice.

+ *We try but fail.* Even those better ways that are valid are not easy to implement. Often an entire project or even an entire organization has to adopt the better way. That is true, for instance, of object-oriented technology and systematic software component reuse. This takes champions, time, investment, and persistence.

+ *We are stifled by the competitive economic system.* On the one hand, our economic system pushes organizations to improve. On the other hand, it removes from marginal organizations the resources needed to support long-range improvement efforts.

So, process improvement is going to be difficult. It is going to take a period of years. It is going to replace organizations that lag with those that modernize. But creative destruction is a painful way for humankind to advance.

Let's Search for a Better Way

Let me make just four points.

Use Valid Process

There are a dozen or so well-regarded methodologies. However, certain basic principles should underlie a process that is going to work:

+ Do the hard stuff first—key requirements, core architecture, major risks, ballpark estimate, feasibility, the rest of the risks, the remaining architecture, main-build estimate.

+ Have a method for ascertaining the requirements, sorting out the ones that are key to the several stages of requirements and transposing the requirements into the first stage of analysis.

+ Since there is an order in which to accomplish the hard stuff, base the process on a series of iterations.

+ Since successive teams of developers must pick up the iterations, document them. Take a look at the Unified Modeling Language standardized by the Object Management Group last November.

+ Since development occurs in an economic framework, collect metrics, maintain a database of them, base estimates on them, and control the execution of the process—actuals against plan—with them.

Communicate the Process

We especially need to reach two audiences. *Sponsors,* those who finance new ideas, need information tailored to the functions they perform in adopting and financing new ways of working. The CS Press Executive Briefings series is a case in point. *Practitioners,* those actually applying the new ideas, need detailed books, manuals, short courses, helpful supervision, and mentoring. They also need software tools to do what tools can do better than people.

Simplify the Implementation

In spite of the obstacles, new ideas do sometimes get to the point of being applied, only to have the implementation fail. Object-oriented technology may be a long-standing example. I wonder how many executives on encountering the term *polymorphism,* have grunted "This stuff is not for us."

Every new idea seems to be born complicated. The challenge for those who would see it applied is to simplify it. Some complications can be incorporated in tools, out of a user's sight. Developers, after all, have the complexity of their applications to occupy them. They do not need the complexity of the new way of working at the same time.

Even after simplification, there will still be a lot of changes to implement. Leading companies understand that implementation takes

+ investment money up front (sometimes for years before payback begins),
+ a champion,
+ dedicated people, and
+ consistent management, dedicated to long-term financial support.

Establish Metrics

The accomplishment to which the new idea leads has to be evident to all, and demonstrated by some type of metrics. The ultimate drivers that influence practitioners and management alike to pursue a difficult course are results that establish the course's success.

To paraphrase Jane Austen, it is a truth yet to be universally acknowledged that no amount of well-meant drum-beating can replace valid process, bring an understanding of that process to sponsors and practitioners, simplify difficult-to-apply parts of it, and capture pertinent measurement of its results. The rewards can be enormous. Dare developers delay using better ways any longer?

Article by Ted Lewis, Computer, July 1998

Joe Sixpack, Larry Lemming, and Ralph Nader

Windows 98 is upon us like the plague. Consumers are poking at their Web browsers to download copies of Microsoft's cash cow as Intel and Microsoft rake in the profits from hardware and software upgrades. It is techno-treadmill time once again. But in the excitement we forget one small detail: These may be damaged goods.

Microsoft has quietly downplayed its damaged goods. It no longer claims its products are 100 percent Y2K bug-free, according to Jason Matusow, Y2K strategy manager at Microsoft. But consumers shouldn't tolerate the soft-shoe routine. Maybe we are a bunch of ignorant Joe Sixpacks who don't know any better? Or else, we are Larry Lemmings: Simply to best our neighbors (who also run Windows on their built-to-order Wintel boxes), we tumble off the cliffs of beautiful Puget Sound, clutching boxes of Windows 98. Clearly, we would not tolerate shoddy goods and their companion problems from Coca-Cola (vomiting), Sony (electrical shock), Panasonic (spontaneous combustion), Amana (Honey, I froze the kids!), or Toyota (engines that require rebooting several times per day).

Speaking of cars, Ralph Nader should stop worrying about Microsoft-the-Monopoly and start worrying about Microsoft-the-software-developer. Nader gained fame by turning in General Motors when someone reported that Chevrolet Corvairs weren't safe for Joe Sixpacks out on a Sunday drive: Corvairs could flip around and run down the highway backward without warning. Why hasn't the consumer crusader picked up on damaged software goods? Where is the consumer advocate when we really need him? Sadly, Ralph has his mind on populist politics instead of consumers. Or maybe he uses a Macintosh!

How Damaged Are They?

Microsoft executives told attendees of a closed-door meeting of OEMs (original-equipment manufacturers), ISVs (independent software vendors), and VARS (value-added resellers) back in March 1998 that Windows 98 fixes 5,000 bugs that plagued Windows 95! This is no typo; 5,000 bugs were shipped in 50 million or so copies of Windows 95, and nobody mentioned it. That is a total of 250 billion insects crawling around inside our PCs. Ring up untold effort, cost, and heartbreak as consumers realize that computers aren't like washing machines (Lisa Dicarlo, "Win98 Plans Shape Up," *PC Week,* March 23, 1998, p. 10).

The U.S. Navy adopted Windows NT because it is certified as a level C2 secure system. Yet a study by Shake Communications Pty. Ltd. identified 104 vulnerabilities in Microsoft Windows NT, which hackers can use to penetrate an organization's network. Many of the holes are very serious, allowing intruders privileged access into an organization's information system and giving them the ability to cause critical damage—such as copying, changing, and deleting files, and crashing the network (see Peter G. Neumann's Risks Forum at Usenet comp.risks or RISKS-request@csl.sri.com).

In another example of damaged desktop goods, correcting the Year 2000 problem on PCs will consume 15 of the $600 billion global tab to fix all Y2K problems. Y2K problems invade not only the BIOS (basic I/O system), but also a lot of the data stored in Access, Excel, and Filemaker files (Bruce Caldwell, "Year 2000 Efforts Falling Short," *Information Week,* March 23, 1998, p. 24). Ring up $90 billion due to more damaged goods.

Can anything be done? Is anything being done?

Gonzo Projects

The Standish Group surveyed $250 billion worth of software development started by U.S. companies in 1995 and found that 31 percent of the 175,000 projects were canceled before completion. Ring up another $81 billion in damaged goods, giving a running total of $171 billion so far (Patrick Porter, "Projects Gone Bad," *Software,* Apr. 1998, p. 8). Of the remaining projects, 52 percent ran over budget by an average of 189 percent. In 1995, this amounted to $59 billion more. Patrick Porter, editor of *Software* magazine, estimates the loss at $185 billion in 1998. Ring up another pile of money for a total of $356 billion. Big companies bring in a mere 9 percent of projects on time and under budget, while the industry as a whole succeeds in only 16 percent of all projects!

These are what I call *Gonzo Projects:* Projects that have gotten out of control and/or produced damaged goods as a result of poor workmanship, design, or both. (I extend my apologies to Nearly Normal's Gonzo Cuisine in Corvallis, Oregon.) And Gonzo Projects beget Gonzo Products. A Gonzo Product might simply crash and lose your files. Or, if it is hooked up to an airport, it might crash an airplane and cause you to lose your life. Fortunately, it hasn't come to that—yet. But there are more Gonzo Projects than non-Gonzo projects, and the disparity seems to be growing.

If Windows 95 has truly contained 5,000 bugs for all of these years, it qualifies as a Mega Gonzo Product. Further, if we could recoup the lost $365 billion from Gonzo Projects in the U.S. alone, we could make computing more reliable for Joe Sixpack and Larry Lemming. For example, Ralph Nader could just about buy all three computer monopolies—Microsoft ($200 billion), Intel ($135 billion), and Cisco ($65 billion) for $356 billion. Then he could divert money from marketing and litigation into software quality assurance, fixing Windows before we lose our files, proving Intel's hardware correct, and making Cisco's Internet switches 100 percent fault-tolerant. In short, Nader could force the computer industry to live up to the same product quality standards expected of other industries. Or, is this even possible?

California Dreamin'

A m I dreaming, or is the problem of software quality unsolvable? Of course, we all learned the Halting Problem, which translates into the undecidability of program correctness. Even so, it seems as though Windows 95 has more termites than it should. And what is the prospect for Windows 98? Maybe we will never be able to write perfectly correct programs, but is it possible to do better than Windows 95?

To get the answer, I turned to Capers Jones' ("Software Estimating Rules of Thumb," *Computer,* Mar. 1996, pp. 117–118). His rule number five says that raising the number of function points to the 1.25 power estimates the defect potential of a new software product. Lacking any indication that Microsoft uses function points to gauge program size, I will use Jones' rule for converting LOC into function points: One function point is about 100 lines of code. We can use these rules and LOC estimates to decide if Microsoft Windows deserves credit or blame for being either elegant or damaged goods.

Running the Numbers

R eportedly, Windows 95 contains 15 million LOC. Dividing by 100, I estimate the size of Windows 95 at 150,000 function points. Raising this to the 1.25 power yields a potential 2.95 million bugs!

Bug potential isn't the same as number of bugs. Rather, it is a way to estimate how much testing to do. Again, Capers Jones says (in rule number six), that the learning rate is 30 percent for each inspection or test step. Thus, 70 percent of the defect potential remains after each step. To reduce Windows 95's defect potential from 2.95 million to 5,000, as Microsoft must have done, requires 18 test iterations. Jones recommends six to 12, so Microsoft's software practice appears to exceed the industry

The Mathematics Behind This Article

Several readers have asked for more details on derivations and "laws" that appear in this column. This section is for the curious practitioner who wants to apply my techniques to their own projects. The rest of you can skip over this stuff!

Capers Jones' defect potential rule can be written as

$$B(0) = FP^{1.25}$$

where *FP* is the number of function points, and $B(0)$ is the defect potential of a new software product. For an enhanced software product, use a 1.27 exponent in place of the 1.25. To convert LOC into *FP*, use Jones' recommendation: Divide LOC by 100. Thus, in this article, 15,000,000 divided by 100 yielded an *FP* equal to 150,000. Raising 150,000 to a power of 1.25 yielded 2,951,985 potential defects.

Jones' defect-removal rule gives a formula for computing the remaining potential defects after *k* test-and-fix steps as follows:

$$B(k) = B(0) \times R^k$$

where learning rate $R = 0.70$, and *k* is the number of test-and-fix iterations. Now, if you want to know how many iterations to perform, solve for *k* using

$$k = -\log[B(k) / B(0)] / \log(R)$$

For example, substituting $B(k) = 2{,}951{,}985$, $B(0) = 5{,}000$, and $R = 0.70$ into the equation yields $k = 17.89$, which I rounded up to 18 in the article.

Now, define software product quality as

$$Q = 1 - [B(k) / B(0)] = 1 - R^k$$

Figure 24.2 plots quality *Q* versus *k* for three learning rates *R*.

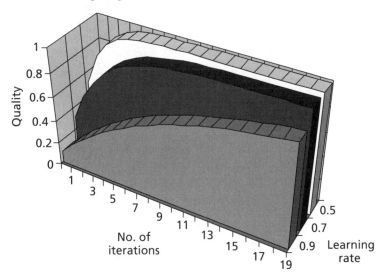

Figure 24.2 *Software quality surface showing the relationship between test-and-fix iterations, learning or improvement rate, and quality.*

norm. A total of 42 steps would be required to reduce the defect potential from 2.95 million to one.

Software quality is a nonlinear function of the number of test-and-fix iterations performed before launching a product. It is simply hard work. Microsoft could attain a higher level of quality by doubling its test effort. Software quality is no California Dream—it is very much within the realm of possibility. So, why isn't Windows 95 bug-free?

To Release or Not to Release

It is easy to criticize Microsoft (or any other software company) for not performing enough testing. But software companies cannot always afford to test their products twice as much as they currently do. It costs money and delays product launch. One thing we know for sure: Fast versioning leads to success in the software industry. High-quality products lose out to quick-and-dirty products because Joe Sixpack isn't a discerning consumer. Also, enough brain-dead Larry Lemmings will follow the market leader, so Microsoft could produce a lot of Gonzo Products before its bottom line began to sink. The Hollywood atmosphere of Silicon Valley keeps the Joe Sixpacks and Larry Lemmings buying software because of its popularity rather than its reliability!

The situation begs the question: When should software be released? Should it be held back, like fine wine, or churned out like sausage? The market determines this. For example, Windows NT is aimed at the enterprise, where few Joe Sixpacks remain. Here, software quality and reliability take on an importance lacking in the consumer space. Over 60 percent of the VARS polled by VARBusiness Research [*VARBusiness*, Mar. 16, 1998, p. 8], cited bugs as their main concern in deploying Windows NT. In their view, Windows NT is relatively early in its product development cycle and doesn't measure up to Unix. Perhaps this is why Microsoft has delayed the launch of Windows NT 5.0 until later this year. Microsoft cannot afford to unleash 5,000 bugs in Windows NT, and the company knows it.

Contrary to the *VARBusiness* results, Windows NT isn't anything new. Microsoft has invested seven years and hundreds of millions in development dollars in Windows NT. There are over 500 people working on it and the most recent estimate of code complexity lies between 22 and 27 million LOC. To bring the quality of Windows NT in line with that of Windows 95, Microsoft has to run NT through approximately 20 test iterations. And to drive out all but one bug will require 44 iterations.

An off-the-top-of-my-head guess is that each iteration costs tens of millions of dollars. (I base this on 500 people times $200,000 per person-year: $100 million. Suppose each iteration consumes 10 percent of everyone's time. This amounts to $10 million per test iteration or $200 million for 20 iterations.) No wonder software companies release beta-test copies on the Internet; they want free testers!

The problem is that good testing takes time, costs money, and cannot be properly done by customers and students. It requires professionals. Will Microsoft support professional, bug-free, product development? Windows 98 is a bellwether of Microsoft's willingness to prioritize quality over a quick buck. If, like its predecessor, Windows 98 turns out to be damaged goods, Microsoft's secret will be out: The company isn't really serious about the consumer market. If Windows 2000 also turns out to be a dog, we can only conclude that the company isn't serious about software.

PART FOUR

When Radical Is Chic

CHAPTER TWENTY-FIVE

Innovation and the Next Big Thing

By 1994 many of the leading-edge companies realized that the Internet was going to radically change communication. But they weren't sure exactly how. The big network infrastructure companies like Cisco, Bay Networks, and Nortel were cashing in on switches, and electronic commerce was rapidly spinning up, but what would this entire infrastructure be used for? Which really big killer application would come along to make people flock to the Internet?

Some people thought it would be video. The telephone companies envisioned the picture-phone, the Netheads envisioned Internet TV, and the conservative business world envisioned video teleconference systems that made closed-circuit TV a practical reality. In one form or another, video would come of age, and everyone would be able to see, as well as hear, everyone else. This is how video became the Next Big Thing in 1994.

But like so many other technological innovations, video never really made it. At least it hasn't made the mainstream as of this writing. Telephone companies struggled to provide bandwidth for Internet access from home, the TV industry nearly self-destructed over half-baked ideas called video-on-demand, and the conservative business world failed to make a business case for closed-circuit TV. The Next Big Thing soon faded as people lost interest. It was an idea whose time had not yet arrived.

This is the story of innovation and how companies manage it. Innovation is like food to Silicon Valley, and nobody wants to go hungry. But when an idea misses its mark, nobody gets overly concerned, either, because they know another wave is right behind the current one. Silicon Valley only begins to worry whenever there is a lull in the steady stream of ideas. The trick is to never allow the flow of radical ideas to stop. Therefore, radical behavior is encouraged. In fact, radical is considered chic. Work becomes part revolution, part conspiracy, and part sweat.

Netscape Communications was considered a good place to work for a while, because employees were allowed to bring their pets to work. Pets-at-work was considered only mildly radical. A few blocks away employees might be throwing themselves against a Velcro wall, just to see who can stick the longest! Skydiving clubs proliferated for a while, and everyone simply had to attend the Burning Man ritual in Mendocino, or somewhere out in the desert. (The Burning Man is a metallic giant that is set afire once each year in a tribal ritual attended by tens of thousands of engineers, marketers, and managers from Silicon Valley.) The famous pirate's flag over Apple Computer came down long ago, but the company still values cleverness over personal appearance and hygiene.

Innovation and risk-taking are so highly valued that it is constantly studied and evaluated. Circuit speakers and high-priced consultants sell creativity, and theories of its origin, like so many pounds of beef. Managers eat it up like Dilbert cartoon characters. One week it might mean rewarding employees with free racing bicycles, and the next week it might mean herding employees into an auditorium to listen to a series of seminars on topics like, "Regaining Your Good Karma," or, "How You Can Leverage Your Feminine Side to Become a Better Manager." There is as much innovation in the art of innovating as there is in dreaming up new technology.

Innovative ideas start in someone's head and through a long process of maturation end up as a Next Big Thing. If the idea gathers enough momentum, it might become as successful as Java. If it doesn't gain ground rapidly, it is forgotten very quickly, like the picture-phone. Nobody can predict which will be the case for a given idea. Rather, let the market decide which idea lives and which one dies. It is more important to generate ideas than to waste time trying to divide them into winners and losers.

Innovation is about exploiting the Next Big Thing. It is about guessing which technology will win and recovering from failed guesses. It is about managing smart people and unexpected events. It is about pushing the limits—and sometimes going beyond them—in order to get a jump on the competition.

In 1994 I found it difficult to believe that video would soon be the Next Big Thing because it couldn't compete effectively against the telephone. Six years later, video is still languishing. Why? People don't want to see themselves on the tube unless there is a value-add. And so far, the killer application that requires face-to-face communication over a wire hasn't been invented. This is the way it is with a number of clever technologies.

What will be the Next Big Thing in 2001? Will it be the Internet Appliance? Will it have something to do with TVs, refrigerators, and cars all connected to the Internet? Nobody knows. Instead, we can learn how companies stimulate new ideas and exploit the resulting opportunities. And we discover that technology sometimes delivers more than consumers want.

Article by Ted Lewis, Computer, October 1994

The Next Big Thing

In between issues of *Computer,* I often contemplate the meaning of life, diabolical ways to reduce my taxes, and what might be the next big thing in computing. Alas, I lag far behind those daring silicon sharpies in Hillsboro, Oregon, and the white labcoats in Murray Hill, New Jersey, who have our computing future all mapped out. It's video, stupid!

Any pizza lover knows better than me where the computing action is. Pizza Hut of Santa Cruz, California—where apparently there is an unusually high concentration of crust-loving piazzi animali—has pioneered a WWW (World Wide Web) Internet home page for ordering your favorite toppings. Any bit wizard connected to the Internet can use PizzaNet of Wichita, Kansas (the center of the pizza universe) to order takeout from his neighborhood Hut.

So what does this have to do with Intel and AT&T? Big companies looking to hook their profits to the Infobahn star are serious about consumer products based on network groupware, especially if it plays video. Stuff like this gets AT&T and Intel to fall into each other's arms to speed up the waxing of their surfboards, as they say in Santa Cruz. (Actually, the pizza-ordering example was demonstrated by Larry Ellison of Oracle during the unveiling of the Oracle video server. I can't put all the blame on AT&T and Intel.)

Worldworx is AT&T's worldwide network service for video teleconferencing. ProShare is Intel's $99 software that makes your PC work with Worldworx. These products are the tip of the next-big-thing iceberg for Intel, AT&T, Oracle, Silicon Graphics, Apple, Microsoft, and a number of other companies hoping to push their revenues to new highs.

Nobody bought AT&T's $999 PicturePhone, so the theory is that maybe someone will buy Intel's $99 surrogate. After a year of secret work together, the two have announced a combined product that will allow your boss in Philadelphia to set up a three-way conference call with you, her, and your client in Dallas, while you are taking a holiday with your family in Honolulu. The two business suits on the mainland can see you in your swim trunks in front of the Mai Tai Bar, and together you can share some bonding and a Lotus spreadsheet.

The thing is, you could have done this years ago if you had bought RTZ Software's (Cupertino, California) conferencing software or simply copied MBone (see *Computer,* April 1994) from the Internet. Or better yet, you could have ripped off the kids at Cornell University who developed CU-SeeMe and donated it to the Cause. CU-SeeMe and MBone are free, but RTZ Software charges a few bucks per client for Macintosh and Windows.

Free is a pretty good price, so why isn't it working? Let's examine why video is in trouble, and why Intel and AT&T will have a long wait for their ROI (return on investment for those who slept through Harvard Business School).

The first thing you have to realize is that video is network TV. (How many of us really want to be on the 6 o'clock news with a 5 o'clock shadow?) This is not your father's telephone. It is live from your office or bedroom, and it ain't necessarily pretty. Second, the bandwidth requirements are more than a voice telephone can handle even with current compression technology. Thus, you need an ISDN line or an ethernet connection. These are not lying around the house, further limiting the number of people you can see and speak to. Current compression technology yields about 200-to-1 lossy compression; hence, a 128-kbps ISDN line is really equivalent to about a 2-Mbps ethernet. A 10-Mbps packet-switched ethernet is really good for about 2–4 Mbps (when shared), so this limits usefulness to only a few players in the right ballpark.

The third thing about the technology is that point-to-point conferencing is not much fun. It is only slightly sexier than using the ancient telephone and unsophisticated e-mail. Have your recorder call my recorder and leave a message for us to do lunch. Like the audio bridges used for conference calls, there are video bridges that can handle multipoint calls, but they cost $80K from Promptus Corp., Sunnyvale, California. You can buy time on a bridge for $1.25/minute/person from AT&T (Aha!) or third-party providers like ConferTech International in Westminster, Colorado. This cuts down the size of the customer base by another factor of 10. In fact, users are probably limited to bytemeisters like myself who are ethernetted to Internet and get their software for free via WWW from the same people who are buying all that pizza after midnight.

It is a wonderful (cyber)world out there. I used MBone between Corvallis, Oregon, and Monterey, California, to conduct two MS-degree final exams. I saved money, they saved time, and both students passed.

MBone, as you recall from your studies, is a broadcast protocol, meaning that it fans the message as each router or bridge is crossed. Like airwave TV, it indiscriminately fills the Internet with frightened graduate students defending their theses.

It is a reflector world out there, too. CU-SeeMe uses reflector technology, which means there is a server somewhere that repeats back to all subscribers whatever it receives. Thus, given an IP (Internet Protocol) address, a CU-SeeMe client on the Internet dials in to the reflector, and voila, everyone who has subscribed to the reflector is in a virtual meeting room. The advantage of a reflector is that it can be restricted to just you, your boss, and your client in Dallas. It does not fill the packets of the world with embarrassed silence when your client asks tough questions in full view of your boss.

CHAPTER TWENTY-SIX

FutureBusiness

The original innovation company is Hewlett Packard, known in Silicon Valley simply as HP. HP has not only survived, but also thrived on change since its founding in 1938. It is the grandparent of all hi-tech companies in Silicon Valley. Therefore, it is fitting to begin the following series of essays on innovation by looking in on the culture of HP. The "HP way" has been copied by many companies hoping to become just as rich and successful as HP.

My familiarity with the company comes from living next door to the Corvallis, Oregon, facility. Corvallis is where the handheld calculators, printers, and some silicon chips are either designed and/or made. In addition, I have visited corporate headquarters in Palo Alto, a few blocks away from the Stanford University campus off Page Mill Road. Page Mill Road is where the research labs and bean counters are; it is the center of the empire. HP invented Silicon Valley casual. Suits, ties, and offices to match the paychecks of managers are banned inside of HP. This classless culture is evident at both facilities: supervisors have the same open cubicle offices as workers, and decision-making is by consensus, not edict. Pencil-protectors are a badge of honor, not a source of ridicule. Happy employees are creative employees, so HP condones time-wasting birthday parties and company picnics, which build a sense of belonging. And it is this sense of community that sets the stage for creativity.

But understanding how hi-tech companies innovate requires a deeper knowledge of company culture than open offices and liberal pet policies. The innovative company lives in a friction-free economy where everything is temporal. Markets come and go with increasing speed and the Next Big Thing is always lurking around the corner—waiting to take your market away from you. Market velocity forces the innovation-based company, like HP, to constantly reinvent itself. While technology

Info Age Principle	FutureBusiness Response
Information technology drives everything toward a commodity price: Things get cheaper.	Branding: "Intel Inside."
Inverse economics: Quality gets better even as prices decrease.	Davidow's law: Be first; render your own products obsolete.
Narrowcasting: The fall of mass marketing.	Individualization: Yes, there is a "market of one." Find the niches.
Flexible manufacturing: Market pull vs. market push.	Personalization: "Customer delight." Custom-fit to consumer's desires.
Retrograde agrarianism: Tribal consumerism.	Mainstreaming: Market saturation in real time (within a decade or less).

Table 26.1   Principles of the Info Age and how FutureBusinesses respond.

drives new products, reinvention of the corporate culture drives new organizations, cultures, and ideology.

Corporate management mantras come and go in Silicon Valley almost as fast as technology changes. To get ahead of the competition, a company must anticipate the future and be ready for the Next Big Thing, both technologically and culturally. In other words, long-term survival depends on short-term flexibility. Flexible companies rapidly adapt to change in the friction-free economy. They are called Future-Businesses, because they live in the future. They stay slightly ahead of their time.

So innovation is stimulated as much by the friction-free environment as it is by corporate mantra. This environment is governed by a set of principles, which have been summarized in Table 26.1. Obedience to these principles have helped HP be highly successful through six decades and perhaps four major transitions: from vacuum tubes to solid-state devices, centralized mainframe computing to decentralized computing, from decentralized minicomputers to desktop PC computing, and finally from desktops to distributed network and Internet computing. Each of these transitions had the potential to kill competing technologies and the companies that exploited them. HP's earlier competitors in the instrumentation business are literally out of the race because they failed to make one or more of these transitions. Tektronix, for example, went from $2.5 billion in sales in 1982 to $1.5 billion in 1997. Epson and Xerox stumbled in their core printer business as HP excelled. Sure, HP's printer business took everyone by surprise.

But isn't this how the Next Big Thing operates? Changing the rules as well as the technology is innovation in action. HP's acumen in processors, workstations, and PCs has consistently placed it in the top three or four "computer companies." In the late 1990s it is in the forefront of the transition from complex instruction set processors to RISC (Reduced Instruction Set Computers), an initiative it began with Intel earlier in the decade. HP and Intel are partners in the next generation Merced chip business—a business that will define computing for at least the next decade. How did HP know that it would need to be in this position more than 5 years in the future? In the next essay I discuss technical and managerial reasons for HP's success. Then I offer a handful of general principles that any company may apply to their own success. Having a handful of guiding principles is the first step toward becoming a FutureBusiness.

Article by Ted Lewis, Computer, November 1995

HP Means High-Powered: FutureBusiness, Side A

This episode continues the Info Age series with an example or two of companies that have made the grade in the toughest Info Age Future-Business of all—the commodity-driven computer business. I claim that corporate survival depends on how well a company executes one or more basic Info Age principles, as listed in Table 26.1. You may want to review the first two episodes (*Computer,* September and October) in this series.

Winners and Weenies

Who are the winners and weenies in the computer industry? Let's look at the so-called box builders—the manufacturers who create platforms for doing FutureBusiness—and see if we can learn anything. (Using real companies is more fun—I get more letters that way!)

Consider Digital Equipment, IBM, Sun, Compaq, and HP: Figure 26.1 summarizes revenue stream percentages for each company, showing, for example, how a so-called PC company like Compaq compares with a so-called workstation company like HP.

Digital is a strong service company competing with IBM and HP. Sun is a workstation company, Compaq is a PC company, and IBM is marginally a software and services company. Figure 26.1 may not surprise

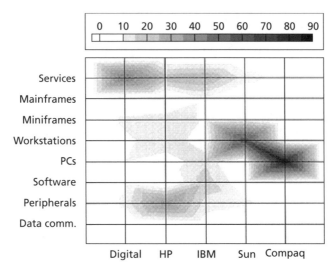

Figure 26.1 *Contour diagram of some representative computer companies and where they make their money. Lighter areas correspond to low percentages, and darker areas correspond to high percentages. All verticals add up to 100 percent.*

any computer jocks, because it is based on percentages within each company rather than total dollars generated in each category. For example, IBM may derive only a small percentage of its income from software, but it is still a very large and powerful software company—surpassing Microsoft in software revenues ($12 billion compared with Microsoft's measly $5 billion last year).

Figure 26.2, also provided for your viewing convenience, shows revenues and profits over the past decade. (Thanks to "Hoover's Company Profiles" on America Online, anyone can do what I do—enlist downloaded facts to support wild conjectures.) Looking at the curves, we see that even though IBM is rolling in cash flow, it stumbled in 1991, along with Digital and a number of other big players. Now both companies are trying to get on the comeback trail.

Sun's revenues look good, but its income as a percentage of sales has slipped from 7.4 percent in 1985 to 4.2 percent in 1994. Compare this with HP, which delivered 6.4 percent on sales of $24 billion in 1994. Sun may dominate workstations, but it doesn't take much cash to the bank.

Compaq's income as a percentage of sales soared from 5.3 percent in 1985 to an astounding 8 percent in 1994. Not only does Compaq vie for leading PC company, but it also makes its elders look like street-corner peanut stands.

Clearly, HP and Compaq are not just winners, but standouts. HP's growth rate is incredible for such a large company. Recently, HP has

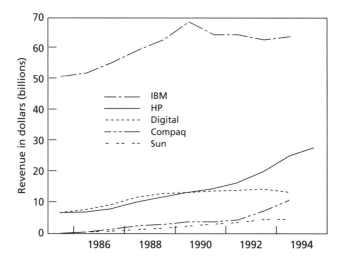

Figure 26.2 *Gross revenues since 1985 for Digital, IBM, Compaq, HP, and Sun. Only HP and Compaq show major upswings in revenues.*

been turning in growth rates in excess of 20 percent on a $20-billion base. This is like growing an Intel or a Microsoft every two years!

It takes a lot of power to move a mountain. HP means high-powered. The question is, why?

Rockin' and Rollin'

L et's face it, HP is a happening company. In a *Datamation* poll (June 1, 1995, pp. 38–39), users gave HP top ratings in product quality, support, and "customer delight" (see Table 26.1). "HP's users rate the vendor highest in almost every market sector in which it competes; . . . if there are people out there who don't love their LaserJets, we couldn't find them."

HP is a prime example of FutureBusiness. From its beginnings in 1938 through the 1990s, HP has reinvented itself many times: first as an Industrial Age business, then as a Post-industrial Age business, and now as an Info Age FutureBusiness. Table 26.2 shows how the company uses Info Age principles to achieve high-powered returns, renew itself, and turn novelty into profit.

HP is principally a printer company, if we believe the data in Figure 26.1. Note that 33 percent of its revenues come from "peripherals." This reminds me of the good old days (way back in the 1980s) when engineers at HP-Corvallis showed me a parallel transputer supercomputer used to design ink jet nozzles. I thought it kind of unusual for an instrument company to invest in fluid-flow research. But this research was more than rock 'n' roll, because it enabled the ink jet printer to become a big revenue generator. At

HP Response	FutureBusiness Response
Sell on HP's reputation for quality and performance, not lowest price.	Branding = HP name.
First handheld calculator 1972, first desktop mainframe 1982, LaserJets in the 1990s.	Davidow's law = Be first; render HP printers obsolete before anyone else does.
HP 95LX palmtop PC for specialized market segments, and specialized ($1.3 billion) Tactical Advanced Computer contract with federal government, 1995.	Individualization = Niche markets. Aim for individuals, federal government, small businesses.
Even though HP gets top ratings for quality and "customer delight," it can improve personalization of its PCs by taking note of Compaq and Dell "bundling."	Personalization. HP misses the mark with its PCs and workstations because they are more or less a commodity. As a consequence, Compaq and Dell are ahead in PCs, and Sun is ahead in workstations.
HP printers are as mainstream as the VCR. Can HP achieve mainstream status with its home computers?	Mainstreaming = Achieve market leadership. HP owns 71 percent of the laser printer market.

Table 26.2   Hewlett-Packard responds to the Info Age.

HP, R&D spending is around 8 percent of sales, and more than half of HP's 1994 orders were for products introduced in the past two years.

The truth is, this kind of investment in far-out technology often pays off for HP. A willingness to experiment, smart acquisitions, and curiously laid-back people built the house of Hewlett and Packard. (These gentlemen still own nearly 22 percent of HP.)

The Vision Thing

Perhaps the company's strongest asset is its management. HP managers were quick to realize that they are in the honest-to-gosh computer business, not the electrical instrument, medical gadget, or printer business. Seems obvious now, but back in 1975 it took vision. HP managers distinguish themselves from their competitors by "the vision thing." Here's what Gloria Tsao, an HP employee, said about HP management in the *San Jose Mercury News* (Aug. 21, 1995, p. D5): "Part of the reason why I've stayed at HP is because of their management. They have really opened my eyes to what good management can do to make a good product and a dynamic workforce."

Good management, indeed! From the outside, it looks like waste and inefficiency. One of my inside moles, John Bertani, said

The InkJet Group has all the fun! They had a party using downtown Corvallis this past year. Another group had a team-building exercise where they went to Florence (Oregon) and rented dune buggies and rode all over the dunes. Then there is the HP summer picnic, which is a family affair—free food, gifts for the kids, games, entertainment, and so forth. The management is the best that I have ever worked for.

Jeez, talk about loyalty!

Compare HP with early rival Tektronix, circa 1980. Both were in the same "instrument business." Both were about $2-billion companies. HP management had a vision and motivated employees; Tek management had heartburn and disgruntled employees. Today, HP has grown to 10 times its 1980 size, but Tek is a mere shadow of its former self. A clueless-in-Beaverton management ruined Tek, while HP's management began acting like post-computer-age visionaries.

Accidents Do Happen

Take a peek inside the company. Visitors often wonder how any work gets done. There seem to be a lot of coffee-heads sharing groovy experiences in the cafeteria. Telephone answering machines cover while software teams celebrate Bill Yoder's birthday. You have to look hard to find someone doing what looks like work. (Contrast this with sweatshop Intel or the salt mines of Microsoft.) The question is, where does the legendary HP performance come from?

Intel stumbled into the PC processor business by way of accidental tourist Datapoint Corp. Maybe HP is not quite *that* lucky, but it has had its share of serendipity. For example, in 1986 then-President John Young's five-year, $250-million open-systems effort (starting in the early 1980s) produced a high-performance RISC-based line able to run the Unix operating system, eventually making HP second only to Sun in workstation market share. (OK, OK, buying Apollo was a big factor, too.)

Other people below the top level of company president are leading laid-back HP into profitable FutureBusinesses. Ted Wilson came out of HP Labs to head up COSE and CDE (Common Open Software Environment and Common Desktop Environment) development in Corvallis. Martin Griss is dragging the company into object technology. Call them coffee-heads, but these people are the secret to HP's success.

But let's face it: There is also an element of luck at HP. Not everything the company does is according to plan. Sometimes HP means "hyped product." Some products have not worked out so well for the company. The HP-85 was a dud. The HP NewWave expansion of Windows got the company into a legal battle with Apple Computer. How many of us are using NewWave today? Pocket calculators were a good idea back in the 1970s, but where are the big bucks from pocket rockets in 1995? Steve

Jobs begged HP engineers to take the first Apple Computer box off his hands, but HP could not visualize a market for personal computers.

Living in Real Time, Circa 2000

In 1938, two Stanford engineers, Bill Hewlett and Dave Packard, encouraged by their professor, Frederick Terman (the founder of Silicon Valley), started HP out of a garage in Palo Alto, California, with $538. One of their first sales was an order of oscillators to Walt Disney for use in making *Fantasia*. Sales reached $1 million in 1943. HP instantly thrived as an instrument company.

Then, using inverse economics (quality products at commodity prices), HP reinvented itself as a computer company. By the late 1970s, computers accounted for half of HP's sales. But the company did not settle in as a computer company. In addition to operating several other businesses, HP is a premier peripherals company. It is also fashionably global. In 1994, HP derived more revenue from non-USA sales than from within the US. What next?

HP passed the $10-million sales mark for its DeskJet line in 1993 and paid about $50 million for a 15 percent stake in Taligent in 1994. In 1995, HP beat out rivals Hughes and DEC for the contract to build the US Navy's $1.3-billion Tactical Advanced Computer. Will these adventures in FutureBusiness be a boon or a bust? Who knows? This sounds like a topic for discussion at the next HP summer picnic.

CHAPTER TWENTY-SEVEN

Learning Curves and Strategy

The home PC market stalled at 35 percent adoption in American homes in the mid-1990s, because only the richest one-third of the population could afford to buy a $3,000 PC for their family. Then technology improved according to a learning curve called Moore's Law, and the same PC could be profitably sold for $2,000. This caused the penetration into the American home to rise to 40 percent. To reach 50 percent penetration, the computer industry brought on the $500 PC. And there is no end in sight. Eventually, a portable PC will become a commodity as inexpensive and pervasive as a TV. I fully expect to see sub-$100 PCs sometime within the next five years. This is inevitable because technology rides a tiger called the price-learning curve.

Price-learning curves dictate the success or failure of most consumer electronics markets, because consumers are the most price-sensitive segment of the population. People want the best product possible for the lowest price. Dell Computer struggled and then rose to become the second largest PC manufacturer in the United States by tuning itself to sharp price-learning curves. Dell shaved 5–10 percent off the purchase price of its PCs by selling direct to consumers. A 5–10 percent advantage wasn't much, but it was enough to get millions of people to buy from Dell instead of Compaq and IBM. Interestingly enough, Dell did this while at the same time giving its customers more choice. Dell maintains a 5–8 day backlog of orders, which reduces its inventory costs—another way to capture consumer's at the cash register.

Dell Computer illustrates *inverse economics*—things get cheaper as they get better. And inverse economics is a consequence of technology learning curves. This is unlike anything else before it. Never before has it been possible to make things better and cheaper at the same time. Today, inverse economics is a requirement. High-tech consumer products like computers, digital cameras, recorders, and printers have to be rendered obsolete by inverse economics because they don't wear out. Instead of replacing a PC because it fails, consumers replace PCs to get a faster one for less money than they paid last year. Thus, manufacturers are on a technology treadmill just like their customers. They are constantly being called upon to make products faster, smaller, and cheaper—all at the same time.

Relentless inverse economics is but one force that drives FutureBusinesses to extremes. Another is the need to rapidly mainstream your products. In the Internet Age a company is valued according to the number of customers it has rather than the profits it makes. This extreme condition was brought on by the positive feedback of increasing returns theory, which says the more products a company sells, the more it can sell. Consumers are too busy to fully evaluate product A versus product B, so they rely on market-leading brands to decide for them. Nobody gets fired for buying Microsoft, IBM, or Sony. A typical consumer will buy a PC from a popular vendor before he or she will buy a better PC from an unknown. And as your brand becomes more widely available, more people recognize it, which leads to more sales! This merry-go-round continues until a company becomes a monopoly. It made Microsoft a monopoly, and it can do the same thing for any other company. That is, monopoly power is within reach of companies that rapidly gain a commanding share of the market. This idea is what propelled early Internet companies like Netscape Communications to do the unthinkable—give away the company jewels. This brings us to the Nethead Gang, a group of companies that tried to dominate the Internet through sheer force of increasing returns. The company that had the largest number of Internet users was supposed to win the Nethead Gang leadership award, and go on to become the next Microsoft. This was the theory behind Netscape Communications back in 1995, but it was a technique practiced much earlier by John McAffee, who created a company by the same name until Network Associates bought it. McAffee gave away his anti-virus software for a long time before he made any money. After millions of users became addicted to his software, he reeled them in by charging for upgrades.

Rapid gains in market share lead to more gains in market share. It is the theory that made McAffee, Netscape, Microsoft, and others. The theory works today, even though America Online, Inc. has absorbed Netscape Communications, and Network Associates have absorbed McAffee's company. AOL especially, is still playing the Nethead Gang game, but the rules have changed because AOL is already the dominant Internet player. Today, AOL must use strategies of the strong because, with over one-third of the market, it is the dominant Internet company.

How does a company mainstream its products? By giving them away! This is the conundrum of the friction-free economy: How can a company make any money if it gives away its product? In the next two essays I first explain how a small niche company can win in the friction-free economy, and then go on to show how a more established company can win in a mature market. There are two fundamental strategies governing Silicon Valley. One is a strategy of the weak, and the other is a strategy of the strong.

> Strategy of the weak: Give away your product and sell updates and revisions. This razor-and-razor-blade strategy is for the weak because it rapidly builds market share.
>
> Strategy of the strong: Absorb-and-extend the market-leading product. This strategy only works for the strong because it takes a lot of money, market presence, and product development power.

Innovative companies play on one or more of these strategies. In other words, competition is a game of strategy. The only question remaining is: How do we keep score? This is where the New Lanchester Strategy comes in, and is the launch point for the second essay. Mature companies can play the New Lanchester Strategy game and rapidly build market share my merging and/or acquiring competitors. We see this activity in action every day on Wall Street.

Article by Ted Lewis, Computer, December 1995

The Nethead Gang

Other People's Money

With sales barely more than a Microsoft engineer's pocket change (est. $12M), 16-month-old Netscape Communications Corp. (NSCP) was instantly valued at $2.8B when it went public in August—that's *billion*, not million. Referring to the rise of NSCP stock that day, *Inter@ctive Week* said, "The stock market created its own version of artificial reality." Eager investors were either being scalped by the NAS-DAQ, or the Netscape Netheads had convinced Wall Street that the little company in Silicon Valley was on its way to becoming the next Microsoft.

The idea that a fly-speck of a company off the well-worn freeways of economically depressed California could topple Microsoft from its perch atop the food chain is intriguing, to say the least. The Lake Washington crew has turned Apple Computer into its research lab for windowing products, thumbed its nose at IBM/Lotus with Exchange, and continues to melt down entrenched Unix with NT. Neither a penchant for incrementally copycat products nor the scoldings from a toothless Department of Justice can turn back a merry Christmas for the red-meat eaters of Redmond. So why would anyone bet their retirement account on a small company from the other end of Highway 101 when WinTel has the world by the short hairs of the mouse?

Milking the Cash Cows

The trend lines shown in Figure 27.1 and the learning curve of high tech shown in Figure 27.2 are where we look to find the answer. First, the trend lines. Microsoft has been taken completely off guard by what is happening in Figure 27.1. The Internet and "interactive media" are where the next big company will make its millions. Video game consoles and office suite software are just the appetizer to a much bigger bounty. Soon, consumer on-line access and multimedia content will surpass video games as the cash cow of software capitalism.

Microsoft, in its haste to impress corporate MIS managers, has misgauged the power of consumerism. Its coffers may be filling with revenues from licensing Windows and selling upgrades to its Office suite, but this is about to end. Neither has much to do with Figure 27.1 trends. Microsoft Office generates less than $2B/year in revenue for the company—only a fraction of what Netscape hopes to generate in revenue from the interactive media business by the turn of the millennia. After everyone in mainland China has a pirated copy of Office, then what?

Learning the Learning Curve

But how does one go about turning the software business upside down? The hardware business is a good model. George Gilder shows how Silicon Valley technocapitalists play the hardware game in his 1990 book *Microcosm*. According to Gilder, the winners are the ones who burrow deeply into the quantum world of the microcosm. They understand learning curves. They slide down the learning curve faster than losers.

Gilder's high-tech learning curve says that price declines along the curve $P (.7)n$, where P is the initial price and n is a number that is incremented by one whenever the *accumulated volume* of a product doubles. That is, the price of a product, service, or idea decreases by 30 percent each time the production doubles. Companies that "learn how to drive prices to a commodity level" win because they drive out slower competition.

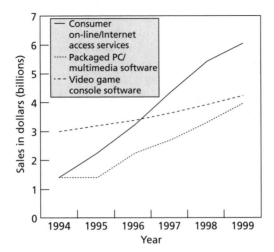

Figure 27.1 *Revenue forecasts for interactive multimedia software and access. Video game machine sales are leveling off; Internet and PC multimedia are still climbing. (Source:* Inter@ctive Week, *August 14, 1995, p. 42.)*

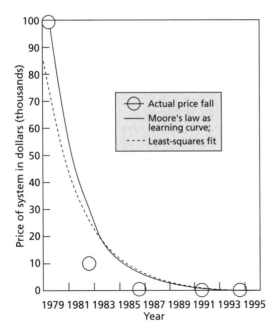

Figure 27.2 *Comparison of the actual price fall of a computer system from 1979 to the present versus Moore's law expressed as a learning curve, P $(.675)^t$. Actual data points are shown as large circles because they are very approximate. The least-squares fit is shown, yielding P$(.715)^t$.*

Gilder's learning curve is just another name for Moore's law: Processor performance doubles every 18 months. Here is the proof. Such a rate of doubling is equivalent to a 48 percent annual compound rate of increase. If we hold performance constant, Moore's law says we can cut the price of a processor chip by $k/(1.48^t)$, where t is time, measured in years, and k is some constant. Now, it turns out that $1/1.48 = 0.675$, which is close enough to 0.7 for engineers.

Figure 27.2 shows Moore's constant-performance law versus the actual price of a computer system (for constant processing power) over the past 15 years. The actual data and Moore's law fit Gilder's learning curve like data in a PhD thesis.

Figure 27.2 works because the hardware wizards have been extremely clever and industrious. Encouraged by huge profits, they pursue Davidow's law with a vengeance, rendering their own products obsolete and getting the next-generation microprocessor to market before their competitors. By being first, as demanded by Davidow, the winner increases market share, sells more chips, and doubles its accumulated volume. Having reached double volume before anyone else, the victor drops prices by 30 percent, attracting more customers. The accumulated volume shoots up, and around we go in the vicious circles of high tech.

Software Learning Curves

How might this work for software? Achieving an accumulated volume is critical, because with it you can slide down the learning curve faster than your competitor. Achieving commodity prices propels your product to even greater levels of market share, often reaching "best seller" status. At the end of the rainbow are the privileges of mainstream status and lush IPOs.

Suppose we illustrate this important principle of the Info Age with a hypothetical example. Company N is unheard of and without any installed base of customers, but it has a software product that can be distributed at very low cost. It also has a big bad Power Ranger on its doorstep in the form of a well-established software company, which we will call company M.

At first, N computes the marketing costs of advertising its product, adds packaging and production costs, and then sets the lowest price it can to undersell M. Its goal is to reach an accumulated volume of 100,000 customers in its first year so that it can cut prices further and undersell M even more. This is a very bad approach.

Traditional approaches won't dislodge M, because M can also slide down the learning curve and match the price cuts. Instead, N must leapfrog ahead of M by doubling and quadrupling its accumulated volume on the first day of business. What to do? The fastest way down the learning curve lies in the quantum microcosm. N gives its product away over the Internet.

Mainstreaming

Company N has discovered one way software can achieve mainstreaming—by establishing its product in over 50 percent of the market. Because the Internet is cheap and pervasive, software can reach mainstream status at very low distribution and marketing costs. Qualcomm's e-mail package Eudora became the number one e-mail client in the world because Eudora was given away over the Internet. When Netscape went public, it had 70 percent of the WWW browser market.

What about company N . . . er, Netscape? Jim Clarke (Netscape cofounder) said in *Upside* magazine (October 1995, p. 34)

> *I suppose the dissemination of the client electronically with no charge to some extent was influenced by the knowledge that Microsoft had a huge installed base. But it wasn't just Microsoft. It also was because Mosaic was already out there. In some sense we were really competing with the thing that these guys created as students, and we felt we had to displace it. And the one way to do that was to give away our client.*

In the Info Age, reaching the mainstream means sliding down the learning curve.

The War Chest

With Christmas Past already a done deal and Christmas Future profits dangling in front of the big bad Power Rangers, all challengers must move fast. 'Tis the season for the software equivalent of Davidow's law.

Netscape is dominating the WWW client-server business by applying Davidow's law. How? It contributed to the rapid change in Internet and WWW standards by shipping Netscape 1.1 with HTML 3.0 before it was established as a generally agreed upon standard. The company sailed down the learning curve, picked up big bonus points for obsolescing its own product (and Mosaic, too), and carried away more market share. Clarke says, "We know that Microsoft isn't going to be standards-based. So that's the one leverage that we have against Microsoft."

An integral part of Netscape's strategy is to meld other companies' products into its own platform, and to do so quickly enough to establish yet more moving-target standards. By fattening NSCP's war chest with other people's money, Clarke can buy more standards and more accumulated volume at the same time. First, Clarke did a deal with Macromedia to get Director's multimedia playback capability. Then he went across the freeway to get Adobe's Acrobat so that Netscape will have a universal file format. Soon after, Netscape added Sun's Java to counter Microsoft's Visual Basic. CollabraShare was purchased to offset

Lotus/IBM, changing the standards once again. A small search company was quietly added to nullify the hotrod guys at ArchiText. Spending other people's money wisely, Netscape is ready to fend off the ominous Blackbird (Microsoft's response to Navigator, due out in spring 1996) from the boisterous laggards tipping grog at Hector's in Kirkland.

Netscape is not the only company that can play this game. Joining in the Nethead Gang's fun is Adobe, which earlier doubled its accumulated volume when it bought out rival Aldus. Then Adobe (named after the creek that runs through Gescke and Warnock's neighborhood) bought Frame Technology to get a fast start on HTML. The once-little PostScript company is now the third largest PC software company in the world. With revenues of $390,000 per employee, Adobe doesn't need other people's money.

The New Lanchester Game

Others have been lining up to take a swing at Microsoft. Sun brought Java out from the back room just in time to join the Nethead Gang. Macromedia had already done its homework, engaging in a series of mergers. Over 60 percent of multimedia titles are created on a Macintosh, and most of them use Macromedia Director and/or Adobe Photoshop. It will take years for Windows 95 to catch up. Or is Microsoft in the early stages of its downfall?

If Netscape and the Nethead Gang are to displace Microsoft, they must understand learning-curve strategy. One of the oldest works on strategy, yet one of the most important for Info Age competitors, is the New Lanchester Strategy.

In 1916, Frederick William Lanchester (1868–1946) wrote *Aircraft in Warfare, the Dawn of the Fourth Arm*. Lanchester's work was introduced into Japan in 1952 in a book by W. Edward Deming. Subsequently, Nobuo Taoka applied Lanchester's theories to sales and marketing. Since those early days, through the efforts of several Japanese strategists, the Lanchester model has evolved into the "New Lanchester Strategy" (see *New Lanchester Strategy* by Shinichi Yano, Lanchester Press, Sunnyvale, CA 94086, fax (408) 732-7723).

Article by Ted Lewis, Computer, January 1996

Computer Business or Monopoly?

How to Keep Score

The computer business is like one big Monopoly game with a global playing board. However, in place of the die and the Community Chest cards, the computer business game uses the scientific approach pioneered by Lanchester, Koopmans, and Nobuo Taoka. The rules of the game are simple yet surprising, especially when applied to hardware and software companies. The path to the winner's circle is shown in Figure 27.3.

Companies with market share in excess of 73 percent are said to hold a monopoly share of the market. It is not necessary to achieve 100 percent, 90 percent, or even 80 percent to win the game. In fact, it may be dangerous to exceed 70 percent, because according to the New Lanchester Strategy, several things happen when a company's market share exceeds 73 percent:

1. It becomes difficult to stimulate more demand.
2. The company invites competition from other industries or specialty companies.
3. The correlation between market share and profitability disappears.

Does Microsoft's 80 percent market share of the PC operating system segment put it in jeopardy?

When a company's goal is to dominate its competitors, it usually attempts to gain at least 50 percent of the market. The New Lanchester Strategy refutes this, saying that only 41 percent is needed. Therefore, the target of a market leader should be to capture more than 41 percent of the market. Why? The gap in profitability between the market leader and its rivals widens when the leader's market share exceeds 41 percent but is less than 73.9 percent.

A company is secure in its leadership if it is the only company to achieve a 41 percent market share. McAffee Associates recently achieved 41 percent market share of the PC network-management-suite market by merging with Saber Software Corp. McAffee is clearly using mergers as a strategy for achieving market leadership.

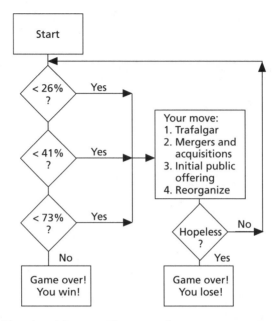

Figure 27.3   *The rules of the game. The game ends as soon as someone gets 73 percent of the market.*

A company with more than 26 percent of a market but less than 41 percent is considered a player. To maintain its position as a competitor, such a company must stay above the 26 percent minimum.

A firm's viability as a profitable company weakens if its market share dips below 26 percent. This is the case with all manufacturers in the desktop PC industry (see Figure 27.4). No PC manufacturer owns more than 26 percent. Companies in this category are called unstable players; that is, a company's position can be easily reversed by a competitor.

Once a company's share exceeds 26 percent, it begins to break away from the crowd. Its profitability increases along with its market share. From Figure 27.4 it is clear that the desktop PC industry is unstable. None of the players are leaders, and none show any trend toward capturing a higher market share.

Using Strategy

We might wonder why one or more of the PC companies shown in Figure 27.4 haven't adopted a strategy to break out of the pack and strive for 41 percent of the market. In fact, they have. Rumors continue to circulate about a takeover of Apple Computer by IBM, HP, Canon, or some unexpected bidder from Japan or Europe. Even in its

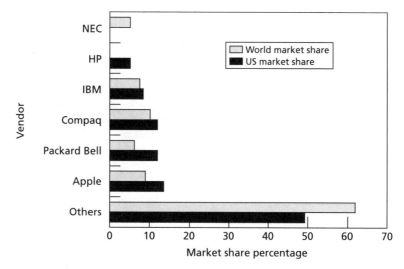

Figure 27.4 *Market shares of the top PC vendors in the US and the world. All are unstable; none are players, leaders, or a monopoly. The largest category is "others," with 48 percent of the US market and almost two thirds of the world market.*

current state of disarray, Apple remains a strong competitor, placing number one in US market share and in the top three of the world.

The theory assumes a constant-size market, but in reality most computer industry markets are rapidly expanding. Therefore, unstable players, like those found in the rapidly expanding PC business, are less likely to feel threatened by a sub-26 percent share, because competition is not as important as shipping product. However, when market expansion slows or stops, unstable players must either surpass their competitors or merge with one another to exceed the 26 percent threshold. Market stagnation will cause a shake-out of unstable players.

Figure 27.3 suggests some strategies for making a move in the game. The Trafalgar Strategy, discussed below, is named after the Battle of Trafalgar, in which Lord Nelson defeated a much larger fleet by focusing his small band of warships on the weakest point of the French and Spanish armada. The other strategies are well known: mergers and acquisitions, IPO for using other people's money through a stock offering, and that old favorite, reorganization of the company.

Shooting-Range Theory

When a company wants to take away other companies' business, it might use the Trafalgar Strategy to target a single competitor's weak point. Finding and targeting an opponent's weakness is called finding the shooting range. According to the shooting-range theory

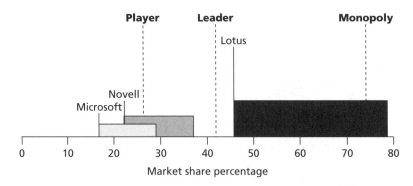

Figure 27.5 *Shooting-range diagram for groupware market. Lotus is clearly a market leader with Notes; in fact, monopoly is within shooting range. Microsoft and Novell are unstable players. Both are within range of becoming a player.*

1. In a two-company battle between companies A and B, if A has a market share three times that of B, A is in an irreversible position. Conversely, if A has a market share less than three times that of B, then either A or B may see its market share reversed.

2. In an *m*-way battle among companies A_1, A_2, . . . A_m, any two companies that are within $\sqrt{3} = 1.7$ of one another—that is, each other's shooting range—may have their positions reversed.

The PC industry is ripe for reversals. Strategists can use a shooting-range diagram like those in Figures 27.5 and 27.6 to analyze their chances of gaining share. In these diagrams, 1.7 is used as the shooting range (shaded areas to the right of company name).

Shooting-range theory is a kind of game theory. Accordingly, the visually impaired can use a game theory matrix like that shown in Tables 27.1 and 27.2 to plan their competitors' downfall.

In Table 27.1, for example, the first row and column contain the name of the competitor. The second column contains the market share for each company. The diagonal is marked with the label corresponding to the company's current status. Thus, Microsoft's share of the groupware market is 17 percent, which makes it unstable, and Lotus has 46 percent, which makes it a leader.

The numbers lying below the diagonal are the sums obtained by combining the shares of the row + column companies. Thus, if Lotus and Novell were to merge their groupware products, they would achieve 68 percent. The label above the diagonal designates the result of a merger. Hence, Lotus plus Novell equals a leader.

A reading across the rows of Table 27.1 suggests that Microsoft can go from unstable to player by buying Novell's market share, and become a leader by buying Lotus's share. Unfortunately, IBM is not interested,

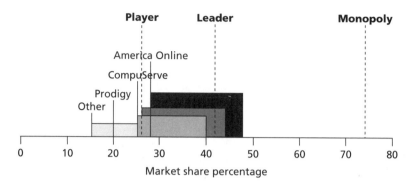

Figure 27.6 *Shooting-range diagram for on-line services market. America Online is the only player, but it is not a market leader. AOL is within shooting range of both CompuServe and Prodigy; moreover, leadership is within shooting range for CompuServe. All "other" players are unstable and not within shooting range. It is perhaps too late for some "other" services, such as Microsoft Network, to enter this market and become a leader.*

Company	Market Share %	Microsoft	Novell	Lotus
Microsoft	17	Unstable	Player	Leader
Novell	22	39	Unstable	Leader
Lotus	46	63	68	Leader

Table 27.1 Merger and acquisition matrix for the groupware market.

Company	Market Share %	AOL	CompuServe	Prodigy
AOL	28	Player	Leader	Leader
CompuServe	25	53	Unstable	Leader
Prodigy	20	48	45	Unstable

Table 27.2 Merger and acquisition matrix for the on-line services market.

but Novell may be willing to sell off its Groupwise product to Microsoft. Conversely, Lotus cannot end the game through a merger, because none of the combinations add up to 73 percent.

Table 27.2 shows that all online companies except AOL (America Online) are unstable. However, a merger of any two would propel the resulting business into a leader position. AOL has the least to gain by a merger, but if in the future the market stagnates, merging may be advantageous. Right now, a merger is unlikely for leadership status because the market is expanding too rapidly.

Company	Market Share %
Toshiba	15
NEC	13
Compaq	12
IBM	10
Apple	8
AST	2
Dell	2
Epson	2
Other	36

Table 27.3 The portables market is unstable. No single vendor is a player. What does the shooting-range theory recommend? (Source: International Data Corp., first quarter of 1995.)[1]

Company	Market Share %
Sun	−27
HP	16
Santa Cruz Operation	12
IBM AIX	9
Digital Unix	7
Silicon Graphics	4
Other	25

Table 27.4 Nobody leads the Unix market, but Sun is a player. (Source: Dataquest, 1995.)[2]

Where Do You Want to Go Today?

The data presented thus far is rather obvious. There are some less obvious markets that may prove surprising, however. It is always good to start the new year with questions that challenge the popular wisdom. The following analysis is designed to make you think.

Shocker #1. From Table 27.3, we can conclude that Toshiba, NEC, or Compaq should merge their portable-computer divisions. The resulting business would be a player. If all three merged, they would fall short of being a leader.

Shocker #2. From Table 27.4, we can conclude that HP should buy out the Santa Cruz Operation instead of Apple. The resulting merger would make HP a player just like rival Sun, but it would not place HP in a leadership position.

Shocker #3. From Table 27.5, we conclude that the game is over in several markets: In color prepress Macintosh won; in word processing

Platform	Color Prepress Professionals (GD)	Motion Video Production/ Playback (GD)	Word Processors (SPA)	Spread Sheets (SPA)	Integrated Software (SPA)	Home Edutainment (SPA)	Desktop Publishing (SPA)	Illustration/ Image Editing (SPA)
DOS			3.6	2.5	2.2	7.6		
Wintel	19.8	52.2	90.0	91.3	64.5	68.2	70	47.9
Mac	76.2	43.5	6.4	6.0	33.2	24.0	30	52.1
Unix		4.3						

Table 27.5 Platform market shares within various software segments. (Sources: SPA = Software Publishers' Association figures for first half of 1995; GD = Griffin Dix.)[3]

Platform	Web Servers	Home Page Publishing
Wintel	14.2	28
Mac	17.0	41
Unix	31.4	25
Other	37.4	16

Table 27.6   Platform market shares of Internet Web servers and Web publishers. (Source: Mirai.)[4]

2D Tools	Market Share %
Adobe Photoshop	50
Fractal Design Painter	25
Alias Sketch	9
Wavefront Composer	9
Other	7
3D and Video Capture Tools	**Market Share %**
Autodesk 3D Studio	32
Alias	20
Adobe Premier	15
Wavefront Gameware	12
Microsoft Softimage	10

Table 27.7   Image-editing market shares. Notice that Adobe is a leader in 2D but not in 3D and video; Autodesk is the only player in 3D, but nobody is a leader; and purchase of Wavefront, recently acquired by SGI, would have propelled Adobe to player status in 3D. (Source: NewMedia.)[3]

and spreadsheets Wintel won. The game is *nearly* over in home edutainment and desktop publishing: Wintel is winning. But the game rages on in video and image editing.

Shocker #4. From Table 27.6, we conclude that the Macintosh is the leading Web publishing platform and that nobody dominates the Web server market.

Shocker #5. According to Table 27.7, Adobe leads in 2D but lags in 3D. Autodesk is a player in 3D but not in 2D. A merger of Adobe and Autodesk would form a monopoly of the image-editing segment of the software market and end the game.

The next time you read about a merger between two fierce competitors in the computer industry, remember the Lanchester **Strategy and the** rules of the game. The winner is the one that ends up with a 73 percent market share. Using other people's money to buy companies is perhaps the easiest way. But it all depends on where you want to go—up or down?

References

1. "Top Portable Vendors," *Information Week,* Oct. 16, 1995, p. 44.
2. "No One Dominates the Unix Market," *Information Week,* Oct. 16, 1995, p. 54.
3. "New Looks for Media 100 and After Effects," *NewMedia,* Oct. 1995, p. 29.
4. A. Mello, "State of the Mac," *MacWorld,* Jan. 1996, p. 17.

CHAPTER TWENTY-EIGHT

The Limits of Innovation

By 1996 the computer industry was getting used to the idea of living in Internet time. Products were developed, manufactured, distributed, and then phased out in a 3–4 year cycle. If the Next Big Thing didn't take off within 18 months, it would never take off. Silicon Valley companies had to cope with extremely rapid learning curves. From introduction to peak marketing opportunity in less than 2 years, and back down the adoption curve in another year—that was the way it was—and still is.

Short life cycles leads to futurism. Small companies were warned to keep their ears to the ground and large companies hired expensive futurists simply to keep one step ahead of the competition. Rather than wait for the Next Big Thing to come along, smart companies learned to anticipate them. They institutionalized futurism and prognostication became a business tool.

Meanwhile, the competition was doing its own market research the expensive way, by building and selling products. Companies on the very leading edge took even bigger risks by simply guessing what consumers wanted, built it, and then coaxed consumers to come to them. Apple Computer made the point: instead of studying psychographics to find out what mobile businessmen and women would really buy, Apple secretly designed and built the world's first PDA—the Newton Message Pad. It was something entirely new and innovative. In fact, it was so innovative that few people knew what it was good for. Even fewer bought it. When it flopped, the company learned the hard way what was wrong with it! It was too big and too expensive. But, unlike a true

FutureBusiness, Apple Computer didn't follow-up with a smaller, less expensive model. In fact, the company took far too long to follow up with anything.

Sales of the Newton stagnated as Palm Computing observed and learned from Apple's mistake. The original design of the Palm Pilot was circulated on the Internet to garner feedback. Thousands of people told Palm what was wrong with the Newton. Apple may have ignored customer feedback, but Palm took in the information like a sponge. What was the top requirement of users? Size. Consequently, the Palm Pilot PDA (Personal Digital Assistant) was designed to fit into a shirt pocket. Instead of packing the Pilot full of innovative technology, Palm focussed on the first lesson learned from the PDA experience—keep it small. So a less innovative product succeeded where a more innovative product failed. There are limits to innovation after all!

Palm Computing (a.k.a. 3COM) emphasized form factor over function. Sacrificing handwriting recognition, integration of functions, and expandability (it had no PC card slot or infrared interface like the Newton), the original Pilot did only one thing well, it kept names, addresses, phone numbers, and dates. The Pilot wasn't very powerful, so it had to be very specialized. But most importantly, it fit into a shirt pocket. Bingo! The Palm Pilot became the first successful PDA.

Apple Computer made its reputation on innovation. It made the first commercially viable graphical computer. It led the personal computer world in networking and multimedia. Most PCs today are still only an approximation of the original Apple Macintosh. But innovation can be a trap. Apple could not bring itself to sacrifice a single innovative function of the Newton, which would have been necessary to make it smaller and cheaper. The Newton had to buttress Apple's reputation as an innovator or else it couldn't be sold under the Apple brand. As a consequence, the Newton died because it exceeded the limits of innovation.

Technical products like the Newton must be designed to keep up with, but not exceed, the industry learning curves that trade functionality for cost and the reverse. As the industry learns this balance, companies learn to exploit various technology/cost points along the learning curve. Highly successful exploitations of the curve lead to volume production of products, which in turn leads to an accelerated learning curve. Feedback increases the rate of expansion of the industry by enabling other companies to target lucrative points on the learning curve. Thus, the technology treadmill works on itself.

Companies must read learning curves like a fortune-teller reads tea leaves. Like I said, everyone must become a futurist. Innovation and the exploitation of innovation beget more innovation. Feedback speeds everything up, but it is possible to get too far ahead of the curve. This idea is explained, in greater detail in the next essay, where I describe a number of learning curves. Of particular interest is my prediction that Microsoft would return to the PDA party, which it eventually did. And so did Apple Computer. Microsoft was obviously put off by the contemporary limits of innovation. But once those limits had been probed by Palm Computing, Microsoft rejuvenated its Windows CE project. Looking back now, it is clear that the success of the Palm Pilot cleared the way for Microsoft. But back in the spring of 1996 the PDA industry didn't look very promising. And here is why.

Article by Ted Lewis, Computer, April 1996

The Limits of Innovation

FutureBusinesses must learn at high speed, because the faster a company learns, the sooner its products achieve mainstream status. The computer industry is full of FutureBusinesses chronically hooked on mainstreaming: If a software company fails to gain a Lanchester share of its market in less than two or three years, the stockholders dump their shares, profit-sharing executives leave in droves, and the press goes wild. Look at what happened to Apple Computer when its momentum stalled. (See *Computer,* Dec. 1995, p. 10, and Jan. 1996, pp. 10–13, for an explanation of the New Lanchester Strategy.)

Are there limitations to living in real time? There sure are. In fact, the most dangerous limits are the tricky limitations of innovation—the juice that keeps Siliwood going. (Siliwood isn't a place; it's a state of mind combining the innovation of Silicon Valley and the trendiness of Hollywood.) Innovative products like PDAs have been a big disappointment because they sputtered right past the 2–3 year time limit in which a computer product is expected to flood consumerland. An examination of the PDA segment of Siliwood is a good case study that shows how the limits of innovation can spoil a perfectly good business plan.

Bang for the Buck

The basic unit of mainstreaming is the market share, measured as a percentage of the overall market (either in terms of units sold or dollars of revenue). Marketers gauge their effectiveness in terms of "bang for the buck"—what it costs to gain a point of market share. Think of this bang as a kind of Nielsen rating for capitalists. The more bang for the buck, the more effective a product or service is. When it works, marketing is a wonder, but when it doesn't work, it is a major drag on the bottom line. When bang for the buck just doesn't materialize, people get upset, companies die off, and capitalism gets a bad name.

Look at two extreme segments: disk drives versus PDAs. The disk drive segment has had outrageous success—achieving mainstream status with each generation because its price learning curve reduces prices at an annual compound rate of more than 62 percent. The high degree of innovation in the disk drive segment is what has made this possible. On the other hand, the PDA segment, which also has a relatively sharp learning curve, is struggling to mainstream. The problem? PDAs are plagued with too much innovation.

PDA Envy

Actually, the PDA market is alive and thriving. People all over the world are clamoring for the Psion 3a from Psion Computer, a United Kingdom manufacturer that has sold over 2 million miniature DOS-like organizers. HP is selling its HP 100LX and 200LX like cholesterol at McDonalds. The new HP OmniGo could fatten HP's coffers even more, and the Palm Computing Pilot is gaining momentum at the low end ($299). Just about every geek in Siliwood either has or is getting a pocket computer.

If the PDA market is so hot, why have the Apple MessagePad, Motorola Marco, Motorola Envoy, and Sony Magic Link done so poorly? There are maybe 250,000 MessagePads, 30,000 Magic Cap-based machines, and even fewer Envoys and Marcos in circulation. Why the big difference in PDA sales? Simply put, the poor-selling PDAs have gone over the wall of innovation.

The Wall

Over-the-Wall rule: Any consumer product or service that changes too many things at once cannot mainstream. Microsoft, for example, knows that lots of innovation at once tends to scare away sales. So the giant software company dribbles out incremental improvements over long periods of time. MIS directors and corporate paper-pushers can handle only so much change at once. Anything that involves more than incremental tweaking from one release to the next turns off the green eyeshades.

Most of the really cool PDAs have violated the Over-the-Wall rule. The Apple MessagePad pushed technology in too many directions at once, leaving early buyers in a technology daze. Even the techno-elite are staggered by the array of innovative technologies one must comprehend when buying a MessagePad or Magic Link. These techies can be found poring over *Byte* articles describing the differences between Magic Cap and Newton Intelligence. Handwriting recognition, functional languages, wireless networking, novel user interfaces, and a new class of applications all add up to overstimulation of the cerebral cortex. If the geeks can't get it, then how are Cyber Simpsons going to cope?

Too Much Tech

The best selling organizers from HP, Psion, and Sharp are miniature DOS machines with keyboards so small that trained fleas have trouble writing home. But these machines use traditional programming languages, operating systems, and packaging. They work pretty much like a 1985 PC, except for a few icons placed here and there to give the appearance of a modern user interface. Packaged like a wallet instead of a plastic brick, they fit into purse or shirt pocket. They weigh less than the batteries of a MessagePad.

Sure, some of these products are starting to include a pen instead of the too-small keyboard. But most of the pen-based PDAs use Graffiti— a handwriting code sort of like shorthand. The user must learn Graffiti rather than the other way around. Only the Apple MessagePad 120 has real handwriting recognition.

The Magic Cap operating systems from General Magic has the most advanced graphical user interface. It simulates a desktop (common applications), hallway (file system), and village (workspaces), and effectively handles communication, pen input, and other advanced functions. This machine changes everything—operating system, programming language, user interface, and so forth. Accordingly, it is the poorest selling PDA on the market. Magic Cap PDAs are even rarer than MessagePads.

Apple's new MessagePad 120 has a novel programming language called NewtonScript, which is probably more advanced than anything taught in graduate-level courses on functional/object-oriented programming. It makes Java look like warmed-over decaf. Its Newton Intelligence operating system is object-oriented, multitasking, and small— leaving better known systems in the Stone Age. It can recognize handwriting and download WWW pages via wireless, and it includes a ton of software right out of the box. So why is it the village idiot of PDAs?

Learning, Again

Clearly, the more technology a company pumps into a new product, the more difficult it is for product managers to get a bang for their buck. There are two reasons for this: (1) technology is expensive, and (2) the more things you change, the more customers you have to educate. Machines based on radically new ideas, such as the General Magic, Apple, and Motorola PDAs, have a long marketing road ahead simply because they go beyond the current limits of innovation.

Bear with me while I apply mainstreaming to prove my point. Any product or service that tries to meet the objectives of mainstreaming must overcome consumer resistance by offering reduced prices, training, maintenance, or social ridicule for *not* owning the product or service. Companies do this by learning how to produce a low-priced, easy-to-use product that requires little maintenance and has great appeal to an increasingly tribal society. PDAs are no exception to this rule. The engineers who designed the Newton and Magic Cap machines raised, rather than lowered, barriers to mainstreaming by incorporating too many technologies all at once. As a consequence, the consumer perceives that there is little bang for lots of bucks.

The Many Faces of Technology

A new product uses many technologies in combination, and each technology tracks a separate learning curve. Therefore, a new computing device will ride several learning curves—each contributing to the device's overall learning curve. Table 28.1 lists some formulas used to model the learning curves of these fundamental technologies. A contemporary PDA uses all but the disk storage technology. Its overall learning curve will be the sum of the individual curves.

Table 28.1 reveals some very interesting secrets. First, software and packaging are major barriers to PDA advancement because they have high "prices" and low learning rates. A high value of B, the learning rate, means that little learning goes on; a low value of B equals a high learning rate. B ranges from zero to one. (B is a fraction $0 \leq B \leq 1$ that defines the improvement in price. $P(t) = P*B^t$ is the formula.) High values of P (the constant in the learning curve) and B are bad news because they prevent a product from achieving mainstream status. The result: not much bang for the buck.

You Say You Want Pictures?

Figures 28.1 and 28.2 show the effects of learning rates on the ability of a technology to muscle its way into the mainstream. A sharply declining learning curve in Figure 28.1 corresponds with a rapidly rising mainstream curve in Figure 28.2. Without low values of P and B, a technology such as software or packaging gets nowhere fast. Stuck in low gear, it is left behind by some other technology.

Technology	From 1970: *P* and *B*	Learning Price 1995
Processors	*P* = 1,370; *B* = 0.73	*P* = 0.525
Disk storage	*P* = 200,000; *B* = 0.625	*P* = 1,000
Software (OS and language)	*P* = 1,046; *B* = 0.956	*P* = 340
Wireless	*P* = 58,622; *B* = 0.60	*P* = 0.17
Packaging	*P* = 7,300; *B* = 0.91	*P* = 691
DRAM	*P* = 1,371; *B* = 0.675	*P* = 0.07
Networking	*P* = 58, 622; *B* = 0.56	*P* = 0.03

Table 28.1 Learning curve, $L = P^*B^t$, for some fundamental technologies in the computer industry. These parameters are estimated by curve fitting data collected from 1970 to 1995. The barrier-to-mainstreaming value is shown as *P* in the "From 1970: *P* and *B*" column. The "Learning price 1995" column is a recent calibration of the curves.

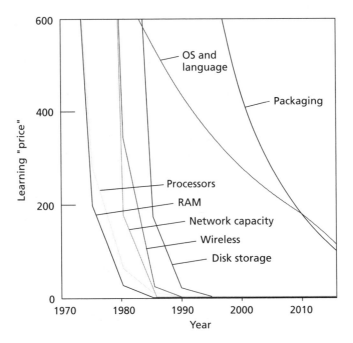

Figure 28.1 *Learning curves for some important technologies. The curves were derived from the parameters in Table 28.1.*

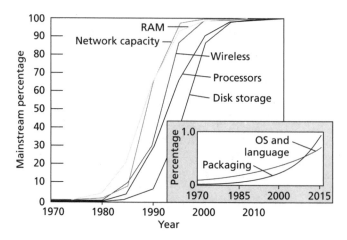

Figure 28.2 *Mainstreaming curves derived from Figure 28.1. Some technologies simply take too long to mature and thus impede an innovative product. (Note: The scale in the shaded box is one hundredth of that in the larger box.)*

Innovation Hyperspace

Think of each technology listed in Table 28.1 as an axis in an *innovation hyperspace*. A product is represented as a point in such a hyperspace. Low innovation corresponds to a product point near the origin. Conversely, a product point located a long way from the origin may mean that a product lies outside its limits of innovation. The problem with over-the-wall products like PDAs is that they lie too far from the origin in innovation hyperspace.

Can we make a mainstream PDA? Current technology forces designers to compromise product utility, which has held back the PDA market. Essentially, PDA design is a trade-off between packaging (weight, size, power) and functionality (software, processor speed, networking, wireless).

The most exotic PDAs are languishing on store shelves because they require the consumer to absorb too much innovation. Compare the HP 200LX with the Apple MessagePad. The HP machine will run for upward of 100 hours on a battery charge, but the MessagePad is gasping after 8–10 hours—typically 3–4 hours.

The Psions, Sharps, and HPs are primitive machines compared with the Sony Magic Link and Motorola Envoy. But the dull machines easily connect to wireless services, making pager and e-mail connectivity as easy as placing a phone call. Conversely, getting my e-mail from AOL into my Newton is about like changing into my red-and-blue Superman suit while inside a phone booth. I can do it, but why wear tight pants?

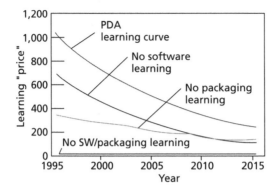

Figure 28.3 *Learning curves for various combinations of foundation technologies and their use in a PDA. If we ignore software learning, or packaging, or both, we get better forecasts.*

High-tech companies are good at squeezing novel products out of silicon, but making *compelling* products is a lot tougher. Innovation to hyperspace is a rough neighborhood. When engineers combine fundamental technologies to create a new product, they must add together the learning curves to determine whether the resulting product is capable of mainstreaming. That is, L = the sum of all $P*B^t$ values corresponding with each technology. This sum was used to obtain the graphs in Figures 28.3 and 28.4.

Microsoft Returns

The number-one problem of PDA design is packaging. These devices need to fit into your purse or pocket, last a long time on a single shot of electrons, and feel good in your hand. In addition, a best-seller must have the power of a real computer, connect to both wires and wireless, and enable developers to easily build applications that make money.

Unfortunately, these are conflicting requirements. Figure 28.3 shows that packaging and software learning curves simply do not support the needs of the market. In Figure 28.4, we see that progress will be slow unless we can speed up the slow advance of packaging and software. It will probably be another decade before the public consumes PDAs as it does televisions and cars.

The limits of innovation have held down the PDA market and will continue doing so until the technology catches up with the dream. Given time, the PDA market will revive. Microsoft dropped out of the Pen Windows business a few years ago because it could not make enough bang for the buck. Now Microsoft is back with a highly secret project that will exploit Apple-like or Magic Cap-like technology at just the right level of

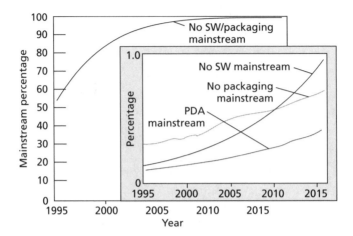

Figure 28.4 *Mainstreaming curves corresponding to Figure 28.3. Of course, the best forecast is obtained by ignoring both packaging and software—two of the major drags on PDA technology (Note: The scale in the shaded box is one hundredth of that in the larger box.)*

innovation. The company must sense that the PDA market is about to revive. But don't wait for Microsoft to shrink Windows 95 and put it in your palm; go out and buy a Sony Magic Link, Apple MessagePad, or Palm Pilot and drive the future today.

CHAPTER TWENTY-NINE

The Borg

Contemplating the downfall of Microsoft was a popular pastime of journalists in 1997–98. The company was getting too big; buying up too many innovators, and acting more and more like a monopoly with each passing day. It was so competitive that many people equated it with the race of half-human, half-machine *Borg*, of the popular science fiction movie *Star Trek*.

The Borg menaced the human race by absorbing—taking over and then merging with every intelligent life form it encountered. The similarity between Microsoft and the *BORG* was not only amusing but also surprisingly accurate. Microsoft had over $10 billion in cash in 1997, and was not averse to buying anyone who got in its way. Whether Microsoft purchased companies to get technology, people, or simply to get them out of the way is not clear, but the company acquired part or all of nearly a dozen companies that year. It was enough to get the attention of the U.S. Department of Justice anti-trust division.

The subject of cocktail party chatter was increasingly Microsoft and its business practices. I encountered an employee of a Microsoft rival during one such party in Carmel-by-the-Sea. We commiserated on the sad state of the software industry as we both dived into a creamy salmon cheese dip on top of an exquisite slice of bread from tony Il Fornio—the best bakery in Carmel. "You think Microsoft is voracious, the guy down the hall from me just pocketed a $3 million signing bonus to go to work for the *Borg*," he said with a voice stuffed full of Il Fornio's best. The *Borg* was absorbing!

Nowadays it is clear that the best strategy of the strong is absorb-and-extend. Microsoft has become a master of this strategy. Whenever a competitor gets ahead of you, absorb-and-extend is a two-step strategy for catching up. In step one, the competitor's product is copied. In step two, the copied product is extended or modified to make it better. The strategy works best for strong companies because they must have the resources to beat a competitor at its own game.

Microsoft had successfully absorbed and extended a number of technologies on its climb to monopoly status. Windows 95 is a clear example of how Microsoft copied the graphical user interface of the Apple Macintosh, and then extended it. Apple lost most of its GUI advantage over Microsoft when its legal battle against Microsoft (and Hewlett Packard) failed in court. Apple could not convince a non-technically savvy judge that its GUI was copyrightable. Microsoft's multimedia software even went so far as to copy some of Apple's QuickTime multimedia code, which prompted another legal challenge by Apple. Microsoft managed to side step a number of other legal challenges from Apple by paying off the Cupertino company with a $150 million investment. Apple subsequently dropped all lawsuits and Microsoft agreed to continue to develop applications for the Macintosh. It was almost as if Apple was the research lab and Microsoft was the product development department! But Microsoft did not restrict itself to raids on Apple. Microsoft's Internet Explorer absorbed and then extended Netscape's Navigator. Microsoft's Windows 2000 was designed with UNIX in its sights. I guess imitating a competitor's product is the sincerest form of flattery.

Throughout the remainder of the 1990s the computer industry vacillated over which one was better: submission to the dominance of Microsoft, or fighting the giant to the bitter end. Being bought by Microsoft was not such a bad exit strategy for investors. WebTV cost its investors about $40 million 15 months before they sold out to Microsoft for ten times as much! Most people were well rewarded for being absorbed.

Others imagined an end to innovation if Microsoft were allowed to continue absorbing and extending. They wanted to put limits on Microsoft rather than see the computer industry stagnate. If the U.S. Department of Justice couldn't divide Microsoft into "Baby Bills," at least they should restrict the behavior of the *Borg,* according to its foes. By 1999 the question of what to do about Microsoft had not been resolved. But once it is resolved, the industry will still practice the best strategy of the strong—absorb-and-extend. Resistance is futile!

Article by Ted Lewis, Computer, May 1997

Absorb and Extend: Resistance Is Futile!

Much of my understanding of the computer industry comes from watching sci-fi movies. Movies like *This Planet Earth, The Thing,* and more recently, *Star Trek: First Contact* can tell us a lot about contemporary culture. For example, in the 1950s, movie aliens would say something like "lecto brackto" as they stepped from their flying saucers. Upon hearing such nonsense, earthlings usually offended the poor, misunderstood creatures, who either turned on humanity or exited in a huff. Simple strategies led to simple plots.

Today, the popularity of movies like *Independence Day 4 (ID4)* suggests that our society no longer views aliens as mild-mannered, benign presences; these aliens are definitely diplomatically challenged. They are diabolical, often English-speaking adversaries—that is, more like humans. In *ID4,* aliens want what earthlings have so badly they are willing to exterminate us to get it.

Strangely enough, a similar transition is going on in Silicon Valley, in the form of the absorb-and-extend thinking prevalent today.

We Are the Borg; We Absorb

The worst bunch of nonterrestrials ever portrayed is the Borg, the villain from *Star Trek: First Contact.* This half-machine/half-organic life-form has only one purpose in life: to absorb all other life-forms and in the process spread its civilization throughout the universe. The Borg's absorb-and-extend strategy includes more than dictatorial takeovers—it involves physical assimilation and eventual extermination. The Borg will not stop until it has absorbed everything in the universe. Resistance is futile!

The Borg's feeding pattern is not unlike that of hi-tech corporate organisms. Do movies reflect reality or vice versa? Assimilation or, as Microsoft calls it, absorb and extend, has become the leading strategy among hi-tech competitors. The idea is this: when you fall behind, absorb your competitor's technology as if it were your own. Then quickly extend it, turning out new products based on the absorbed technology faster than the originating company. The absorbed technology soon becomes the laggard; the extended technology becomes the market leader. The result is almost always a reversal of fortune.

Paradoxically, absorb and extend is a strategy most often adopted by the weak that is now used by the strongest. And paradoxically, it turns what used to be a strength—innovation at a deliberate pace—into a weakness. The rules have changed: winners make better, cheaper, faster, smaller products based on the same technology as losers. Like the Borg, the winners get stronger as they consume the resources of their vanquished competitor. It works for the Borg, and it works for companies like Microsoft: Windows 95 absorbed the Mac OS; Windows NT is absorbing Unix and Novell NetWare, Microsoft Money is attempting to absorb Quicken, ActiveX with J++ is attempting to absorb Sun's Java, and so on.

One interesting counter example: Apple Computer continues to demonstrate exactly the opposite strategy. It absorbs market-lagging technologies and quickly falls even further behind. Apple absorbed market loser Next and is attempting to propel itself into the forefront with a product that lost to Wintel many years ago. Apple continues to act like an arrogant market leader and as a consequence will become a shadow of its former self.

On the other hand, powerhouse Microsoft has repeatedly used a strategy of the weak. Clearly, Bill Gates and his strategists are not too proud to use catch-up techniques even when not necessary. In the hands of a powerful competitor such as Microsoft, absorb and extend is dangerous to the universe, locking customers into proprietary systems. Is such a competitor unbeatable?

Only one thing stopped the Borg. What was it? Netscape knows. Oracle, IBM, and Sun are learning. Adobe, Novell, and Apple don't have a clue.

Stopping the Borg

Here is where years of watching sci-fi comes in handy. Only the Borg can stop the Borg. The best way to fight fire is with fire. In *Star Trek: First Contact,* the biomechanical humanoid named Data saved the day using a fire-against-fire strategy.

Data stopped the Borg by getting inside of the Borg's decision loop and changing the rules. For a short time, he first became one with the Borg. Once he understood the enemy, he betrayed it by doing something entirely out of Borg in character. Once absorbed, Data was supposed to use Borg-like cunning and brutality to defeat Captain Picard and the Enterprise's crew. Instead, Data went against the rules: He out-Borged the Borg.

When Radical Is Chic

In the battle for enterprise (pun intended), a competitor that does the unexpected can defeat Microsoft. By changing the rules and acting out an

Metaphor	Explanation/Example
Mathematics	Fortran numerical analysis computation
Literature	Pascal literate programming software engineering, discovery-oriented computer science
Direct manipulation	Macintosh OS, Windows 95, object-oriented programming, invention-oriented software development
Simulation	3D virtual worlds, networked simulators, movie making, author-oriented application development
Reality	Concreteness delegation invisible technology, agent-oriented information system development

Table 29.1   Computing metaphors, past and future.

uncharacteristically radical plan, a competitor can overcome the absorb-and-extend strategy. But it has to be very radical. Half measures won't work.

Oracle, IBM, and Sun are trying to change the rules by introducing an entirely new device—the network computer—and an entirely different software platform based on Java and Java Beans. Netscape also wants to change the rules faster than Microsoft can absorb its browser business. Netscape's Communicator product and renewed intranet emphasis is aimed squarely at a market segment that took Microsoft by surprise. IBM/Lotus is doing the same thing to Microsoft and Netscape: Lotus Domino is rapidly absorbing features from Microsoft Exchange and Netscape Communicator, in an attempt to out-Borg both companies.

One or more of these companies may succeed against the Borg, but most will not. Some will fail because they do not take the time to become part of the Borg—even for a short period—so they won't fully understand what the Borg would do. Others will fail because they cannot execute their plans. But most will fail because they will make plans that are not radical enough. None of them have proposed the biggest rule change of all: a change in metaphor.

Machine as Metaphor

The metaphor engineers of the late twentieth century have clearly been computer scientists. For 50 years, we have proposed, tested, and commercialized metaphors, all of them borrowed from other sectors. I have listed two classical metaphors along with two unconventional metaphors of computing in Table 29.1.

The early computer industry mimicked mathematics: Fortran was math on a typewriter. Most applications were implementations of various numerical-analysis algorithms and the computer was little more than an adding machine with big round-off errors.

This metaphor was replaced largely by the computer-as-literature machine. From about 1965 through 1978, programmers based the computing metaphor on the 500-year-old book. They wrote in an elegantly structured textual language, and their machines began to push text around as well as numbers. Donald Knuth even coined the term *literate programming* and borrowed heavily from the book paradigm. Programs should be written with the reader in mind instead of the hardware, Knuth said. I don't think many disagree with this observation, but Knuth's metaphor eventually wore out.

It was replaced with the graphical user interface, as mainstreamed by the Macintosh. Direct manipulation of icons, menus, pictures, text, numbers—just about everything—became the norm, and various representations of the physical world as a desktop became the metaphor. "Look and see," "point and click," and other cute phrases remind us of the direct-manipulation metaphor, clearly the era we are in now. Except that Microsoft now dominates. The computer industry has reinvented the Macintosh about four times over the past decade, and lack of imagination will probably condemn us to another decade of Mac knockoffs.

But let me go out on a limb here and suggest that we may be entering the fourth metaphorical machine age: simulation. Applications now take on a greater degree of reality, as three-dimensional virtual worlds become the objects manipulated by programmers and users alike. Object-oriented programming, like movie making, is being pushed to its limit. Applications are "authored" instead of "developed." The computer industry takes on a Hollywood atmosphere as money changes hands, introducing the consumer as a dictator of technology's direction. The Borg is vulnerable to rapid adoption of this metaphor, but we should consider yet another metaphor.

Walking further out on a limb, I speculate that the next metaphor beyond simulation will be reality itself. In this stage, symbols no longer represent something else; instead, they represent themselves. In other words, metaphorical computing goes away and is replaced by reality. The best technology is invisible to the user. Sure, technology lurks in the background but plays a subservient role. Users/programmers describe and delegate instead of formalize and implement. Some call this agent technology, some call it artificial intelligence. I call it reality. At this point in computing's evolution, it is unclear what computing as reality means, but a rapid transformation from where we are today to concrete reality would stun the Borg. It might not even be able to survive.

Adversaries can defeat the Borg by riding a new metaphor. Microsoft's competitors can defeat it by pioneering an entirely new metaphor, just as Microsoft rendered IBM meaningless by pioneering the PC. If you want to win the war of the worlds, forget about the GUI and hook your wagon to an emerging metaphor. Get real.

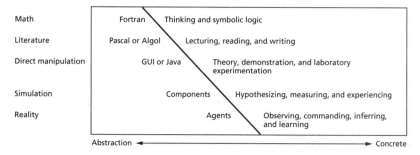

Figure 29.1 *As computing becomes more concrete, objects become more tangible and the technology dissolves.*

Tangible Objects, Invisible Technologies

In the past, computers derived their power from metaphor. In a sense, these computers were tools for building metaphorical systems. Companies that were able to leverage skills within the context of the current metaphor became winners. Everyone else became losers or at least minor-league players. I believe this trend will continue. So, if you want to go beyond Microsoft, hop onto the next metaphor.

In the future, the metaphorical computer will disappear. Concrete systems will manipulate the real world instead of symbols. Figure 29.1 illustrates this trend and shows how metaphor dissolves into reality. As metaphors that represent things abstractly give way to concreteness, our computing machines become invisible. They melt into the real world of tangible goods.

Because our educational system has been slow to adopt new metaphors, I will use it to illustrate these ideas. I labeled Figure 29.1 with keywords that best describe a progression from teaching symbolic logic to truly imparting knowledge.

Suppose I want to become a surgeon. In the symbolic era, I would discover medicine by reasoning within the Hippocratic system. This system attempts to find a logical explanation for everything in the world. It seeks explanations that the rigid logic of mathematics can express. Of course, hands-on experience (opening up a cadaver or two, for instance) supplements logic, but the main effort is to understand the mechanical nature of the human body through reasoned logic.

The progression from logic to experience and eventually to real learning follows a path as shown in Figure 29.1. If my education takes place in the literate era, I read lots of books. If it takes place in the direct manipulation era, I perform laboratory experiments and supplement my education by listening to lectures that explain the theory. At each level, my education edges ever closer to concreteness.

In the simulation era, medical training becomes even more concrete: I hypothesize cause and effect, but mostly I probe, measure, and try things (on even more cadavers). I advise, "take this and call me in the morning." Experiential learning is highly interactive and based largely on cause and effect, the major activity in simulation. Of course, I keep reading, observing, and experimenting, but the experiments become more lifelike. Logic and reason must share space with keen observation and hypothesis testing.

In reality-based medicine, I am connected to operating rooms around the world through unobtrusive machines that permit me to see, hear, feel, and manipulate real objects. In "learning mode" I can merely go along with someone else—watching, listening, and feeling one or more surgical operations as others perform them miles away. Lectures, laboratory experimentation, reading, and writing become supplemental activities rather than central activities. Learning takes place largely through observation and inference.

Going further, technology makes it possible for me to be connected to thousands of operations occurring simultaneously throughout the world. Doctors can use software agents to improve diagnosis and operating techniques. After some time, they can tell these agents what to do. When computing reaches this level, the human "programmer" gives commands instead of detailed instructions. Whether or not this is a form of programming, I do not know. It certainly changes how people interact with metaphorical machines.

As the manipulation of symbols becomes the manipulation of tangible objects, the learning experience becomes more like everyday life with one exception: the rate of experiencing, observing, and commanding must become thousands of times greater. Otherwise, we cannot learn fast enough. In such a world, everyone will use invisible technology to increase the rate at which we learn.

Language designers are searching for greater and greater levels of abstraction. They equate abstraction with a language's power and hence technical progress. I believe this is an abuse of abstraction and is wrongheaded. Programming languages have become more concrete rather than more abstract. They have become abstract only in the sense of distancing themselves from machine language. The ultimate machine language is the Turing machine, and I cannot think of anything more abstract than a Turing machine. So the notion of abstraction has lost its meaning when used to describe programming languages. Instead, I submit that the more concrete a language is, the more successful it is.

The task of programming a computer will continue to become more concrete. Object orientation is one step in that direction. Although it is not possible to hold a programming object in your hand, most objects at least represent a tangible object of some kind. In the future, we may program by manipulating tangible objects. This is already a reality in the world of industrial robotics, where spray-painting machines are programmed by mimicry. Borland's Delphi and Adobe's Director use a weaker version of mimicry.

The next winning metaphor—and possibly the successor to Microsoft's Mac knockoff—could be a product based on modeling and simulation. And the next big company might be the one that perfects simulation as the metaphor for all of computing. In the long run, computers will disappear as computing adopts reality as its world model. Winners will beat Microsoft to reality. Resistance is futile!

PART FIVE

Techno-Society

CHAPTER THIRTY

The Age
of Information

The rise of Netscape, Yahoo!, America Online, Microsoft, and other Information Age companies illustrates a modern day fact of life: traditional economics is ill equipped to describe valuation in the age of information. After all, what is the value of data? When data is organized into information, then what is its value? How should the Information Age be characterized? Information may be manufactured and packaged like other goods, but it isn't valued like a loaf of bread or a box of cereal.

How can a dollar value be placed on information? This was one of the burning questions that crossed my mind as I watched Internet company after Internet company achieve astronomical valuations as they went public through 1995, 1996, 1997, and 1998. In many cases, such as Amazon.com, valuations exceeded that of much more established companies even while Amazon.com lost money! In a sense, Amazon.com's book value was worth an infinite amount! Why?

There is an explanation, but it isn't possible to understand the explanation given traditional Machine Age thinking. This is due to the intangible nature of information. Asset valuation is no longer based on tangible goods like it used to be. Asset valuation is based on value-ad, and value-ad is based on a number of intangibles like brand name, speed, learning rate, and who your partners are. Information is more difficult to value than any tangible good known before it.

To grasp the meaning of money in the Information Age, we have to assign monetary value to intangibles like speed, brand, and the leverage value of information. In the Information Age, currency and fashion are as important—and valuable—as owning a large manufacturing plant. To make matters worse, information is perishable. Its value changes over time. Yesterday's stock quote isn't as valuable as today's. Combining data in new and novel ways to create new information can enhance its value. For example, combining information about a new car with other information about financing, insurance, and service adds value to the car information. This form of aggregation adds value, often more than proportional value. Finally, information increases in value when it is integrated with other things, e.g., when the location of nearby stores is integrated with virtual stores found on the Web.

Information is most often found in the heads of intelligent people. So people are even more important and valuable in the Information Age than in the Machine Age, because only humans can turn data into information. Sure, they may use computers to help, but human insight is what makes the Information Age go around. Peopleware, as it might be called in today's new-speak, are the ultimate source of value. The smarter and quicker your peopleware is, the more your company is worth. That is why brain power, and the means of getting it, is so critical to the Information Age. Thus, "side B" of the following essay describes how the Information Age will transform education as radically as it is transforming business. The next 20 years should prove interesting because just about every institution we know of today will undergo a similar transformation. The Information Age is as big and important as all of its predecessors.

In just five short years since I wrote the following essay on "What is the Information Age?" most of the blueprint summarized in Table 30.1 has been implemented in one form or another by a variety of Internet companies. The notion of personalization, targeting, and fashion are clear examples. The notion of aggregation of content (turning data into information) is the basis of just about every Web business today. In short, the age of information is happening faster than expected. But then, isn't speed one of the features that distinguishes the Information Age from all others? I guess we will have to get used to it!

Age	Length, T yrs (Term)	Rate of Interaction, R mph (Technology)	Time to Circle Earth, yrs (Travel Time)
Agrarian	3,000–5,000 (age)	3–5 (human)	3–5 (years)
Industrial	300–500 (revolution)	30–50 (horse-auto)	0.3–0.5 (months)
Post-industrial	30–50 (trend)	300–500 (airliner)	0.03–0.05 (days)
Info	3–5 (fad)	3,000–5,000 (network)	0.003–0.005 (hours)

Table 30.1 The ever-shrinking length of successive ages correlates with accelerating technology.

Article by Ted Lewis, Computer, September 1995

Living in Real Time, Side A (What Is the Info Age?)

What is the Info Age? Everyone uses the term, but nobody defines it. So here goes. In this and subsequent essays, I formulate the principles of the Info Age and use the computer industry as proof of its existence. In this series, I answer some burning questions: What is the Info Age, how does it differ from the Machine Age, where is it leading, and what does it have to do with computers?

A Civilization on Speed

The single most important factor in shaping modern society is the relentlessly accelerating tick of the technological clock, a clock that boosts the rate of change in modern society to greater heights each day. Projects that once took a decade now take a month; tasks that used to take a day now take mere seconds. We no longer live by the biological clock but rather by the constant flow of information, services, and products that envelop the globe in a 24-hour business day on which the sun never sets.

But further increases cannot be sustained indefinitely. Within the next 10 to 20 years, we will have reached a kind of terminal velocity, marking civilization's passage from Machine Age to Info Age—an age in which people live in real time. Even the rampant increase in microprocessor speeds will taper off in about 10 years, if we believe in physics and assume it takes at least one atom to make a transistor (see Figure 30.1).

This series examines what it means to live and prosper in a constantly changing world, defines the principles of an Info Age, and examines the Computer Age in the context of business warfare. After all, the computer industry is the best example of a civilization on speed.

Predicting the Future by Understanding the Past

Civilization evolved through at least three, and perhaps four, generally recognized overlapping stages characterized by their dominant mode of human activity: Hunter-Gatherer, Agrarian, Industrial, and

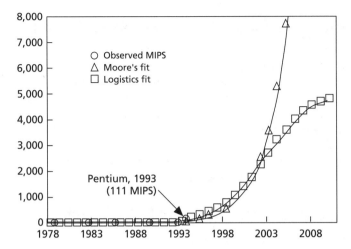

Figure 30.1 *Observed MIPS performance, past to present, is compared with Moore's law and Info Age logistics growth-curve forecasts of microprocessor performance over the next 15 years.*

Post-industrial. The Industrial and Post-industrial Ages are often lumped together into a single Machine Age, but I argue that they are two distinct ages. The current rage is the so-called Information Age, or Info Age for short. I claim that the Info Age has yet to begin, will last perhaps no more than one or two decades, and will be the last of the major ages.

Why is the Info Age the terminal age? Let's look at the data in Table 30.1. The Industrial Age was 10 times shorter than the Agrarian Age; the Post-industrial Age was 10 times shorter than the Industrial Age. The duration of these periods obviously correlates with basic transportation and communication technology. In fact, we can estimate the length of an age from the formula 15,000/R, where 15,000 is derived from the time required to circle the Earth and R is the rate of interaction that can be supported by transportation and communication technology. Ideas, products, and services spread around the globe at a pace determined by technology. After they are globally dispersed, the stage is set for their decline and replacement by new ideas, products, and services.

This process has accelerated to the extent that we now face an Info Age that may be so short that it ceases to be an age at all. Civilization is reaching a terminal velocity—a rate of change so voracious that it is limited by the human capacity to absorb it. In this final age, rate of change hits the wall and is metered by human cycles of sleep, thought, and communication. At terminal velocity, change and the rate of change are constants.

Having a Good Old Real Time

The major characteristic of living in the Info Age is constant, unrelenting, maximum change. Like the rhythmic ticking of an ancient grandfather clock, change occurs with such regularity that nobody even notices. It is an ongoing part of life. The Atomic Age, the Space Age, the Computer Age; the Lost Generation, the hippie generation, Generation X: these and other designations for periods become passé; they no longer matter because cultural phenomena come and go with such frequency that in the future we will no longer have time or labels to designate them. This is what I call living in real time.

Characteristics of the Ages

Table 30.2 lists some distinguishing features of past and current ages. Here are just a few observations.

In the Post-industrial Age, power is rooted in organizational and managerial skill because without them a large, hierarchical organization cannot function efficiently and produce products and services ever faster and faster. The Post-industrial ideas of total quality management (TQM), the "one-minute manager," and reengineering of business processes reflect classical Post-industrial thinking. TQM and process reengineering are designed to make bureaucracies work faster and more efficiently, but they cannot cope with the creativity, fashion, and personalization that will characterize the Info Age. When Post-industrial managers apply such concepts to Info Age systems, it leads to disaster.

Software development is a good example. Post-industrial techniques for making programmers more efficient and tools for making the programming process "cheaper and quicker" have not succeeded. On the contrary, programming is more of an individual activity than ever before. Instead of becoming an assembly-line manufacturing process, programming is increasingly becoming the subject of fashion. Today, object-oriented programming is the latest and greatest technology. Next year it might be functional programming or perhaps visual programming.

John Trudel ("Management Insights," *Upside,* May 1995) complains about the mismatch between Post-industrial Age management tools and the needs of the Info Age. He says, "They call it the Information Age, but I doubt there has been a time when there was so much frenzy and so little thought. [Managers] don't read to learn and change. They are drowning in data, but starved for knowledge. Business performance and personal lives suffer from an Alice-in-Wonderland existence, where people run ever faster to stay in the same spot." This is typical Post-industrial Age rhetoric. He goes on to express one of the conceptually distinguishing features separating Info Age managers from those of the Post-industrial Age: "Rather than doing things faster and cheaper, [managers] will invest to be

Machine Ages

Feature	Agrarian	Industrial	Post-industrial	Info
Basic value	Land, human labor, livestock	Weight, size, energy	Efficiency, speed	Information
Symbol of power	Land ownership, might	Material possessions	Organizational skill	Fashion, currency, popularity
Means of production	Individual craftsmanship	Hierarchical, large-group, mass production	Networked, small-group projects, flexible production	Individual craftsmanship, flexible production
Means of distribution	Individual barter	Large-group distribution channels	Small group, targeted just-in-time inventory, specialized mail-order	Individual barter, data storage, electronic transmission
Basic technology	Ritual, tradition	Discovery, scientific method	Inverse economics: faster, better = cheaper	Computerized search inference, creativity
Legal system	Military might	Patents and copyrights	Litigation	Trade secret, obsolescence
Economic drivers	Family bloodlines, seeks ecological balance	Capital formation seeks balanced supply and demand	Government prints money, seeks stability	Highly educated work force seeks novelty, more information
Government	Chieftain tending toward dictator	Centralized, representative, industrial republic tending toward socialism	Decentralized, representative, informed consent tending toward social republic	Direct democracy tending toward anarchy
Education	Apprenticeship, one-on-one, authority-based, home-learning, just-in-time	Factory assembly line, group batched, authority based, institutionalized, one-shot event	Factory assembly, line, group modular, expert based, efficient, institutionalized, life-long learning	Apprenticeship, individualized, expert based, anywhere-anytime, just-in-time, automated
Religion	Shaman spiritualism	Organized mass religion	Decentralized major religions	Personalized, diverse beliefs
Social structure	Clan, extended family	Urban, nuclear family	Disintegrated, non-nuclear family	Virtual community, special-interest groups

Table 30.2 Features of the ages.

different and better." Finally, he shows his understanding of the Info Age when he says, "we need new methods for business. The new ways will be as different from linear, reductionist, Machine Age business as quantum physics is from Newtonian physics."

Inverse Economics

Automated factories produce an abundance of material things with mechanized precision and efficiency. But it is no longer sufficient to produce a high-quality, inexpensive car, television, cellular telephone, or videotape recorder. To succeed in the Post-industrial Age, smoke-stack relics of the Industrial Age have had to emphasize efficiency, speed, and customer satisfaction. A Post-industrial company cannot survive unless it builds products that sell cheaper, run faster, and cost less to maintain. This is inverse economics—a feature being carried over into the Info Age. Indeed, it is one of the centerpieces of the Info Age.

Through inverse economics, everything plunges toward a commodity; technology merely accelerates this plunge. How, then, are Info Age businesses (which I call FutureBusiness) to survive?

Retro Rockets

The Info Age brings us full circle from the era of old-world craftsmanship to the era of machine production and back again to an era of craftsman-like production and distribution. The Info Age corporation revives many of the features of the Agrarian Age: small-group or individual craftsmanship and individual (electronic) barter.

The use of information technology to increase the efficiency and speed of mass production and mass distribution has peaked and in the Info Age will almost always lead to failure. TQM, business process reengineering, and many other business mantras that have enjoyed their 15 minutes of fame are no match for the new realities of business. Success in the Info Age means learning to use technology to individualize and personalize services and products.

A Vapor Trail of Litigation

Lawyers do not understand technology; therefore, the technology of efficiency and speed, leading to low-cost, out-sourced production, makes the legal system more litigious and less decisive. Plea bargaining, out-of-court settlements, and appeals are the norm in Post-industrial legal circles. These are all legal devices for delaying the opposition rather than deciding on a proactive course of action. In the Info Age, legal procedures will be too cumbersome and too expensive to accommodate the rate of change.

The disruption of the Industrial Age legal system that began in the Post-industrial Age becomes more pronounced in the Info Age. Technology is no longer based on economies of scale, patent protection for discovery, or copyright protection for the expression of an idea. It is based on speed and customization.

The Real Weapon of FutureBusiness

The swiftness of an electronic marketplace will force the legal system to change. The mechanisms for protecting Info Age property (information) are trade secrets and obsolescence. Apple Computer remains competitive by being a technology leader even though its innovations are ultimately co-opted by other firms. Intel wants to be the first company to render its own microprocessors obsolete. Trade secrets may delay copycat competition, but the real weapon of the Info Age is obsolescence.

The basic technology of the Info Age is computerized search, inference, and creativity. An individual sitting at a home computer can sift through the World Wide Web to create a new product from raw information easily accessed by anyone. The resulting product can be distributed over the same network; through individual barter, the traditional mid-level distribution channel can be eliminated. When goods and services are sold at electronic speeds, obsolescence takes effect before a competitor can litigate.

Age Without End

In the absence of successive ages, the future beyond the Info Age will be characterized by instant celebrity, fashion, fad, and cycles of creation followed by rapid obsolescence. (In fact, we are seeing some of this already.) For more on this subject, read John Petersen's *The Road to 2015* (The Waite Group Press, 1994) or Frank Koelsch's *Infomedia Revolution* (McGraw-Hill Ryerson, 1995). For an in-depth discussion of how Info Age technology returns to agrarian notions of personalization and individualization, read Howard Thomas's *Global Expansion in the Information Age* (Van Nostrand Reinhold, 1995).

The computer industry is the vanguard of FutureBusiness, where products and services are made more personal instead of cheaper, markets are defined by individual tastes rather than hordes of consumers, and companies race to replace their own products and services with the next version, edition, or model before their competition does. It is a treadmill. It is living in real time.

Article by Ted Lewis, Computer, October 1995

Living in Real Time, Side B (Where Will the Brain Power Come From?)

The Katzenjammer NetHeads

The Agrarian Age student learned from parents, villagers, and the village shaman in order to survive. The Info Age student does the same, but InfoKids use information technology in ways never imagined even 10 years ago. Oddly, education in the Info Age is returning to an Agrarian Age form—one that Machine Age educators thought was extinct. In particular, Info Age education is becoming personalized, individualized, and delivered just-in-time. But unlike their Agrarian Age ancestors, InfoKids learn from machines; in fact, they learn more from machines than their Machine Age predecessors did. Let's face it, InfoKids are NetHeads.

Before exploring FutureSchools of the Info Age, let's look at what is wrong with the Machine Age schoolhouse.

What Went Wrong?

Education during the Industrial and Post-industrial Ages seemed to take a step backward. Even though an educated person stands a better chance of living well than a dropout (Figure 30.2), Machine Age learning is too regimented, having been modeled on the successful factory system. Students are seated in rows like parts on an assembly line. Knowledge is packaged and force-fed into the learning units far in advance of when those units need to know or want to know. The learning process mimics the batched, authority-based assembly line of the factory.

The Machine Age model rewards conformist thinking, obedience, and socializing behavior. It punishes individual creativity, unconventional thinking, and diverse learning styles. For example, a child who is good with his or her hands but slow to pick up reading and mathematical skills often does poorly in the MachineSchool system. Ironically, this same student often excels in the workaday world of the factory. Conversely, the fast reader and articulate speaker does very well in this system, but may adapt slowly when confronted with technological change. Often, the best

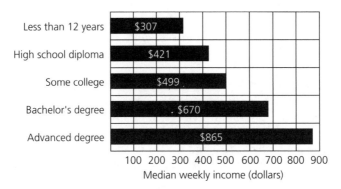

Figure 30.2 *Earning power versus educational attainment. (Source: U.S. Bureau of Labor Statistics.)*

students in either category excel at hacking on the Internet or discovering the ending of the interactive game "Myst" in record time.

The Post-industrial Age school makes things worse. It attempts to standardize learning to make it more efficient and cost-effective. It reengineers the factory model to save taxpayers' money. The "new math" and "new reading" programs that gripped U.S. school systems are examples of efficiency-oriented Post-industrial Age pedagogy. Post-industrial Agers (meaning most of the people reading this article) learned to optimize, categorize, right-size, and turn a phrase with politically correct TQM-isms. Robotically correct thinking may suffice in the optimized technocratic corporation, but it is left in the dust in an Info Age corporation.

What Went Right?

On the plus side, Post-industrial Age education replaced authority-based learning with expert-based learning. Boomers gained a healthier respect for experts than for authorities—a lesson learned even more profoundly by government bureaucrats during the past 30 years. Of course, expertise-based learning is a necessary response to the high-tech, knowledge-intensive help-wanted ads of Post-industrial companies. We learned that authority-based educators cannot explain the scientific and technical world to the satisfaction of the TV generation. Experts can.

Just-in-Time Education

Living in real time means living with too much data. There is simply too much to learn and too little time to learn it all. Therefore, the Info Age student must learn *how* to learn, extend learning throughout his or her entire life, and absorb only what is needed, when it is needed. InfoKids want just-in-time and just-enough learning. Unlike students in other ages, they must filter out the deluge of data and focus on the data needed at the moment.

This changes everything. For one thing, FutureSchool is not a place, but a frame of reference. It returns learning to its apprenticeship-based, individualized, just-in-time, Agrarian-style roots. Info Age citizens need knowledge to survive, but they get it when and where they need it, rather than being forced to acquire it by age 18 and store it in advance for a lifetime.

Another important difference: unlike Agrarian learning, Info Age learning is highly automated and expert-based. High-speed computerized filtering, searching, and sorting capabilities protect students from information overload. Pervasive educational software offers a world of instruction, but in small, digestible, focused chunks. FutureSchool books look more like "Where in the World is Carmen Sandiego?" and less like the manual to Microsoft Windows.

FutureSchool

In "The University of the Future," Donald Perrin (*ED Journal*, Vol. 9, No. 2, Feb. 1995, p. J-10) opens with

> *Imagine a university without walls where you select programs, courses, and mentors from leading institutions of higher learning, libraries, museums, and technical institutes throughout the world. Imagine a university designed for nontraditional learners where learning can take place anytime, anywhere, and where the learner makes the choices. Imagine a university that operates 24 hours a day, 365 days a year where you can participate in live courses or complete the courses in your own time frame. Imagine a university that is truly international, multicultural and multilingual, where courses originate in different countries, cultures, and languages. Imagine a university where computers, interactive multimedia, electronic libraries, and the information superhighway play a major role in providing a full range of interactive courses and services. Imagine a university where the curriculum is oriented to future needs, prepares you for real jobs and initiates placement strategies at the time you enroll. Imagine a university where ingenious, creative and collaborative efforts are rewarded and programs are future-oriented, exciting, and relevant. Note: The University of the Future is a virtual learning environment, not a physical campus or place.*

Perrin is not dreaming. He is director of the Almquist Center for Innovative Learning at San Jose State University, a FutureSchool in the making.

What It Takes

Phrases like personalized, individualized, planned obsolescence, and just-in-time delivery are incantations of the Info Age. FutureBusinesses cannot escape it, and neither can FutureSchools. What happens to universities if everyone has access to any course at any university at any time? Will universities go out of business? Machine Age universities will. What are universities going to do about it?

Just as the Machine Age required assembly-line education, FutureSchools must apply FutureBusiness techniques to survive. A FutureSchool educator realizes that universities are in the knowledge-as-a-commodity business. Therefore, they must use commodity business techniques or risk becoming as irrelevant as the *Encyclopedia Britannica*. For those who missed the announcement, *Encyclopedia Britannica* has become the latest roadkill on the Infobahn, posting large losses each of the past three years. The 227-year-old company failed to recognize the transition of its knowledge business into the Info Age (*San Jose Mercury News*, May 16, 1995, p. E3).

CHAPTER THIRTY-ONE

Tribalism

Consumers are becoming increasingly tribal. That is, they are self-organizing into groups of people having the same occupation, habits, ideas, and interests. Because people are highly mobile and determine their own fate more so than ever before in history, tribalism is a result of self-selection rather than genetic inheritance today. And because people seek community as never before, most tribes are special interest communities. And because the Internet spans time and distance, modern communities are increasingly being melded together by electronic communications. Electronic mail, Web sites, and on-line services are creating tribes of choice, much like the need for shelter, protection, and food created tribes of necessity thousands of years ago.

Merchants are exploiting tribalism among the consuming masses as never before. It is possible to define extremely narrow tribes, a process called *targeting,* such that the payback is enormous. Grocery stores give away awards to loyal customers, airlines give away free travel, and Web stores pay you to visit their Web site. While this may seem like an added expense to the merchant, the truth is that targeting increases sales, diminishes costly inventory, and boosts profits. Targeting is so powerful in the information age that various algorithms for determining the best time, place, and subject matter to hit you with have been patented. It is the age of *narrowcasting.*

Silicon Valley may have been slow to learn the lessons of marketing to consumers, but companies like Intel, Microsoft, and Sony have made up for lost time. Tribes are generally defined by the platform—a certain PC, operating system, programming language, or application. Thus there are Macintosh, Java, Photoshop, and Microsoft Office tribes associated with each of these "platforms." If you buy Adobe Photoshop, you are sure to get junk mail from the Photoshop plug-in vendors. You may even receive a free issue of Adobe's magazine. Join the club.

Conversely, merchants have learned to exploit tribes through extremely targeted promotions. By keeping databases up-to-date on each customer, a department store can promote your favorite product, service, or celebration. Distributing goods and services to a targeted interest group is a form of narrowcasting. And narrowcasting has been shown to be much more effective, in terms of "hit rate," than broadcasting. This all assumes the merchant has good intelligence gathering and analysis capability. In other words, narrowcasting works especially well in the computer age, because computers, databases, and Web sites can automate the process of data mining. Only the purpose of this gold rush is to find consumers rather than gold.

One way to anticipate the Next Big Thing is to follow the platform trends. In the consumer electronics world, this is extremely easy. Simply find the platform with the largest following or tribe, and target some portion of that tribe. Personal computing vendors sell about 75 million PCs per year. Automobile manufacturers sell about 45 million cars and trucks globally. There are about 30 million cell phones sold annually. The market for TVs in the United States is about 25 million per year. Printers and fax machines follow in order of market size. Then there are the various software platforms such as Microsoft Word, PowerPoint, and Access. Each of these has a large but specialized following. These are the tribes that attract the attention of Silicon Valley companies.

In the next essay I speculate on how hi-tech capitalists might try to exploit these tribes. The PC market is still growing, but greed is motivating these capitalists to start thinking about other large installed bases of users. Car, telephones, and toys are among the sugarplums dancing in their heads. If only there was some way to add a microprocessor to a car or telephone in such a way that millions of people become addicted to the platform created by the new combination. This is the challenge facing the industry as it enters the next decade.

Article by Ted Lewis, Computer, November 1997

Cars, Phones, and Tamagotchi Tribes

They are "a little key chain thingy, like a smiley face or a dog, and you have to feed it and take care of it," says Sarah Cook, age 14, of Del Rey Oaks, California (Sedona Callahan, "Virtual Pets," *The Monterey County Herald,* Sept. 4, 1997, p. D1). Sarah is talking about her Tamagotchi—a virtual pet that demands to be fed, disciplined, paid attention to, and taken to the bathroom. As if life isn't already crowded enough with obligations, virtual pets would seem to be at odds with the information age. But cars, phones, and TV-like appliances will become more like Tamagotchis as the friction-free economy once again expresses itself in tribalism.

My premise is simple: The friction-free economy rewards retrocultures that yearn to return to agrarian tribalism. Selling hi-tech products in this new economy becomes ritual, and the greater the ritual, the greater the financial rewards. Some may use different names—database marketing, targeting, or niche marketing—but the key to expanding the computer industry will be to build a tribe around your brand, and flaunt it.

Successful product design and sales will increasingly require targeting products, services, and ideas to various tribes. An idea long understood in the entertainment and services industry, this is only now becoming a computer industry mantra. The question is, how will this impact the design of future computer products? Study the Tamagotchi and other Christmas season best-sellers to find out.

Tribalism Sells

The Extended-Family Database maintained by the Saturn automobile company allows customers to search for other Saturn owners by location and by model. One anonymous owner sent e-mail saying, "I hate cars, but I love Saturns. If I become rich and famous, I won't waste money on fancy, expensive cars, but instead buy a couple of Saturns every year" (*The Friction-Free Economy,* Harper Collins, 1997).

Saturn cars evoke a response often reserved for premium cars like Lexus and Mercedes. But without a high price tag to distinguish itself from the other value-priced small cars, Saturn has to come up with another lever. It has discovered the lock-in that tribalism provides—regardless of price and quality. This is the lesson the computer industry needs to learn.

When Apple Computer got into trouble in 1996, 91 percent of Apple customers said they were confident the company would recover. Even when things deteriorated in 1997, customer loyalty was high. "We are devoted to the Mac," said Betty Baldwin of the Space Science Division at NASA Ames Research. "Our users would die if they told us we had to change from the Mac." When asked why people in companies continued to buy Macintoshes when it looked like Apple was failing, Macintosh tribalism kicked in. David Wu of Chicago Corp. said, "If Apple disappeared tomorrow there would be a lot of depressed graphics artists and publishers." (*Information Week,* May 6, 1996, p. 66).

Apple led the PC industry in repurchase loyalty even though it seemed like the company was not long for this earth. According to a survey conducted by Computer Intelligence InfoCorp, 87 percent of customers who bought a Macintosh purchased another. In his 1997 MacExpo keynote speech, Steve Jobs showed an understanding of tribalism when he said, ". . . you have to think differently to buy an Apple computer . . . we make tools for those kinds of people."

Cars and computers may seem too mundane to get emotional about, but this is exactly what builds a brand. The more emotional consumers become, the more they spend! Saturn and Apple may not threaten Ford and IBM, but they will continue to be profitable companies as long as their tribe is on their side. Feed the tribe and reap the rewards. But it hasn't always been this way in hi-tech.

Asbestos Underwear

Tribalism cropped up early on the Net and its spread accelerated when Wired-World politics appeared for the first time in 1979. In that exciting year, the Finger controversy arose. A Unix command that allowed a user to locate another user and find out personal information, Finger was considered a violation of privacy by some. In any case, it created an uproar, with flaming (heated debate via e-mail) and emotions. Tribal behavior always involves the emotions. A flame sometimes required asbestos underwear, but it also inspired a new subcult.

Soon nongeeks realized that e-mail (and the Internet in general) was an entirely new form of human communication. And it was way-cool technology. E-mail was *not* simply a better telephone, TV, radio, or memo machine. It stood alone as a new techno art form. It had its own sociology. The beginnings of this art form stem from the writings of Steve Crocker, whose job was to document the Internet's technology. His per-

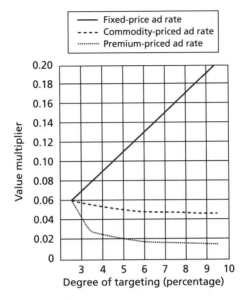

Figure 31.1 *Effect of targeting on the value chain multiplier.*

sonal writing style established a kind of network etiquette—*netiquette*—that became part of the Net culture.

As the subcult grew, Crocker's netiquette melded with the hacker culture. E-mail nomenclature held the network culture together. Shortcuts like BTW (by the way), RSN (real soon now), and icons like:-) and:-(became part of the lexicon. The nethead tribe was born. Now, over a half-million people read *Wired*, the hard-copy digest of this tribe.

Do the Math

I f you do the math, you can see the importance of targeting as a value chain multiplier in Figure 31.1. I have developed this simple model to illustrate my point that the deeper one targets, the greater the return. A premium-priced advertising campaign, such as running an ad on all the television networks at one time, has a lower return as the degree of targeting goes up. Next in line is a commodity-priced ad, for which you've slightly targeted your audience by placing the ad in *Wired, Computer,* or a specialty magazine like *IEEE Software.* This has less value as the degree of targeting increases, because it still misses the point of tribal agrarianism. Only the fixed-price ad that targets a specific tribe has linear value as the degree of targeting increases. In this scenario, the ad uses tribalism to identify a product with a lifestyle, niche, or fad. This, for example, is like ads on MTV hucstering pimple removal ointment to

12-year-olds: It's very narrow. And if the ointment is the same as that used by the members of the band Nine-Inch Nails, tribalism kicks the value multiplier into linear returns, as shown in Figure 31.1.

Culture Clash

By now you get my drift—the Internet has melded technophiles, hackers, and the upwardly mobile digirati into a new tribe. This youthful tribe (somewhere between the ages of 20 and 40 years old) may be small today, but it already has buying power. When it grows up, it will be an economic force not unlike the Baby Boomers. So why haven't more computer companies targeted this group?

For one, the Internet's tribal ritual did not surface until the mid-1990s— to the surprise of staid companies like Microsoft, Intel, DEC, IBM, and Oracle. Maybe Netscape got it, but in general the computer industry was slow to realize the power of tribal marketing. Unwittingly, a culture clash has prevented these staid companies from entering the most profitable of all hi-tech businesses—cars, phones, and the Tamagotchi—not to mention fashion computers and smart appliances of all types. Most of these companies just don't get it.

Intel may have sold 150 million processors over the past decade, but there are 885 million TVs in the world. With TVs turning over approximately every seven to eight years, this represents a market of 100 million TVs per year. U.S. cellular phone sales exceed personal computer sales (30 versus 25 million units), and cars probably come in second, at around 20 million. These are attractive numbers. What will it take to get the attention of Silicon Valley product planners?

Addressing this market will take more than adding obvious features to standard products like phones. Cell phones contain sophisticated digital signal processors today, but think of the enormous market for a computer-in-a-phone appliance that does more than e-mail. Why hasn't someone addressed the telephone as a delivery platform the way Microsoft exploits desktop computers? The telephone is a major untapped platform that has so far escaped the Microsoft monopoly. It will not remain untapped for long, because the market for telephones that "think" is enormous. Someone will notice soon.

Computers as cars are great platforms to sell into, also. Without the American automobile, there would be no McDonalds, shopping malls, and freeways. Forget the old markets; smart cars will create whole new shopping malls and eateries. Currently, the average car has a handful of computers that perform rudimentary functions like adjusting fuel flow and preventing skids in emergency stops. But the great untapped market is for cars with e-mail access, Web browsers, and game consoles. Sales of obvious applications like navigation will be nothing compared with the market for *personalized* information hubs that reside in everyone's cars. In addition, a smart car gets to know its driver and passengers. It adjusts. It soothes and accommodates. Car as Tamagotchi will change the way we get from point A to point B.

So, what's the connection between cars, phones, and Tamagotchi pets? Before consumers will fork over cybercash for a smart car, phone, or TV, companies will have to design products to be more like a Tamagotchi. They have to appeal to the *PIC factor*—personal, individual, and customizable. People don't want just another electronic gadget—they want a personal gadget. They don't want to change their lives to fit the toy; instead, they want the toy to fit their lives. And manufacturers really cannot know in advance of production what individuals do with their smart cars, so they have to design customizable products. In other words, technology must allow for the consumer to complete manufacturing in the form of after-the-sale customization. Sounds difficult, doesn't it? Yet, if Silicon Valley doesn't do it, then Bandai or some other company outside the Valley will. It's inevitable.

CHAPTER THIRTY-TWO

Privacy

Before WebTV Networks was a division of Microsoft, it was a tiny startup in downtown Palo Alto. I was a paid consultant to a large European company when I first met the founders in their office off of Lytton Street. Parking is so scarce in Palo Alto that I had to leave the company CEO's business card in my car window to ward off the tow truck as I spent hours in meetings. There is a 2-hour limit to parking in Palo Alto, even if you move your car. Using computer technology, the city meter maids can track your car as it moves from parking location to new parking location!

WebTV Networks had yet to deliver its first product, but already there were concerns about exporting its set-top boxes to Europe. The boxes incorporated strong encryption, for example, a technology that the U.S. government ruled as munitions for the purposes of exporting outside of the United States. In addition, each device was designed to accommodate a smart card so that user's viewing preferences could be captured automatically. The concern, of course, was how much personalization should be captured and used by WebTV Networks? Isn't this a violation of privacy? In Europe it was, but the United States had no such laws in 1996.

Targeting has a dark side. As Web sites, databases, and customer reward cards increasingly gather more data on consumers, they also become a threat to personal privacy. Take a credit card database as a simple example. A data-mining program can go through the database and identify what kind of restaurants you dine in, what kind of clothes you buy, and how often you travel. This information, when combined with demographics such as your level of income, age, and marital status, can be used to deduce certain buying patterns. A clever merchant can determine, for example, that you like to dine at French restaurants more often in July than November. This information can be used to target you as a potential member of the French Diner's Club. The offer will show up at the right time of the year—July—to entice you the most.

Targeting a tribe for purposes of selling is one thing, but targeting by Big Brother is another. Cars with GPS (Global Positioning System) and Internet connections can report their location upon demand. This might be useful for locating stolen or lost cars, but it can also be used to determining your speed and direction. This information could be sold to police departments, which could save millions by automating the process of issuing speeding tickets. What could be an extremely beneficial Internet service during rush hour (to identify traffic jams and reroute you around them) could turn into a nightmare in the hands of the law.

In the next essay, George Lawton explains many of the ways the Internet could be used to violate personal privacy. Unfortunately, there are even more ways than the ones enumerated by Lawton. Is anything being done about it? At the time of this writing, a number of proposed laws were circulating within the U.S. Congress. None have become law yet. See the second essay, "We Don't Need No Regulation." But the Europeans have already begun to act. They passed a law in 1998 that made it illegal for company A to sell your personal profile information to company B. This will reduce risk of correlating data from different sources in order to deduce information that you want to keep to yourself. At least this is a start.

Article by George Lawton, Computer, June 1998

The Internet's Challenge to Privacy

According to polls by *Business Week* and the Georgia Institute of Technology, privacy is the number one concern people have with the Internet today. Internet users are worried that businesses, the government, or criminals could intercept their communications or gain access to personal or private information.

Privacy is a concern because most of our online communications go across open backbones. Dial-up service providers, backbone Internet providers, governments, businesses, or hackers can either intercept our Internet activities or monitor them via data trails.

Users are particularly concerned because the Internet has become a transmission line and repository for personal information, private corporate data, and financial transactions.

The main areas of concern are electronic commerce, the public availability of private personal and corporate information from online databases, and government access to private communications.

Electronic Commerce

The public has expressed concern about e-commerce because it requires users to put information about their credit cards, bank accounts, financial history, and shopping habits over the Internet.

The Growth of e-Commerce

Many observers contend that concerns about privacy are a significant reason why electronic commerce has not grown faster. According to Ari Schwartz, a policy analyst for the Center for Democracy and Technology, a U.S.-based public-interest organization, fears about privacy play a larger role in limiting electronic commerce than, for example, fears about thieves stealing credit card numbers.

David Medin, the U.S. Federal Trade Commission's associate director for credit practices, said, "Consumers are concerned about online privacy, and they are staying away from the Internet because their behavior could be monitored without their knowledge or consent."

For example, Medin said, consumers fear that once they fill out a form on a Web site, the information could be sold, processed, repackaged, and otherwise used in ways that may hurt them.

However, said Bob Visse, an Internet Explorer product manager at Microsoft, users are becoming more comfortable with privacy-protection technology, such as encryption. Increased trust in such technology will make users more comfortable with activities like e-commerce.

Cookies

As businesses use the Internet not only to sell products but also to gain information about potential customers, additional privacy concerns arise. For example, many companies use cookie technology to glean information about visitors to their Web sites.

Cookies are data structures that pass from a Web site to a client's hard drive. They store information for an organization about visitors to its Web site, such as items the visitors have purchased online and other Web sites they have looked up. Companies use this information to target marketing efforts to individual users. However, opponents say this collection of information from users violates their privacy.

Most Internet visitors are unaware of these cookies. And many who are aware of them don't know they can turn off cookie generators or use programs that let them control cookies.

Online Databases

Online databases from credit bureaus and other information vendors have raised serious privacy-related concerns. Criminals have obtained victims' Social Security numbers and other personal identification information from the Internet, simulated their identities, and fraudulently obtained money or credit.

Public concern focused on online databases in 1996, when it was discovered that Lexis-Nexis, a vendor of information services and management tools, provided information that could compromise personal privacy on its P-Trak database. Lexis-Nexis removed this information, which included Social Security numbers and mothers' maiden names, from its database after 11 days.

Nonetheless, there are still many commercial and noncommercial sources for this information. For example, dozens of databases, many run by government agencies, provide Social Security numbers and related information. In many states, criminals can also obtain personal identification information directly from a state driver's license database.

To illustrate the availability of personal information, the Stalker's Home Page (http://www.glr.com/stalk.html) lists the social security numbers of some of the U.S.'s leading executives. The Stalker's Home Page collected the information from the U.S. Securities and Exchange Commission's Edgar database, which is available freely on the Internet.

However, said Lexis-Nexis spokesperson Judy Schultz, the danger of online databases distributing personal data should decrease when the Individual References Services Group guidelines go into effect on January 1, 1999. (See the sidebar "Addressing Internet Privacy Concerns".) On that date, she said, many sources of information will stop providing material to noncompliant companies that operate online databases.

Government and Privacy

Privacy advocates contend government access to online communications should be limited in order to curtail invasions of personal and corporate privacy. Some organizations contend such abuses already take place. Federal agencies say they sometimes need access to information to protect public safety and national security.

In the U.S., some privacy organizations and industry officials are concerned that the government is eroding encryption technology's ability to protect privacy.

Concerns About the Internet's Effect on Privacy

REASONS FOR CONCERN

Most Internet communications go across open backbones and can be intercepted or monitored via data trails. People are concerned about maintaining the privacy of their online personal information, corporate data, and financial transactions.

AREAS OF CONCERN

ELECTRONIC COMMERCE
• Surveys show that people are concerned about putting their financial information and shopping habits online.
• Businesses are concerned that a lack of trust by consumers could hurt e-commerce's growth.
ONLINE DATABASES
People are concerned about criminals "stealing" their financial identities by accessing their Social Security and driver's license numbers, mother's maiden name, and so on via online databases.
GOVERNMENT AND PRIVACY
People are concerned about government agencies gaining and then abusing access to private online communications.

ADDRESSING CONCERNS

STANDARDS
The World Wide Web Consortium is promoting the Platform for Privacy Preferences, saying it will give users more control over the way their personal information is used online.
LEGAL REQUIREMENTS
The European Union has passed a Data Protection Directive that limits the use and dissemination of private information in Europe.
VOLUNTARY GUIDELINES
• The largest US private information vendors formed the Individual References Services Group and designed guidelines to address the way they handle and distribute private information.
• Japan's Ministry of International Industry and Trade has created guidelines for the collection, use, and distribution of various types of personal data.

A Clinton administration policy, vehemently opposed by industry, says that U.S. vendors cannot export strong encryption technology or products that use strong encryption without the approval of the U.S. Department of Commerce. A recent federal court ruling challenged this policy as unconstitutional, but the government is appealing the decision.

The Clinton administration also wants encryption users to make decryption keys available. U.S. law enforcement and national security agencies could use the keys to decode messages if they deem it in the public interest and can obtain a court-issued warrant to do so.

The Clinton administration says encryption restrictions and safeguards are necessary because criminals or terrorists could use strong encryption when communicating about illegal acts.

Addressing Internet Privacy Concerns

Vendors, standards organizations, and government agencies have used specifications, voluntary guidelines, and legislation to address concerns about privacy over the Internet.

There has frequently been debate about whether the best approach to protecting privacy is legislation or voluntary guidelines. Technology vendors generally argue that voluntary guidelines are the best approach because laws would be designed by government agencies and thus would not give businesses the flexibility necessary to provide the best technology.

On the other hand, some elected officials and privacy advocates argue that legislation is the only way to assure that companies will do what is necessary to protect privacy. Because self-regulation is voluntary, they say, the approach won't provide such assurances.

P3P standard

To address users' concerns about online privacy, the World Wide Web Consortium (W3C), with the support of many companies, is developing and promoting the Platform For Privacy Preferences (P3P).

The W3C has rolled into its P3P project the preliminary work it had done on the proposed Open Profiling Standard. The OPS was a compromise measure designed to let organizations continue to use their Web sites to obtain data from visitors for marketing purposes while letting visitors control what information is provided to organizations.

With P3P, Web sites would declare their privacy practices, such as the manner in which they use the information they gather, in a way that is understandable to a visitor's browser. The standard would also let visitors establish their privacy requirements and limit the information that is collected.

Visitors could let their browsers automatically determine whether a Web site's practices meet their requirements. If so, they could contact the site seamlessly. If not, the visitor would be notified of the Web site's policies and could then decide whether to continue browsing.

To perform these activities, Web servers and browsers must have P3P extensions. Major vendors of servers and browsers, such as Microsoft and Netscape, are now including these extensions in their products.

If an organization uses information it gathers in a different way than stated in its P3P policies, the federal government could investigate it for deceptive trade practices, noted David Medin, the U.S. Federal Trade Commission's associate director for credit practices.

The W3C expects to release the first P3P standard later this year. Some companies are currently working on compliant products. Microsoft has already used a preliminary version of P3P in its Integrated Information Server and Internet Explorer Client.

Although the industry needs to do more work to protect privacy, P3P is a good first step toward giving users more control over their own data, said Ari Schwartz, a policy analyst for the Center for Democracy and Technology, a U.S.-based public interest organization.

In the short term, he said, two key concerns are whether companies will support P3P in their products and whether technology based on the protocol will be easy to use. In the long term, he said, consumer demand for privacy will probably force vendors to support P3P.

Europe: Legal requirements

The European Union's Data Protection Directive, scheduled to take effect in October, limits the dissemination of private information in Europe. The law says that companies can only process personal information about an individual if, for example, that person gave it to them and if they would use the information to handle a transaction, fulfill a legal obligation, or protect the individual's interests.

The law further states that companies cannot send personal data to countries or businesses that don't observe the directive's requirements.

In addition to limiting the trade and sale of information between vendors, some observers say, the directive would also make it illegal for Europeans to give out private information about themselves or someone else over the Internet.

Abrams said he cannot see how the EU could control the flow of such information.

IRSG: Voluntary guidelines

After the 1996 Lexis-Nexis incident, the 14 largest US information vendors formed the Individual References Services Group (IRSG). The IRSG, working with the FTC, designed a set of voluntary guidelines, which take effect January 1, 1999.

According to the guidelines, vendors should make public their policies for using information they gather and should also limit the way they distribute data they collect, said Marty Abrams, vice president for information policy and privacy at Experian Information Solutions, an IRSG member company that provides credit, marketing, and other information services.

IRSG companies wanted to address privacy concerns expressed by the FTC and also comply with the European Union's Data Protection Directive.

Privacy advocates, such as the Center for Democracy and Technology, say the IRSG guidelines are flawed in that individuals won't get to see public records about them that are held by participating companies, and they won't be notified if an organization or individual accesses and uses such records.

Also, privacy advocates say, no one will audit the way IRSG companies actually use personal information, and individuals have no easy way to seek relief if a participating business violates the guidelines.

Japan: Voluntary guidelines

According to Junji Yoshihara, the Japan External Trade Organization's assistant director of technological affairs, his country's Ministry of International Industry and Trade has created a set of voluntary guidelines concerning the collection, use, and distribution of personal data relating to such subjects as health, sexual activities, religion, trade union membership, race, and family origin. The nonprofit Japan Information Processing Development Center has begun certifying companies that adhere to these guidelines.

However, U.S. encryption vendors say strong encryption is available throughout the world, so government restrictions accomplish nothing except to limit domestic companies' ability to compete in the international marketplace. And privacy advocates say the Clinton administration's attempts to gain access to decryption keys would make it too easy for the government to abuse privacy rights.

The U.S. economy is growing and becoming more service-oriented. Both factors require an increasing flow of information. To guard this flow, organizations will demand more protection for privacy, said Marty Abrams, vice president for information policy and privacy at Experian Information Solutions, which provides credit, marketing, and other information services.

However, even though a growing number of people will use increasingly sophisticated technology to protect their privacy, new and more powerful tools for aggregating data will present new potential threats, said the Center for Democracy and Technology's Schwartz.

Because of this, he said, privacy may become an even bigger issue than it is now.

Article by Ted Lewis, Scientific American, November 1997

We Don't Need No Stinkin' Regulation

Politicians will meddle as they have for generations. Now that the Internet is front-page news, what politician doesn't want to appear to be leading the leaders? The problem is, they don't know enough about technology to grasp which wave of public sentiment to get in front of.

An example is the debate over the regulation of encryption. This issue has created a wildly vacillating Congress, judiciary and executive within the U.S. (and consternation among governing bodies worldwide). First, the U.S. adopted a heavy-handed, controlling attitude on encryption. Now it apparently prefers a laissez-faire policy. But maybe not: a plethora of regulatory bills is pending before Congress. This erratic course points out the folly of sluggish governments attempting to keep up with Internet Time.

"The Internet should be a global free-trade zone," President Bill Clinton said in reversing his administration's stance on the export of encrypted computer products. That change led to "A Framework for Global Electronic Commerce" (www.iitf.nist.gov). The report aims to create a uniform code for electronic commerce, to delegate privacy regulation to industry and consumer groups, to let security standards and management be driven by market forces, to address Internet copyright protection issues, and to promise not to tax goods and services delivered by the Internet. Most dramatically, it takes a hands-off stance on content—no restrictions on pornography. The framework's primary author, Ira Magaziner, has been propelled into the limelight as a consequence of this enlightened policy.

So far so good, but the battle is not over. Spanning all nations, the Internet is the biggest machine in history. It is not clear that any single government can control it. Few politicians understand that. The Clinton administration may have shifted, but Congress still doesn't get it. This year no fewer than four bills regarding encryption either went or are scheduled to go before the legislature.

The most liberal proposal went down this past spring. Called the Promotion of Commerce Online in the Digital Era, or ProCODE Act, it was killed by the Senate Commerce Committee, which believed Clinton would have vetoed it. The ProCODE Act was exactly what the civil cyberians wanted—absolutely no export ban on encryption software.

A compromise of sorts is the Secure Public Networks Act, which passed the Senate Commerce Committee on June 19 (now it waits for a House vote and more committee meetings). It restricts export of strong encryption except when manufacturers require "key recovery." (Using more than 56 bits to encrypt a message is considered "strong," but in reality, 1,024 bits are needed to assure secrecy.) Think of an encoded message as a treasure chest with a lock that can be unlocked by only two keys: the one that the originator used to encode the message and the one that the receiver needs to decode it.

This bill would force consumers to store their secret keys in a safe place—in a "key escrow account"—where the government can get the keys and unlock the messages. Of course, the government would need a court order to do that, but even so, the computer industry opposes the interference. Thus, the fight has centered on key recovery—what some have colorfully called the "back door."

In the end, Congress may have to yield to the freewheelers, especially in light of the shenanigans of Phil Zimmerman. He's the cyberhero who a few years ago wrote PGP (for "Pretty Good Privacy"), a very strong encryption software that was posted on the Internet. Now it is all over the world producing strong encryption—up to 2,048 bits—for free.

For a while, Zimmerman was accused of illegally exporting munitions. The feds eventually gave up on him: technically, Zimmerman had not violated the law, because a friend posted the software on the Internet, not him. With similar legal finesse, Zimmerman's company, PGP, Inc., worked out a deal with a non-U.S. company that also sidestepped the embargo on strong encryption.

The Clinton administration's change of heart stems in part from Zimmerman's and PGP's end runs around the rules. Whether such tactics have similarly influenced Congress should become clear soon. A proposal is in the works: the Safety and Freedom through Encryption Act, or SAFE Act. Barring last-minute amendments, this bill may be the best hope for individual freedom in cyberspace. It would lift controls on commercial and personal transactions alike. At press time, Congress was expected to vote on it this fall; it has 134 out of 218 votes needed to pass. This bill stands in stark contrast to the restrictive Encrypted Communications Privacy Act of 1997, which remains bottled up in committee and will probably die.

So it seems that SAFE is the leading candidate for passage, and the battle tilts toward noninterference and free-enterprisers such as Zimmerman. Already PGP, Inc., has secured Commerce Department permission to ship its 128-bit cryptography to a preapproved list of U.S. subsidiaries outside the country. Likewise, VeriFone got the go-ahead to ship overseas its software for secure online credit-card transactions.

If this trend continues, everyone will be able to export secure software. Not only will banks and credit-card companies enjoy security, but you and I will be able to send messages to friends and business associates without concern about invasion of privacy. Zimmerman's PGP has traveled from outlaw to pin-striped suit in Internet Time. Let's hope enlightened governments around the world keep up.

CHAPTER THIRTY-THREE

Technology and the Productivity Paradox

Is technology fundamentally "good" or "bad"? Technological advances have raised the standard of living for billions of people, but they have also caused environmental, social, and cultural upheavals. In each "era" upheaval has dislocated workers, changed mores, and set the stage for political, cultural, and economic change. Sometimes the change has been for the better and sometimes it has been for the worse.

Never before has the world had to face the kinds of changes brought on by technology. These changes pose entirely new challenges to the human race. So history is often useless as a guide. We cannot use the known impact of the internal combustion engine on society to predict the ultimate impact of the modern computer, because one is not a lesson in how to deal with the other. In fact, we cannot determine with any certainty whether good or evil will result for a certain innovation. At this point in time it is impossible to foretell the impact of genetic engineering, artificial intelligence, or global communication on the future of society. As far as we know, Internet communication, biological cloning, and the ever-lengthening human life span, portends both good and bad.

It is perhaps too late to ask these questions because, in a sense, we cannot live with technology, and we cannot live without it. For good or bad, once the choice was made, it became impossible to go back to an earlier, simpler non-technical society. There is no turning back now.

I, for one, am optimistic about the effects of technology. In fact, I attribute most of the wealth of nations to technological advancement. Never before have so many enjoyed such a good life. Technology has given us many more options than at any other time in history. It has provided the potential for the good life, even when that potential has not always been realized.

In the next and final essay, I list the four major driving forces—from technology—that I believe are most responsible for the extremely high standard of living enjoyed by Americans. This era of prosperity will most likely be remembered as one of the best economic growth periods in history. It has propelled Americans into an economic orbit that will last for at least a decade, and when it is done, leave the population in better economic conditions than ever before. This period of prosperity will be remembered for a long time because of its height and duration. And I believe it is due to technology.

But the current era of good times is not unique. In fact, the economy has benefited from advances in technology before. And as in the past the benefits do not always kick in immediately, because it takes several decades for technological change to work its way through society. The time delay between deployment of an innovation, like the personal computer or birth control pill, and its impact on the economy is responsible for the so-called "productivity paradox," a contradiction that asks "Why hasn't investment in technology paid dividends in the form of a better life?"

After every burst of technological advancement, economists try to link the new technology with enhanced or diminished productivity. But the long delay between deployment of technology and the realization of an increased standard of living results in a temporary *decline* in productivity. Productivity goes down during this period of adaptation, which results in a "productivity paradox." It is as if the money was spent on technology without any resulting benefit. But this effect is temporary. The benefits of technology usually take about 20 years to be fully realized. In the meantime, economists ask, "Why hasn't the economy improved?" In their impatience, economists start to blame technology rather than credit it with the expansion of economic wealth. When the benefits begin to roll in 20 years later, everyone is surprised!

In this final essay I answer the question, "Why is the economy so good?" The answer is that hi-tech has changed the world in four fundamental ways: Disintermediation, Integration, Flexing, and One-on-One marketing. The first two, disintermediation and integration, form the basis of reintermediation—the reconstruction of electronic middlemen. Reintermediation will be the most influential ingredient of prosperity well into the next century.

Flexing is what technology has done to organizations, and one-on-one marketing is the process of narrowcasting to tribes. Technology has made it possible for organizations to become much more flexible and adaptable. This has allowed organizations—businesses, governments, and education—to react in real-time. This will be the second most influential impact of technology on the next century. Finally, one-on-one marketing will bring narrowcasting to its ultimate achievement. It will bring back many of the communal attributes of previous ages. It may even bring back the e-Village.

I also address the productivity paradox and note that the good times enjoyed by Americans in the 1990s were the result of investments made over a period of 20 years, from 1975 to 1995. Indeed, this is the third time Americans have benefited from a "productivity paradox." It won't be the last time, either!

Article by Ted Lewis, Computer, May 1998

Why the Economy Is So Good

The U.S. economy has rarely been as prosperous as it is today, and many businesspeople and economists are pressed to explain why. Compared with the past, the recent rise in the wealth of the nation doesn't make sense. How can the United States go on enjoying full employment and prosperity without the threat of inflation? The answer: rocketing productivity. Increased productivity has more than compensated for a slowly rising wage rate amid unbridled consumerism. The late 1990s has the best of both worlds—low inflation and rising prosperity—because, unlike the 1980s, productivity has kept pace.

Many economists don't like the data: more jobs, less inflation, more supply, less spending, and so forth. The data predicts a crash—or what economists politely call a "correction." But disaster never arrives. Indeed, the economy seems to defy common sense, especially as the rosy economic picture gets even rosier.

Will this prosperity never end? Not for another 10 years or so, and here is why.

Measuring Productivity

Classical economists have sold us on the misguided idea of a "productivity paradox" that raises its head whenever cocktail chatter turns to the subject of IT (information technology). The productivity paradox of the 1990s asks why productivity has remained constant even though captains of industry have spent billions on computers and networks over the past two or three decades. If IT is so good, why hasn't it improved productivity? Were these billions squandered?

The measure of productivity may itself be outdated, because it simply tallies the value of products produced by factory workers and divides by average hourly wage. Thus, productivity is measured in how many dollars are produced in relation to how many dollars are spent. Perhaps a better measure for a company is the amount of revenue generated per employee. But such a measurement doesn't account for expenses.

Another metric is what I call the MegaGates. One MegaGate is equal to the market capitalization of Microsoft—currently around $200 billion and rising. The beauty of this measure is that market cap seems to go up and down with perceived productivity.

Still, whatever the metric, most people would agree that current measures do a poor job of gauging true productivity. There is a little publicized fact of life about the infamous paradox that should get more attention: The productivity paradox isn't anything new. It has happened before. In fact, we can gain a much better understanding of why the economy is so good by dissecting previous productivity paradoxes.

In short, the economy is so good because we are enjoying the bumper crop of a third productivity paradox. What were the previous two and how does today's version account for the current state of prosperity?

The First Two Productivity Paradoxes

Everything is going according to plan if you believe in the previous two paradoxes. Figure 33.1 shows adoption rates for three infrastructure technologies: electrification of factories from 1899 to 1939, electrification of city dwellers' homes from 1907 to 1929, and the Webification of American homes from 1993 to the present and beyond. Each of these technologies corresponds to a productivity paradox. The first two happened so long ago that we've overlooked them. The latest one, Webification, is partly responsible for the good times ahead.

The similarity among adoption curves shown in Figure 33.1 is clear: Changes in infrastructure diffuse through society today in much the same way as yesterday, only faster. Technological change—whether it is due to electric motors or desktop computers—sends waves of change throughout society. It happened with electricity, telephony, air travel, and broadcasting, and now it is happening all over again with the adoption of IT.

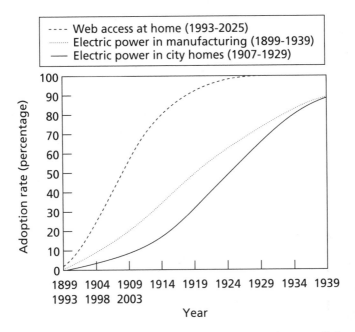

Figure 33.1 *Changes in infrastructure diffuse through society today in much the same way as yesterday, only faster.*

Between 1914 and 1929, industrial-power use increased by 68 percent per year, but productivity barely increased at all. Just like the computer revolution that took place between 1975 and 1990, electrical power transformed manufacturing from a centralized or "mainframe" era to a decentralized network system of personal devices in the form of electric motors that could be distributed to every worker's workbench. And like the decentralization of computing power that characterized the 1980s, electric motors decentralized power, which caused radical changes in the structure of organizations.

In another analog with today's diffusion of IT throughout society, the electric motor found its way into home appliances just like the microprocessor is finding its way into network appliances. Figure 33.1 shows the growth of Web infrastructure in homes, which is really a precursor to the widespread acceptance of network appliances in the years to come.

Electrification of the factory led to the study of the first paradox by economist Paul David of Stanford University. What he discovered applies to today's scene: Power systems evolved over a period of 25 years and gave power to small energy users without a large investment. Cheap power permitted efficient reengineering of industrial processes, but the productivity gains were not realized until much later during the 1920s.

Productivity gains lagged behind the investment in infrastructure by two decades.

We can observe a similar phenomena in homes: Electrification did not increase productivity. Rather, it shifted the burden of work to women, who replaced servants with washing machines and refrigerators, took up machine-assisted strenuous work previously done by men and boys, and increased the amount of time they spent on housework from 51 to 60 hours per week to 60 to 81 hours. Modern labor-saving devices eliminated drudgery, not labor. Thus, the second productivity paradox was observed in the home. Not until 20 to 25 years along the adoption curve did automation begin to show benefits to homemakers.

Information Technology: The Third Paradox

Now we are nearing the end of a two-decade time period of investment in IT that has consumed more money and effort than it has produced. But this third productivity paradox is starting to reverse itself. We are entering a golden age similar to the 1920s, when the 20-year investment in infrastructure and reengineering of processes around the computer is beginning to pay off.

As you can see in Figure 33.1, the period of payoff doesn't begin until adoption exceeds 50 percent. If we use the adoption rate of Web access in homes as our starting point, Figure 33.1 suggests the golden era of the information age will begin around the year 2002. But if we compare this model to adoption of business IT, we realize that the U.S. economy is currently in the midst of the payoff. Indeed, dramatic increases in productivity made possible by large investments in IT is the force underlying today's prosperity.

The industrial revolution was built on top of networks of water, power, telephony, and transportation. These networks required 20 to 25 years of investment before they boosted productivity and led to greater economic prosperity. Similarly, the information revolution is built on top of networks of computers and information processes that took 20 to 25 years of investment to build. This investment has been made and now the U.S. economy is reaping its rewards.

The Four Pillars of It

The introduction of electric motors into factories and homes led to reengineering—a step that is taking place again today. But today, four megatrends are reengineering factories and homes: *disintermedia-*

tion, integration, flexing, and *one-on-one narrowcasting.* These are the pillars of the new economic architecture.

Disintermediation

Disintermediation is the process of flattening organizations. In many cases, disintermediation eliminates the middle party. It permits consumers to buy directly, not through intermediaries but directly from the manufacturer or wholesaler. For example, Amazon.com drop-ships books directly to your doorstep, bypassing the Barnes & Noble retail outlet. Amazon.com grows whereas Barnes & Noble scrambles to open a bookstore in cyberspace.

Disintermediation diffuses throughout an organization in subtle ways. E-mail replaces memos, but it also flattens the organization because e-mail can go directly to the top. Automated workflow systems bypass middle management. Databases and online services replace people managers with process owners. Taken all together, these disintermediated processes accelerate the modern organization by shortening decision loops. And short loops mean greater productivity.

Integration

The other side of the disintermediation coin is integration, which is the process of putting the organization back together again. Today's integration spans multiple organizations, with supply-chain integration being the most dramatic example. Using the Internet, companies can tie together all of the procurement processes needed to manage buying, negotiating, and distributing materials used for products or services.

Wal-Mart integrates its database with the databases of its suppliers, and resultantly cuts costs because there are fewer intermediaries and even less spoilage. Just-in-time inventory becomes extreme—turning mass production assembly lines into mass customization build-to-order cells for companies like Dell Computer. Value-chain partners such as Sony, WebTV, and various ISPs share the risks as well as the rewards of bringing a product to market. Once again, integration reduces costs, accelerates organizations, and increases productivity.

Flexing

Integration paves the way for flexing, which is the business ecosystem equivalent of natural selection in nature. Flexing permits organizations to adapt to change and turn on a dime. IT enables flexing.

Top-down organization charts give way to workgroup charts that change on a project-by-project basis. Sometimes a workgroup organization reorganizes three to four times per year: Some workgroups thrive and grow, while others wither and die. All live for a certain time, eventually fading as their reason for being rises and falls. Flexing organizations are more flexible than matrix organizations.

A flexing design team can span several companies. Beckton-Dickinson & Company combined 110 people from its IT operation with 50 SAP and Deloitte & Touche consultants during a rollout of the company's new information system. No one had a title or an office; everyone in the workgroup worked as peers. After about a year of working together, the workgroup splintered into smaller groups and infiltrated branch offices throughout the world.

Instead of top-down managers, flex companies have product champions; instead of pursuing efficiency, flex organizations pursue opportunities; instead of tolerating slow decision loops, they run through extremely fast decision loops; and instead of building consensus, flexible organizations evolve according to Darwinian principles.

A flexible organization is driven from the bottom up, exploiting emerging behaviors as soon as they are identified. They get the ultimate productivity boost when a billion dollar idea, product, or service emerges from the bottom. Without flexing, top-down managers often never even see such breakthroughs.

One-on-One Narrowcasting

Finally, heightened productivity has propelled us into abundance. The economy of abundance puts the consumer in the driver's seat. Thus, the fourth pillar is the power of the Market of One.

The fact that there is plenty of everything makes one-on-one narrowcasting necessary; that technology can deliver products to a single individual or nearly the same cost as mass production makes one-on-one narrowcasting possible.

Dell Computer dramatically illustrates the BYO (build your own) transformation sweeping the computer industry. But there are many other examples in the friction-free economy. For example, the Web's cookie controversy pits personalization against privacy as software watchdogs track consumers electronically.

The Safeway and Lucky grocery stores have a reward system that works the same way. Every time you buy groceries, you swipe your reward card. The store tracks your behavior and tailors their incentives to you. If you buy enough tofu, sooner or later you will be rewarded with a special price on tofu. You could be the only shopper in the store to receive this reward. After a while, you find yourself going back for more—at the same store.

Modern business is simply exploiting the 20- to 25-year investment in information technology that is now fueling the friction-free economy. The total information technology industry surpassed the automobile industry in its dollar impact on the U.S. economy in 1997. The $5 trillion retail business is up for grabs as the Web makes buying and selling friction free.

This burst of productivity will continue until baby boomers start to die off—somewhere around the year 2008. Consumers reach their buying peak at the age of 46, and the number of 46-year-olds in the U.S. will reach its pinnacle in 2008. But be careful. When 2008 rolls around, the U.S. economy will need to find another engine of prosperity.

EPILOGUE

What To Do About Microsoft

My revisionist history of the computer industry throughout the 1990s cannot be completed as I write this epilogue, because the trial of Microsoft is still in process. This trial will be the most significant legal event of the last 50 years in terms of its impact on the largest industry in the world. It could change everything, or not, depending on its outcome. So, I was contemplating the possible outcomes as I wrote this final essay.

The following thoughts crossed my mind as I drove up highway 101 to Palo Alto on my way to one of the largest legal firms in California. I had been hired as an expert witness. In one corner was Microsoft—the reigning champion of American free enterprise. In the other corner was a small struggling company that had recently been crushed by Microsoft. I was on the side of the loser.

My job as an expert was to convince a judge that Microsoft was attempting to monopolize the software development tools industry through predatory contractual shenanigans. It was a classical David and Goliath story. David had a few patents that Goliath wanted, and Goliath was willing to whack David in order to get them. The small tools company needed some Microsoft Windows DLLs (Dynamic Link Libraries) and interfaces to Windows APIs in order to make its product work with Windows. Microsoft had been licensing these tools to a number of small companies for years. My small company was one of these small fish swimming with the shark.

When it came time to renew its license agreement with Goliath, David was confronted with an ultimatum: either assign all of its intellectual property to Goliath or else go out of business. But as the story goes,

David whacked Goliath with a lawsuit instead of capitulating. Hence, I was on my way to the law offices to deliver a technical declaration that essentially claimed that Goliath would ruin David if it withheld the license.

This story illustrates the inherent dangers of a monopoly. A market dominating company such as Microsoft can demand, and usually get, almost anything from its competitors. It can be your friend one day and your enemy the next day. As long as David enhanced and supported Goliath's products, the big guy was friendly. When disgruntled, Goliath could extinguish David without a fuss. And companies often become disgruntled on their way to a monopoly. As they get closer and closer to 100 percent market share, it becomes more difficult to grow. To compensate, they start feeding off of the smaller fish swimming along with them.

Microsoft is nearing the top end of the adoption curve for most of its products. It is becoming more difficult for it to grow. After all, there are only so many copies of Windows that it can sell, and Microsoft Office is tied to Windows. Together, Windows and Office account for almost all of Microsoft's revenues. Thus it is essential that the company squeeze everything it can from the industry. Otherwise, its growth will slow down. When this happens, its stock prices will fall, and the company will begin to contract. That is, unless it can find new markets to dominate.

The problem with the computer industry is that domination is not difficult to achieve once a company or product gains momentum. It can ride a wave of increasing returns or "network effects" to victory over almost any foe. There is no stopping an increasing returns company once it starts gathering momentum. And because software products, Internet services, and information in general obey a friction-free economy, it is rather easy to gain momentum if you are a first-mover in a new market. Thus, Microsoft came early to the party and stayed late into the night, like some uninvited guest.

What to do about Microsoft? The answer to this question is identical to the answer to, "What to do about increasing returns?" In the following article I note several remedies. But all of them make me uncomfortable because they involve government interference. And we know from history that governments know the least about innovation, entrepreneurialism, and how to increase the wealth of a nation. Thus at the dawn of the twenty-first century we are left with a daunting problem: What to do about Microsoft? At least for the next decade, I expect Microsoft to keep on rising.

Article by Ted Lewis, Computer, September 1998

What to Do About Microsoft

September will go down as the month of infamy or liberation, depending on which side of the fence you sit. The Trial of Microsoft, which begins on September 8, may be a turning point for this wildly successful company. The spectacle is about more than monopolies, although the U.S. Department of Justice (DOJ) bases its complaint on U.S. law as articulated in the 1890 Sherman Antitrust Act. Recall that the Sherman Act expressly sought to contain big oil (represented by John D. Rockefeller), big railroad (the Vanderbilts), and big business (J. P. Morgan and others).

"The difference between John D. Rockefeller and Bill Gates is [that] Gates recognizes no boundaries to his monopolistic drive," says consumer advocate Ralph Nader. Is the Microsoft case a repeat of the Standard Oil case? (See "Who's Afraid of Wintel?" *Computer*, Jan. 1998, pp. 149–152.)

Leveraging a Monopoly

"Unless we're allowed to enhance Windows, I don't know how to do my job. . . . This isn't a country where success and great products should be punished," pleads Gates. In Microsoft's view, the company is simply giving customers what they want.

But Gates may have overstepped boundaries established more than 100 years ago by the Sherman Act. DOJ accuses Microsoft of monopolizing rather than competing against the likes of Netscape Communications and Sun Microsystems. *Monopolies* are legal, but *monopolizing* is not. Section 2 of the Sherman Act, which ". . . prohibits the use of one monopoly to create another," makes the distinction clear.

This rule is at the center of the trial. Microsoft cannot use its monopoly of the OS market to create another monopoly in the browser market. Even if customers deem browsers a necessary part of a modern OS, it is as illegal to leverage Windows into Internet dominance as it is to leverage a gasoline monopoly into dominance of the automobile industry.

Or is it? Aren't consumers better off with bundled software than cumbersome-to-use, stand-alone parts from different vendors?

Joel Klein, assistant U.S. attorney general, intends to find out. He wrote the claim against Microsoft, leading up to the September 8 trial, "This kind of product-forcing is an abuse of monopoly power, and we seek to put an end to it." Subsequent to Klein's charge, several states initiated similar complaints of their own. Samuel Goodhope, an attorney for the state of Texas, says, "This is very Borg-like. Resistance is futile. You will be assimilated." However, U.S. District Court Judge Thomas Jackson combined the states' complaints with the DOJ complaint in an attempt to simplify and expedite litigation.

A blow-by-blow account of events leading to the trial is presented on the following page, but I will not dwell on past events here. Rather, the purpose of this essay is to suggest how the industry might deal with Microsoft. The Trial of Microsoft should answer a simple question: What should be done about Microsoft? But first, what are the charges against the defendant?

Just the Facts

U.S. vs. *Microsoft* will address a number of festering complaints against Microsoft concerning its alleged predatory practices and illegal leveraging of its OS monopoly into a monopoly of Internet access. Specifically, the trial will try to prove that MS

- conspired with Netscape to monopolize the browser market,
- created a second (Internet) monopoly from an existing (operating system) monopoly,
- forced PC makers to take MS Internet Explorer to get Windows and prevented them from modifying the boot-up sequence, and
- employed similar exclusionary practices with Internet service providers (ISPs).

The press often overlooks the last point about ISPs, so it is worthwhile to repeat the DOJ claim. According to paragraphs 78 and 79 of the DOJ complaint, Microsoft forces ISPs to exclude non-Microsoft products (see the "DOJ's Complaint" sidebar for these paragraphs).

In addition, DOJ seeks remedies for monopolizing, because of its negative impact on innovation, which directly impacts the ability of competitors to compete. Paragraph 37 of the claim spells this out in detail.

Again, it is not illegal to be a monopoly. Rather, it is illegal to monopolize. To win its case, DOJ must prove that Microsoft engaged in monopolizing using predatory pricing, exclusionary contracts, and the company's monopoly in Windows to gain a monopoly in another market segment—browsers.

Events Leading to the Trial

June 1990: The FTC begins a secret probe regarding IBM-MS collusion.

February 1993: The FTC takes no action against MS after commissioners deadlock on the collusion charges, 2-2.

August 1993: DOJ takes over the FTC's investigation of MS.

1994: Netscape Communications Corp. incorporates: Dan Rosen, MS Director of Strategic Relations approaches Jim Clark, Netscape cofounder, offering to license Navigator code for $1 million and no royalties. Clark declines, saying, "They will use it against us."

July 1994: MS and DOJ announce a settlement: MS agrees to change its licensing practices. This settlement becomes known as the 1995 Consent Decree.

February 1995: U.S. District Court Judge Stanley Sporkin rejects the 1995 Consent Decree, saying it does not go far enough.

March 1995: Netscape president Jim Barksdale chats with Microsoft's Rosen about cooperation on browsers.

April 1995: Marc Andreessen and Mike Homer of Netscape meet with Rosen and others of Microsoft to discuss licensing. Andreessen says, "I sensed an implied threat: Cooperate or be crushed."

June 1995: DOJ investigates the bundling of MS Network with Windows 95.

June 1995: An appeals court panel of three judges rules that Sporkin overstepped his bounds in issuing the consent decree and sends its decree to Judge Jackson for approval.

June 1995: MS files a petition in federal court claiming "harassment and abuse" by DOJ in regard to bundling MS Network and Windows 95.

August 1995: DOJ extends its investigation to the bundling of IE and Windows 95.

August 1996: Netscape asks DOJ to take action against MS for predatory practices in the browser market.

August 1995: Judge Jackson enters a consent decree, banning MS from linking one product (IE) with another (Windows).

Events Leading to the Trial (continued)

September 1996: DOJ seeks information from MS on bundling IE and Windows 95.

September 1997: Netscape says it will not file suit against MS, but hopes DOJ will persuade MS to "reevaluate its practices."

October 1997: U.S. Attorney General Janet Reno fines MS $1 million per day until it complies with the 1995 Consent Decree.

December 1997: An injunction allowed vendors to remove IE from Windows 95.

December 1997: DOJ says MS should be held in contempt of court for not obeying the injunction.

January 1998: MS complies with the injunction, saying that vendors can remove IE from Windows 95.

January 1998: Netscape announces that its source code will be open.

February 1998: U.S. Senator Orrin Hatch (R-Utah), in a Senate hearing, rails against MS.

March 1998: Attorneys General from 27 states back an injunction against MS.

March 1998: Bill Gates appears before the U.S. Senate Judiciary Committee.

March 1998: DOJ investigation widens to include Sun's suit against MS on the Java license.

April 1998: MS reports a 29 percent-increase in earnings for the third quarter, but warns of a slowdown.

May 1998: Gates meets with U.S. Assistant Attorney General Joel Klein.

May 1998: Sun Microsystems seeks an injunction against the release of Windows 98.

May 1998: An appeals court rules that the December 1997 preliminary injunction does not apply to Windows 98.

June 1998: U.S. District Court of Appeals reverses lower court ruling regarding the 1995 Consent Decree, saying Microsoft may integrate IE + Win95, and that the IE icon may appear on the Win95 screen, lifting the injunction.

The Remedy

Gates prefers the term "innovating" to "monopolizing." Where does innovation end and monopolization begin? Adding Internet Explorer to Windows 95 and calling it Windows 98 is innovation in Gates' terminology, but it is monopolizing according to DOJ.

Microsoft believes it adds consumer value to its products when it integrates them into a working suite or system. The problem with Microsoft's definition is that it leads to anticompetitive behavior. Thus, integration of the TCP/IP stack enhances consumer value, but it may have also put FTP Software out of business. Combining IE with Windows also enhances consumer value, but it may put Netscape out of business. Therefore, DOJ must walk a line between promoting consumer value and promoting competition.

DOJ has the difficult task of drawing a line somewhere between systems software and applications software. This will not be easy but is essential to the outcome of litigation. Most likely, Judge Jackson will rule in DOJ's favor, asserting that it is more important to protect competition than to define a browser as an OS feature. Thus, the court would draw the line on the basis of a legal technicality rather than product definition. The June 23, 1998 decision unexpectedly reversed an earlier ruling on the 1995 Consent Decree regarding bundling of Windows 95 and Internet Explorer, leading some analysts to argue that the DOJ now has a weak case. However, I argue that this decision is narrowly restricted in scope and applies only to the particular instance of Windows 95, but leaves the broader question of competition versus innovation still open.

DOJ perceives the bundling and linking of one product to another as either predatory pricing or the linkage of one market to another for the purpose of monopolizing, or both. Therefore, licensing agreements whereby Microsoft "simplifies" the configuration of a browser to work with a certain ISP is considered improper. But the consumer may interpret such linking as beneficial and therefore desirable. Once again, the court will likely base the decision on legalities. In this case, the court may fine Microsoft for damages caused when it forced licensees to link one product with another.

Path Dependency

The simplistic remedies I've just suggested fail because they don't deal with the underlying path dependency problem. According to the theory of increasing returns, path dependency occurs whenever the success of one product is coupled to the success of another product. In other words, a browser is path-dependent on an OS because browsers require an OS in order to work. Hence, IE is guaranteed success because of the path dependency created by Windows. Netscape Navigator gets left out of the race because, while it also depends on Windows it does not have equal access to Windows.

U.S. vs. *Microsoft* is the first case to use the theory of increasing returns and path dependency as an argument against a monopoly. If the plaintiff's approach proves effective, it could set a legal precedent. The legal community could add path dependence to the list of monopolizing activities, just as the law deemed the use of predatory pricing monopolistic on the part of Standard Oil.

Therefore, the long-term remedy to Microsoft and companies in similar situations lies in regulating path dependencies. If DOJ believes it is the regulator of a fair-market economy, then its response to monopolizing via increasing returns and path dependence should be to

- increase competition in the face of increasing returns,
- break down path dependence in essential-facility products like Windows, and
- overhaul trade secret, copyright, and patent law to protect innovators from predators.

Applying the Theory

How should DOJ apply this theory to *U.S.* vs. *Microsoft?* A simple solution would be to penalize Microsoft for violations (if proven) per paragraphs 37, 78, and 79 and direct the FTC (Federal Trade Commission) to oversee compliance. Microsoft's recapitulation to the 1995 Consent Decree suggests that the company can be reined in through fines and restrictions. After all, the company has changed a number of practices since the lawsuit was filed (see the sidebar). But is this enough?

Probably not. Microsoft is approaching monopoly status in several other markets, because path dependence applies to e-mail, Web servers, databases, and other products. To prevent another browser war, DOJ must come to terms with increasing returns, perhaps taking one or several actions. All the following actions go beyond the Sherman Act, and therefore require congressional approval:

- Enforce section 2 of the Sherman Antitrust Act as it applies to enhancing software products such as Windows, and fine Microsoft if it bundles any other new software products—either physically or contractually—with its other market-leading software.
- Declare dominant products such as Windows to be an essential facility, thereby making it available to all software developers on a timely basis and for a reasonable price.

+ Stop buyouts of companies with path-dependent products. Companies with products that are path-dependent on Windows include Stac Electronics (compression), Netscape (browsers and servers), HotMail (e-mail), Vxtreme (3D graphics), SoftImage (multimedia), and Novell (network directories).

+ Encourage investment in monopolized market segments by accelerating tax deductions (tax incentives) for the development of competing products. Netscape, for example, would receive a heavier deduction for its development costs than Microsoft.

+ Fine any company that sells or gives away its software for a price far below actual marketing and development costs. For instance, Microsoft could not sell IE below its true development cost amortized over a reasonable product life cycle.

+ Adopt a system similar to the Writer's Guild system of Hollywood: Create a software developer's guild that archives technical ideas as legal documents for use in cases of intellectual property theft. Schematics, programs, ideas, and so on could be stored and used as court evidence only if a predator company steals an idea from an innovator.

+ Open essential utility products such as Windows to the industry (via, say, an API), but afford protection of the intellectual property through a mechanism very similar to patent claim disclosures.

Libertarians will not like these ideas, because they lead to a regulated software industry. They favor a free-market over a fair-market economy. Supporters of a free-market economy consider such regulation unfair to a dominant company like Microsoft. But controlling path dependence levels the playing field for smaller, innovative companies. Is leveling worth the price?

The Trial of Microsoft is about more than the abuse of monopoly power. It is also about fear, uncertainty, and doubt. "PC makers won't even talk to us. They're scared to death of Microsoft," says Scott McNealy of Sun Microsystems.

And Larry Ellison of Oracle Corp. says, "The question is, are we looking forward to the Information Age or the Microsoft Age? It's kind of like Microsoft versus mankind, and mankind is the underdog."

"They're hell-bent on dominating the entire information infrastructure of the world, and it scares the daylights out of me," snorts Gary Reback, attorney for Netscape. The Trial of Microsoft won't silence Microsoft's critics, but it might establish a new rule in antitrust litigation: one company, one monopoly.

Even if Microsoft is not found guilty, fined, or reined in by DOJ, it is stuck with the image of a company that bought its dominant position in the industry through fear and intimidation. This is not a good image for a consumer brand as significant as Microsoft's.

Excerpts from the DOJ Complaint

78. In return for attractive placement by Microsoft in its Internet Connection Wizard, or Online Services Folder, ISPs agreed:

a. to distribute and promote to their subscribers Internet Explorer exclusively or nearly exclusively;

b. to eliminate links on their Web sites from which their subscribers could download a competing browser over the Internet;

c. to abstain from expressing or implying to their subscribers that a competing browser is available;

d. to include Internet Explorer as the only browser they shipped with their access software most or all of the time; and

e. to limit the percentage of competing browsers they distributed, even in response to specific requests from customers.

79. Microsoft's agreements with ISPs also require the ISPs to use Microsoft-specific programming extensions and tools in connection with the ISPs' own Web sites. Web sites developed with these Microsoft-specific programming extensions and tools will look better when they are viewed with IE than with a non-Microsoft browser.

37. Microsoft's conduct adversely affects innovation, including by:

a. impairing the incentive of Microsoft's competitors and potential competitors to undertake research and development, because they know that Microsoft will be able to limit the rewards from any resulting innovation;

b. impairing the ability of Microsoft's competitors and potential competitors to obtain financing for research and development;

c. inhibiting Microsoft's competitors that nevertheless succeed in developing promising innovations from effectively marketing their improved products to customers;

d. reducing the incentive and ability of OEMs to innovate and differentiate their products in ways that would appeal to customers; and

e. reducing competition and the spur to innovation by Microsoft and others that only competition can provide.

About the Author

Ted Lewis is CEO, and President of DaimlerChrysler Research & Technology Center, North America, in Palo Alto, CA. Before that he was Professor of Computer Science at the Naval Postgraduate School, Monterey, CA. Prior to 1993, he was a Professor of Computer Science at Oregon State University and Director of OACIS—a University-Industry Research Center created to transfer technology from research into products.

Lewis holds advanced degrees in Mathematics (BS), and Computer Science (MS, Ph.D.), and has over 30 years of experience with computers, starting with vacuum tube machines. More recently, he has designed e-commerce systems, web-zines, web-enabled databases, re-engineered large-scale enterprise systems, implemented video tele-conferencing systems for distance learning, defined software products for information appliances, performed technology and marketing assessments of network appliances, and advised clients on product definitions for World Wide Web products.

He has extensive experience in the technical publishing industry, having served as the Editor-in-Chief of *IEEE Software* magazine 1987–1990, *Computer* magazine 1993–1994, Editorial Board member of *IEEE Spectrum* magazine 1990–1998, and was elected to the Governing Board of the Computer Society, twice. Widely read in the computer industry, Lewis writes the Binary Critic column for *IEEE*

Computer magazine, and has written the Wired Wired World column for *IEEE Internet Computing*. He is also an occasional contributor to *Scientific American, Upside,* and other trade periodicals. He has been a guest of PBS Tech Nation, Ann On-line, Business Commerce Daily, Entrepreneur Magazine, Fast Company, and a number of Silicon Valley TV and radio stations.

IEEE Computer Society Publications

The world-renowned IEEE Computer Society publishes, promotes, and distributes a wide variety of authoritative computer science and engineering texts. These books are available from most retail outlets. Visit the Online Catalog, *http://computer.org*, for a list of products.

IEEE Computer Society Proceedings

The IEEE Computer Society also produces and actively promotes the proceedings of more than 141 acclaimed international conferences each year in multimedia formats that include hard and softcover books, CD-ROMs, videos, and on-line publications.

For information on the IEEE Computer Society proceedings, send e-mail to *cs.books@computer.org* or write to Proceedings, IEEE Computer Society, P.O. Box 3014, 10662 Los Vaqueros Circle, Los Alamitos, CA 90720-1314. Telephone +1 714-821-8380. FAX +1 714-761-1784.

Additional information regarding the Computer Society, conferences and proceedings, CD-ROMs, videos, and books can also be accessed from our web site at *http://computer.org/cspress*

Revised 9 November 1999